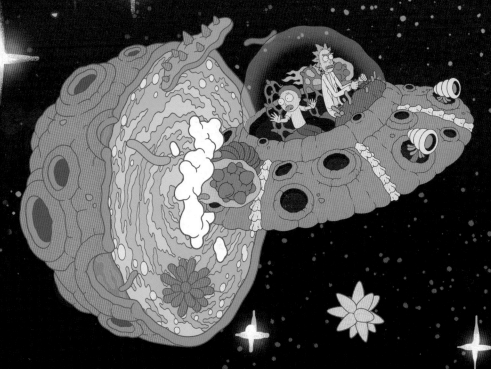

AN ONI PRESS PUBLICATION

[adult swim]

# VOLUME TWELVE

*RICK AND MORTY*™ CREATED BY **DAN HARMON** AND **JUSTIN ROILAND**

RETAIL COVER BY
**MARC ELLERBY** AND **SARAH STERN**

ONI EXCLUSIVE COVER BY
**JULIETA COLÁS**

EDITED BY
**SARAH GAYDOS**

DESIGNED BY
**SARAH ROCKWELL**

ONI PRESS

[adult swim]

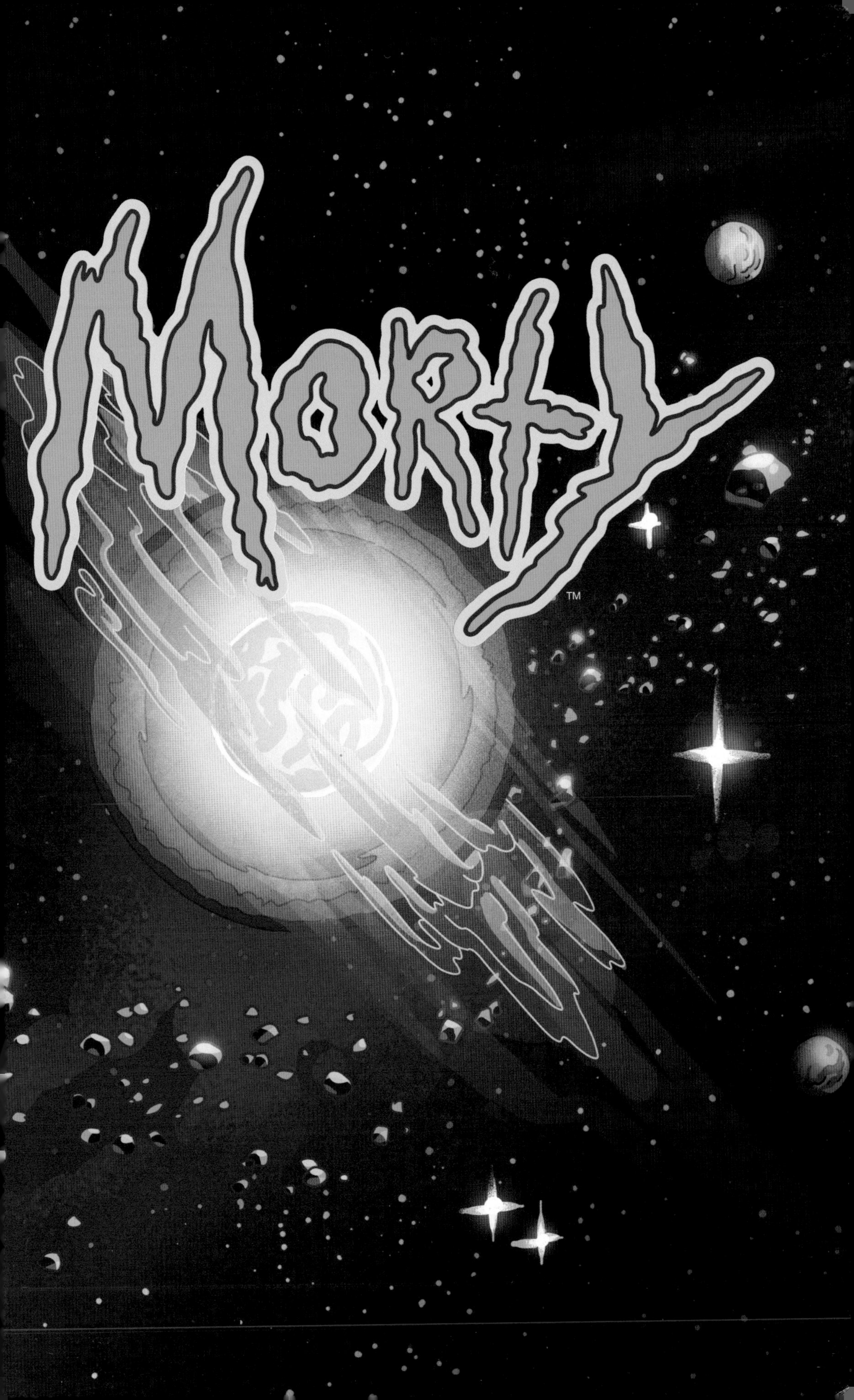
Morty™

# PUBLISHED BY ONI-LION FORGE PUBLISHING GROUP, LLC

**JAMES LUCAS JONES,** PRESIDENT & PUBLISHER

**SARAH GAYDOS,** EDITOR IN CHIEF

**CHARLIE CHU,** E.V.P. OF CREATIVE & BUSINESS DEVELOPMENT

**BRAD ROOKS,** DIRECTOR OF OPERATIONS

**AMBER O'NEILL,** SPECIAL PROJECTS MANAGER

**HARRIS FISH,** EVENTS MANAGER

**MARGOT WOOD,** DIRECTOR OF MARKETING & SALES

**DEVIN FUNCHES,** SALES & MARKETING MANAGER

**KATIE SAINZ,** MARKETING MANAGER

**TARA LEHMANN,** PUBLICIST

**TROY LOOK,** DIRECTOR OF DESIGN & PRODUCTION

**KATE Z. STONE,** SENIOR GRAPHIC DESIGNER

**SONJA SYNAK,** GRAPHIC DESIGNER

**HILARY THOMPSON,** GRAPHIC DESIGNER

**SARAH ROCKWELL,** JUNIOR GRAPHIC DESIGNER

**ANGIE KNOWLES,** DIGITAL PREPRESS LEAD

**VINCENT KUKUA,** DIGITAL PREPRESS TECHNICIAN

**JASMINE AMIRI,** SENIOR EDITOR

**SHAWNA GORE,** SENIOR EDITOR

**AMANDA MEADOWS,** SENIOR EDITOR

**ROBERT MEYERS,** SENIOR EDITOR, LICENSING

**GRACE BORNHOFT,** EDITOR

**ZACK SOTO,** EDITOR

**CHRIS CERASI,** EDITORIAL COORDINATOR

**STEVE ELLIS,** VICE PRESIDENT OF GAMES

**BEN EISNER,** GAME DEVELOPER

**MICHELLE NGUYEN,** EXECUTIVE ASSISTANT

**JUNG LEE,** LOGISTICS COORDINATOR

**JOE NOZEMACK,** PUBLISHER EMERITUS

[adult swim]™

ONIPRESS.COM  LIONFORGE.COM

ADULTSWIM.COM
TWITTER.COM/RICKANDMORTY
FACEBOOK.COM/RICKANDMORTY

THIS VOLUME COLLECTS ISSUES #56–60
OF THE ONI PRESS SERIES *RICK AND MORTY*.

FIRST EDITION: JANUARY 2021

ISBN 978-1-62010-873-4
EISBN 978-1-62010-874-1
ONI EXCLUSIVE ISBN 978-1-62010-894-9

RICK AND MORTY™, VOLUME TWELVE, TKTKTK 2021. PUBLISHED BY ONI-LION FORGE PUBLISHING GROUP, LLC, 1319 SE MARTIN LUTHER KING JR. BLVD., SUITE 240, PORTLAND, OR 97214. RICK AND MORTY, ADULT SWIM, THE LOGOS, AND ALL RELATED CHARACTERS AND ELEMENTS ARE ™ OF AND © 2021 CARTOON NETWORK. ALL RIGHTS RESERVED. ONI PRESS LOGO AND ICON ARE ™ & © 2021 ONI PRESS, INC. ALL RIGHTS RESERVED. ONI PRESS LOGO AND ICON ARTWORK CREATED BY KEITH A. WOOD. THE EVENTS, INSTITUTIONS, AND CHARACTERS PRESENTED IN THIS BOOK ARE FICTIONAL. ANY RESEMBLANCE TO ACTUAL PERSONS, LIVING OR DEAD, IS PURELY COINCIDENTAL. NO PORTION OF THIS PUBLICATION MAY BE REPRODUCED, BY ANY MEANS, WITHOUT THE EXPRESS WRITTEN PERMISSION OF THE COPYRIGHT HOLDERS.

PRINTED IN CHINA.

LIBRARY OF CONGRESS CONTROL NUMBER: 2015940219

1 2 3 4 5 6 7 8 9 10

SPECIAL THANKS TO JUSTIN ROILAND, DAN HARMON, MARISA MARIONAKIS, ELYSE SALAZAR, MIKE MENDEL, JANET NO, AND MEAGAN BIRNEY.

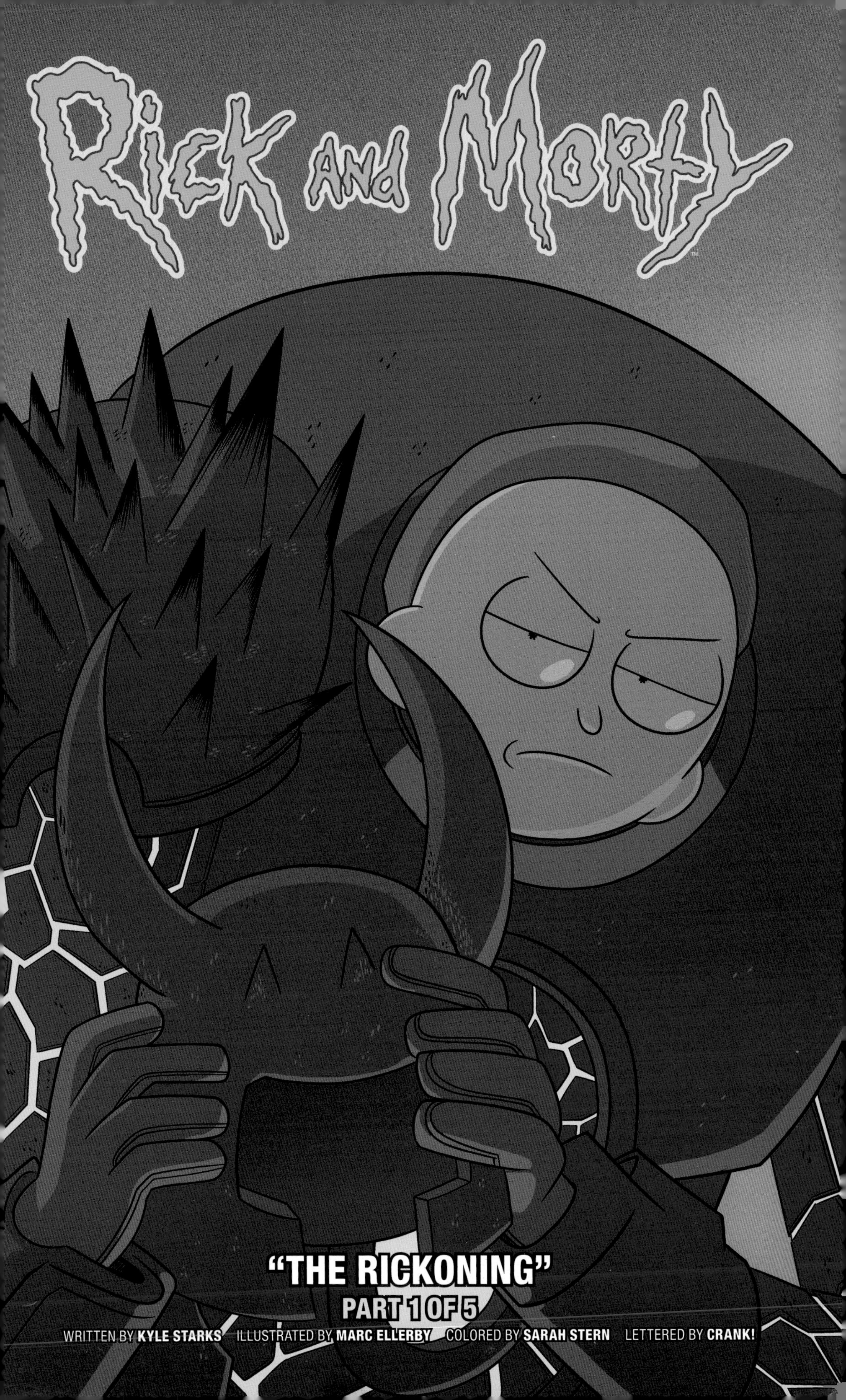
Rick and Morty
"THE RICKONING"
PART 1 OF 5
WRITTEN BY KYLE STARKS ILLUSTRATED BY MARC ELLERBY COLORED BY SARAH STERN LETTERED BY CRANK!

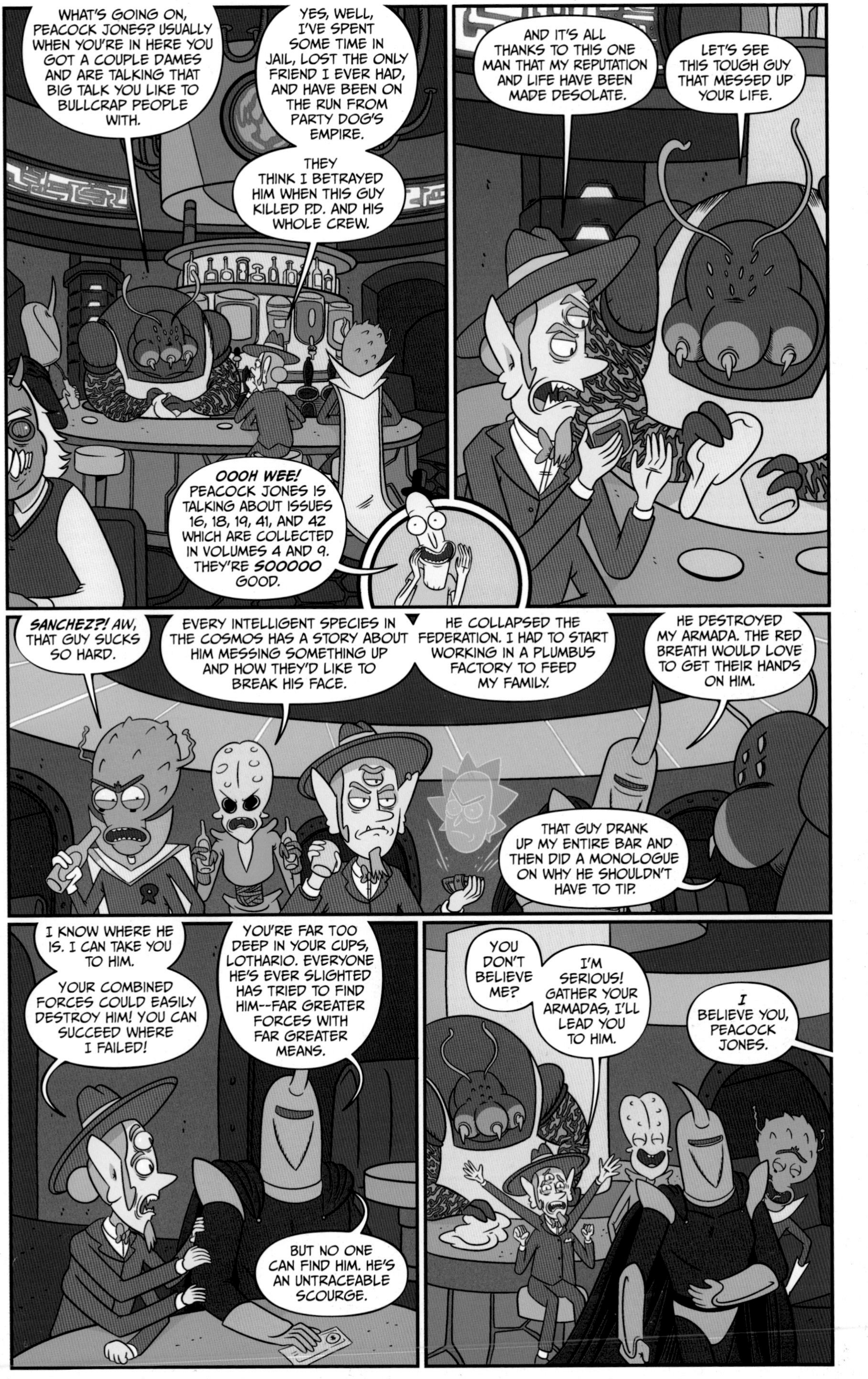

WHAT'S GOING ON, PEACOCK JONES? USUALLY WHEN YOU'RE IN HERE YOU GOT A COUPLE DAMES AND ARE TALKING THAT BIG TALK YOU LIKE TO BULLCRAP PEOPLE WITH.
YES, WELL, I'VE SPENT SOME TIME IN JAIL, LOST THE ONLY FRIEND I EVER HAD, AND HAVE BEEN ON THE RUN FROM PARTY DOG'S EMPIRE.
THEY THINK I BETRAYED HIM WHEN THIS GUY KILLED P.D. AND HIS WHOLE CREW.
OOOH WEE! PEACOCK JONES IS TALKING ABOUT ISSUES 16, 18, 19, 41, AND 42 WHICH ARE COLLECTED IN VOLUMES 4 AND 9. THEY'RE SOOOOO GOOD.
AND IT'S ALL THANKS TO THIS ONE MAN THAT MY REPUTATION AND LIFE HAVE BEEN MADE DESOLATE.
LET'S SEE THIS TOUGH GUY THAT MESSED UP YOUR LIFE.
SANCHEZ?! AW, THAT GUY SUCKS SO HARD.
EVERY INTELLIGENT SPECIES IN THE COSMOS HAS A STORY ABOUT HIM MESSING SOMETHING UP AND HOW THEY'D LIKE TO BREAK HIS FACE.
HE COLLAPSED THE FEDERATION. I HAD TO START WORKING IN A PLUMBUS FACTORY TO FEED MY FAMILY.
HE DESTROYED MY ARMADA. THE RED BREATH WOULD LOVE TO GET THEIR HANDS ON HIM.
THAT GUY DRANK UP MY ENTIRE BAR AND THEN DID A MONOLOGUE ON WHY HE SHOULDN'T HAVE TO TIP.
I KNOW WHERE HE IS. I CAN TAKE YOU TO HIM.
YOUR COMBINED FORCES COULD EASILY DESTROY HIM! YOU CAN SUCCEED WHERE I FAILED!
YOU'RE FAR TOO DEEP IN YOUR CUPS, LOTHARIO. EVERYONE HE'S EVER SLIGHTED HAS TRIED TO FIND HIM--FAR GREATER FORCES WITH FAR GREATER MEANS.
BUT NO ONE CAN FIND HIM. HE'S AN UNTRACEABLE SCOURGE.
YOU DON'T BELIEVE ME?
I'M SERIOUS! GATHER YOUR ARMADAS, I'LL LEAD YOU TO HIM.
I BELIEVE YOU, PEACOCK JONES.

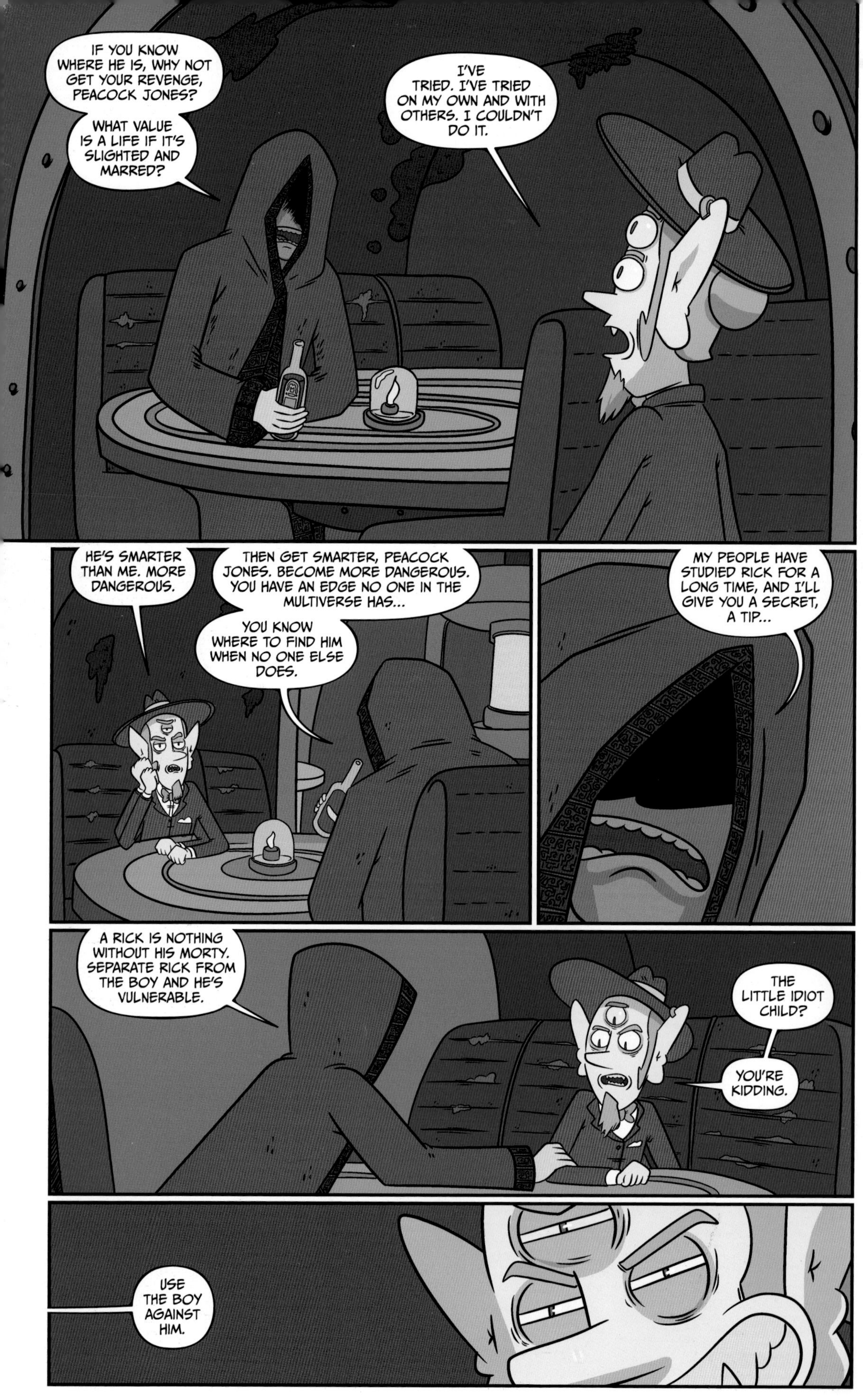
IF YOU KNOW WHERE HE IS, WHY NOT GET YOUR REVENGE, PEACOCK JONES?
WHAT VALUE IS A LIFE IF IT'S SLIGHTED AND MARRED?
I'VE TRIED. I'VE TRIED ON MY OWN AND WITH OTHERS. I COULDN'T DO IT.
HE'S SMARTER THAN ME. MORE DANGEROUS.
THEN GET SMARTER, PEACOCK JONES. BECOME MORE DANGEROUS. YOU HAVE AN EDGE NO ONE IN THE MULTIVERSE HAS...
YOU KNOW WHERE TO FIND HIM WHEN NO ONE ELSE DOES.
MY PEOPLE HAVE STUDIED RICK FOR A LONG TIME, AND I'LL GIVE YOU A SECRET, A TIP...
A RICK IS NOTHING WITHOUT HIS MORTY. SEPARATE RICK FROM THE BOY AND HE'S VULNERABLE.
THE LITTLE IDIOT CHILD?
YOU'RE KIDDING.
USE THE BOY AGAINST HIM.

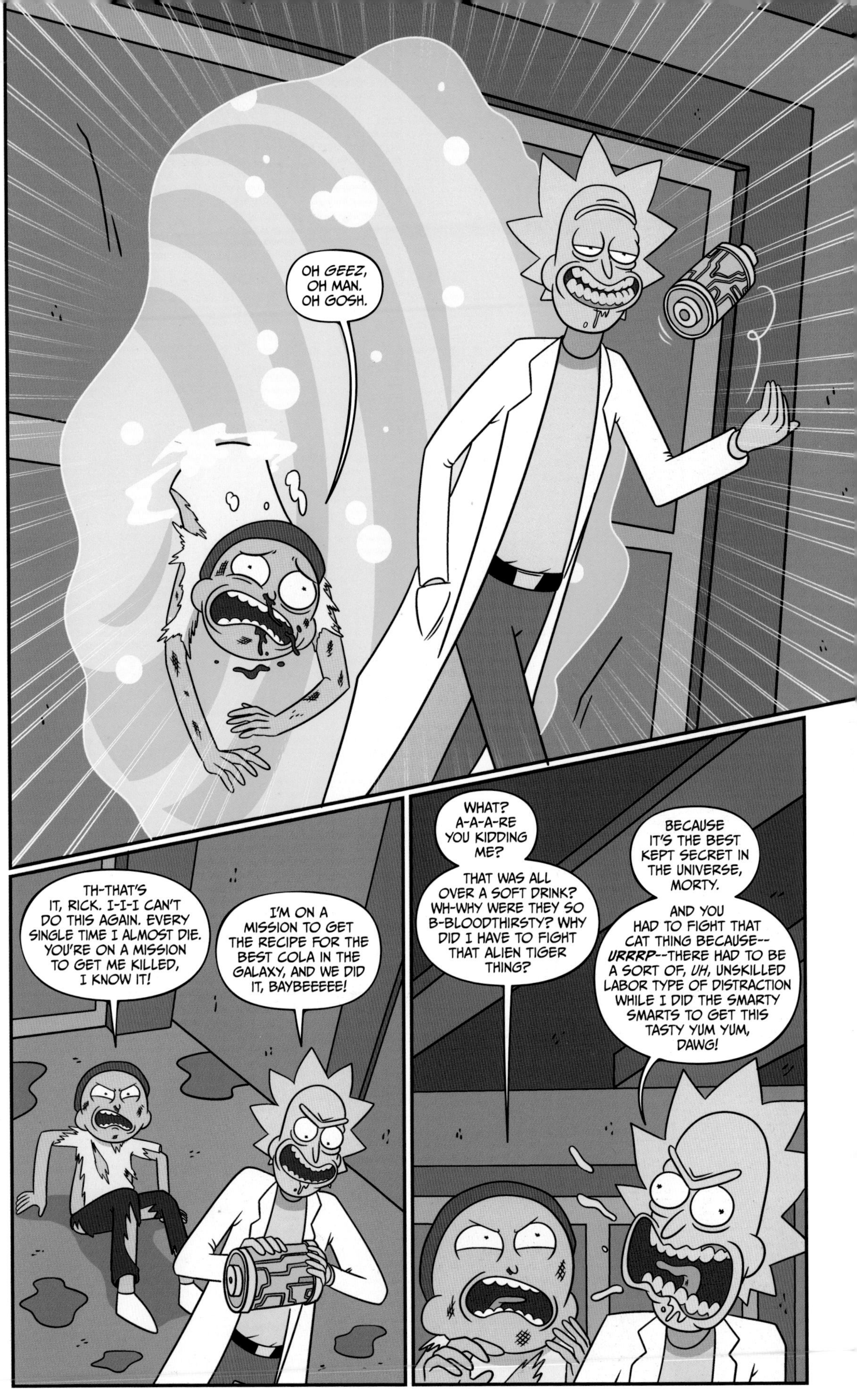

OH GEEZ, OH MAN. OH GOSH.
TH-THAT'S IT, RICK. I-I-I CAN'T DO THIS AGAIN. EVERY SINGLE TIME I ALMOST DIE. YOU'RE ON A MISSION TO GET ME KILLED, I KNOW IT!
I'M ON A MISSION TO GET THE RECIPE FOR THE BEST COLA IN THE GALAXY, AND WE DID IT, BAYBEEEEE!
WHAT? A-A-A-RE YOU KIDDING ME?
THAT WAS ALL OVER A SOFT DRINK? WH-WHY WERE THEY SO B-BLOODTHIRSTY? WHY DID I HAVE TO FIGHT THAT ALIEN TIGER THING?
BECAUSE IT'S THE BEST KEPT SECRET IN THE UNIVERSE, MORTY.
AND YOU HAD TO FIGHT THAT CAT THING BECAUSE-- *URRRP*--THERE HAD TO BE A SORT OF, *UH*, UNSKILLED LABOR TYPE OF DISTRACTION WHILE I DID THE SMARTY SMARTS TO GET THIS TASTY YUM YUM, DAWG!

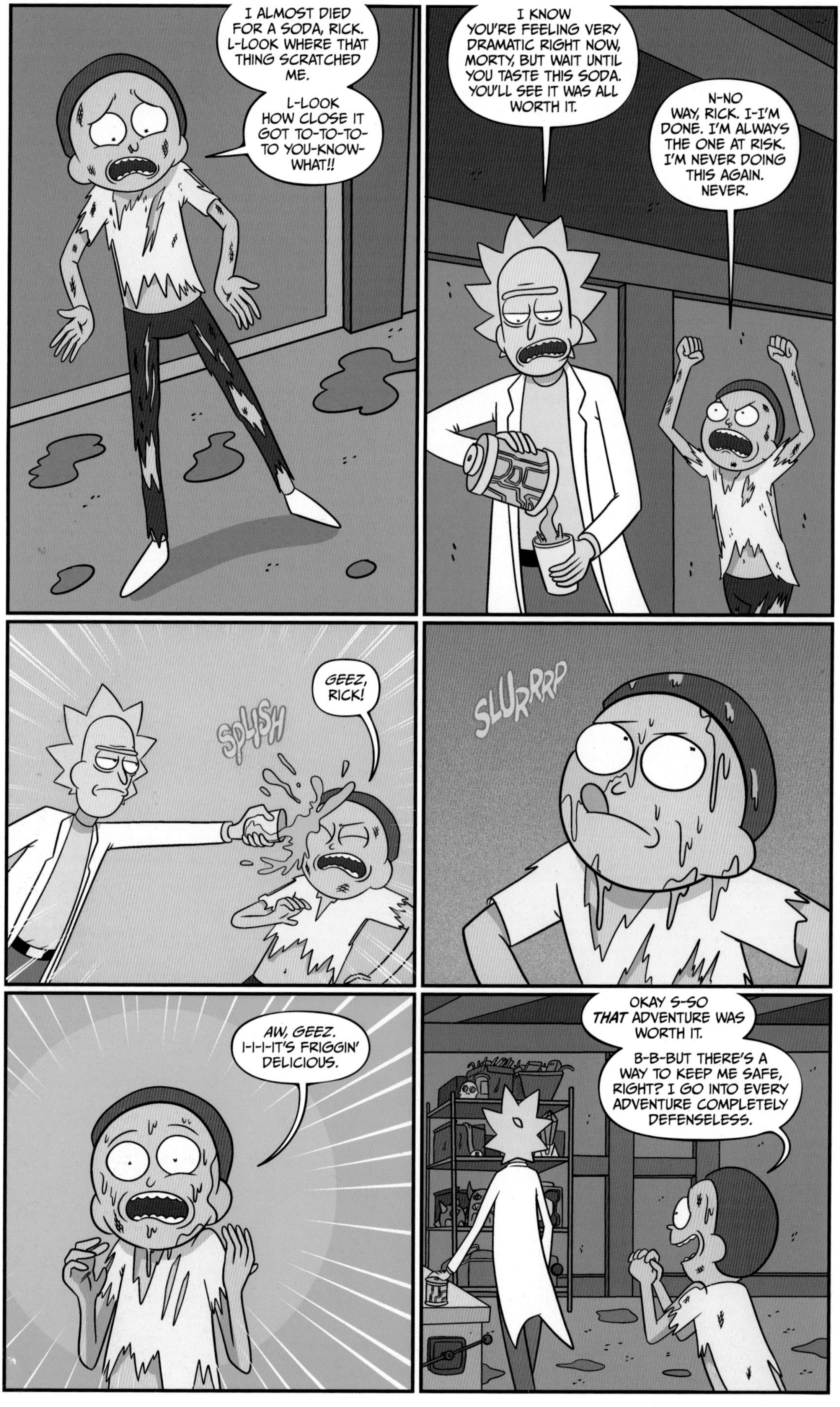
I ALMOST DIED FOR A SODA, RICK. L-LOOK WHERE THAT THING SCRATCHED ME.
L-LOOK HOW CLOSE IT GOT TO-TO-TO-TO YOU-KNOW-WHAT!!
I KNOW YOU'RE FEELING VERY DRAMATIC RIGHT NOW, MORTY, BUT WAIT UNTIL YOU TASTE THIS SODA. YOU'LL SEE IT WAS ALL WORTH IT.
N-NO WAY, RICK. I-I'M DONE. I'M ALWAYS THE ONE AT RISK. I'M NEVER DOING THIS AGAIN. NEVER.
SPLISH
GEEZ, RICK!
SLURRRP
AW, GEEZ. I-I-I-IT'S FRIGGIN' DELICIOUS.
OKAY S-SO *THAT* ADVENTURE WAS WORTH IT.
B-B-BUT THERE'S A WAY TO KEEP ME SAFE, RIGHT? I GO INTO EVERY ADVENTURE COMPLETELY DEFENSELESS.

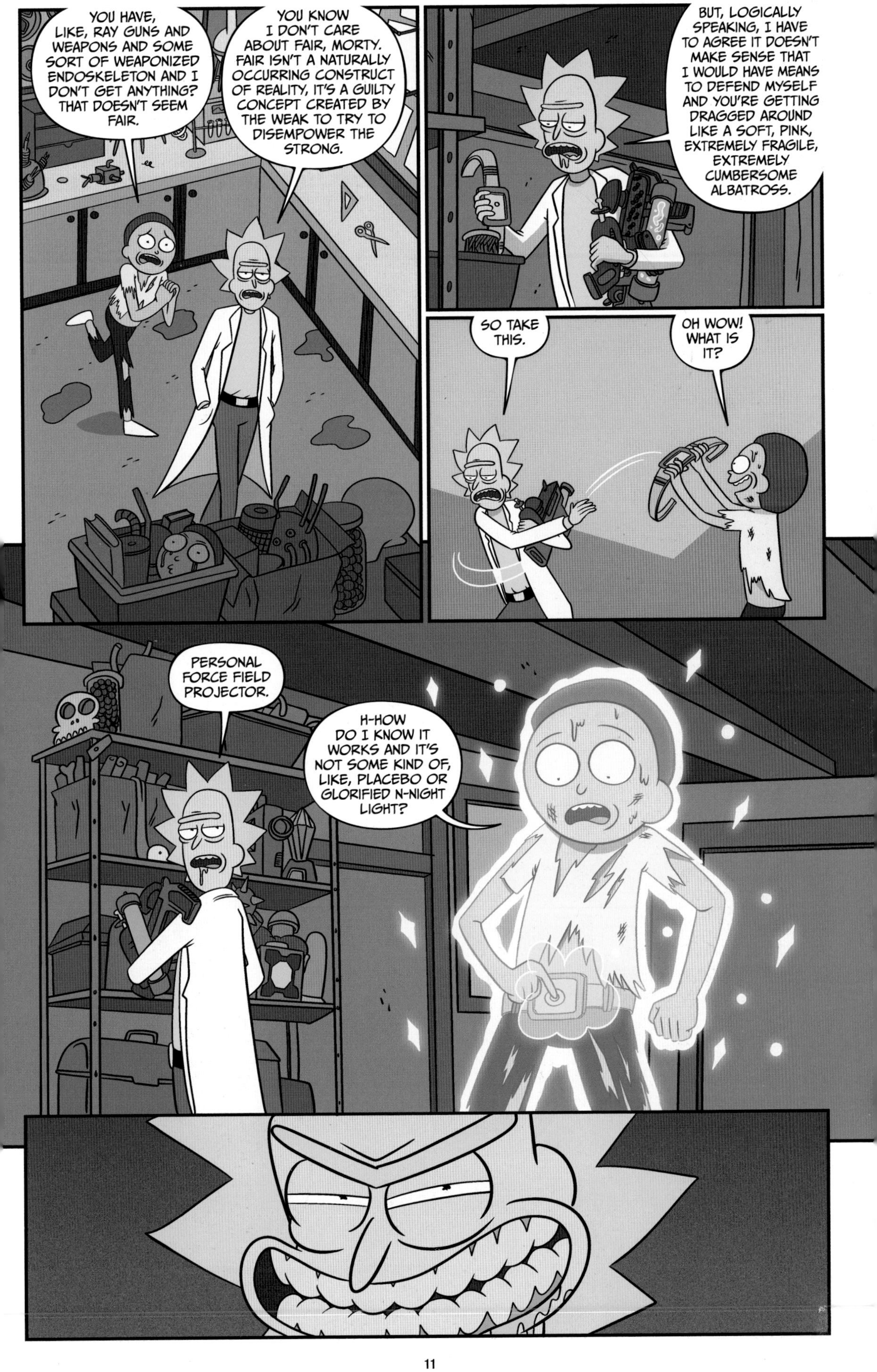
YOU HAVE, LIKE, RAY GUNS AND WEAPONS AND SOME SORT OF WEAPONIZED ENDOSKELETON AND I DON'T GET ANYTHING? THAT DOESN'T SEEM FAIR.
YOU KNOW I DON'T CARE ABOUT FAIR, MORTY. FAIR ISN'T A NATURALLY OCCURRING CONSTRUCT OF REALITY, IT'S A GUILTY CONCEPT CREATED BY THE WEAK TO TRY TO DISEMPOWER THE STRONG.
BUT, LOGICALLY SPEAKING, I HAVE TO AGREE IT DOESN'T MAKE SENSE THAT I WOULD HAVE MEANS TO DEFEND MYSELF AND YOU'RE GETTING DRAGGED AROUND LIKE A SOFT, PINK, EXTREMELY FRAGILE, EXTREMELY CUMBERSOME ALBATROSS.
SO TAKE THIS.
OH WOW! WHAT IS IT?
PERSONAL FORCE FIELD PROJECTOR.
H-HOW DO I KNOW IT WORKS AND IT'S NOT SOME KIND OF, LIKE, PLACEBO OR GLORIFIED N-NIGHT LIGHT?

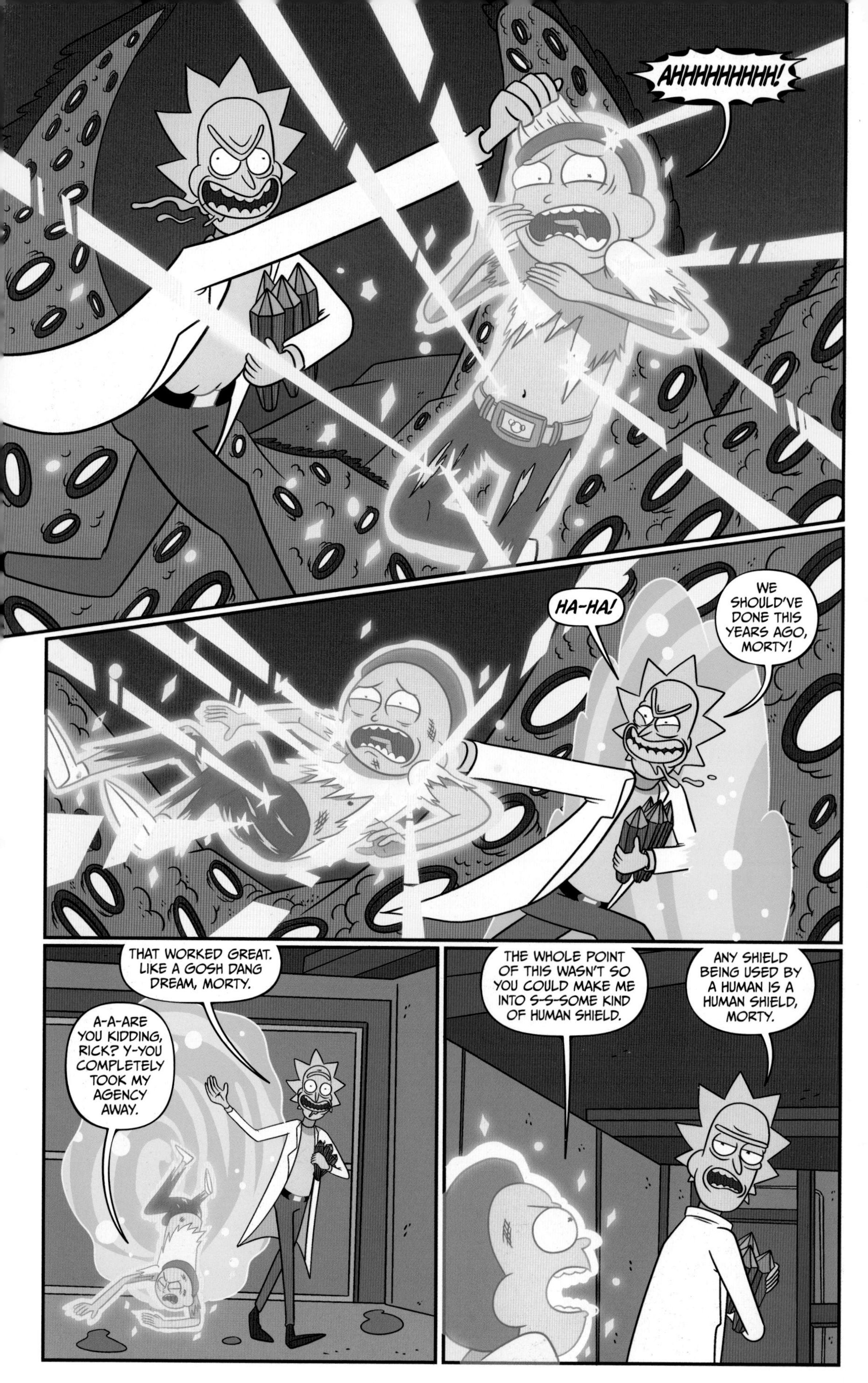
AHHHHHHHHH!
HA-HA!
WE SHOULD'VE DONE THIS YEARS AGO, MORTY!
THAT WORKED GREAT. LIKE A GOSH DANG DREAM, MORTY.
A-A-ARE YOU KIDDING, RICK? Y-YOU COMPLETELY TOOK MY AGENCY AWAY.
THE WHOLE POINT OF THIS WASN'T SO YOU COULD MAKE ME INTO S-S-SOME KIND OF HUMAN SHIELD.
ANY SHIELD BEING USED BY A HUMAN IS A HUMAN SHIELD, MORTY.

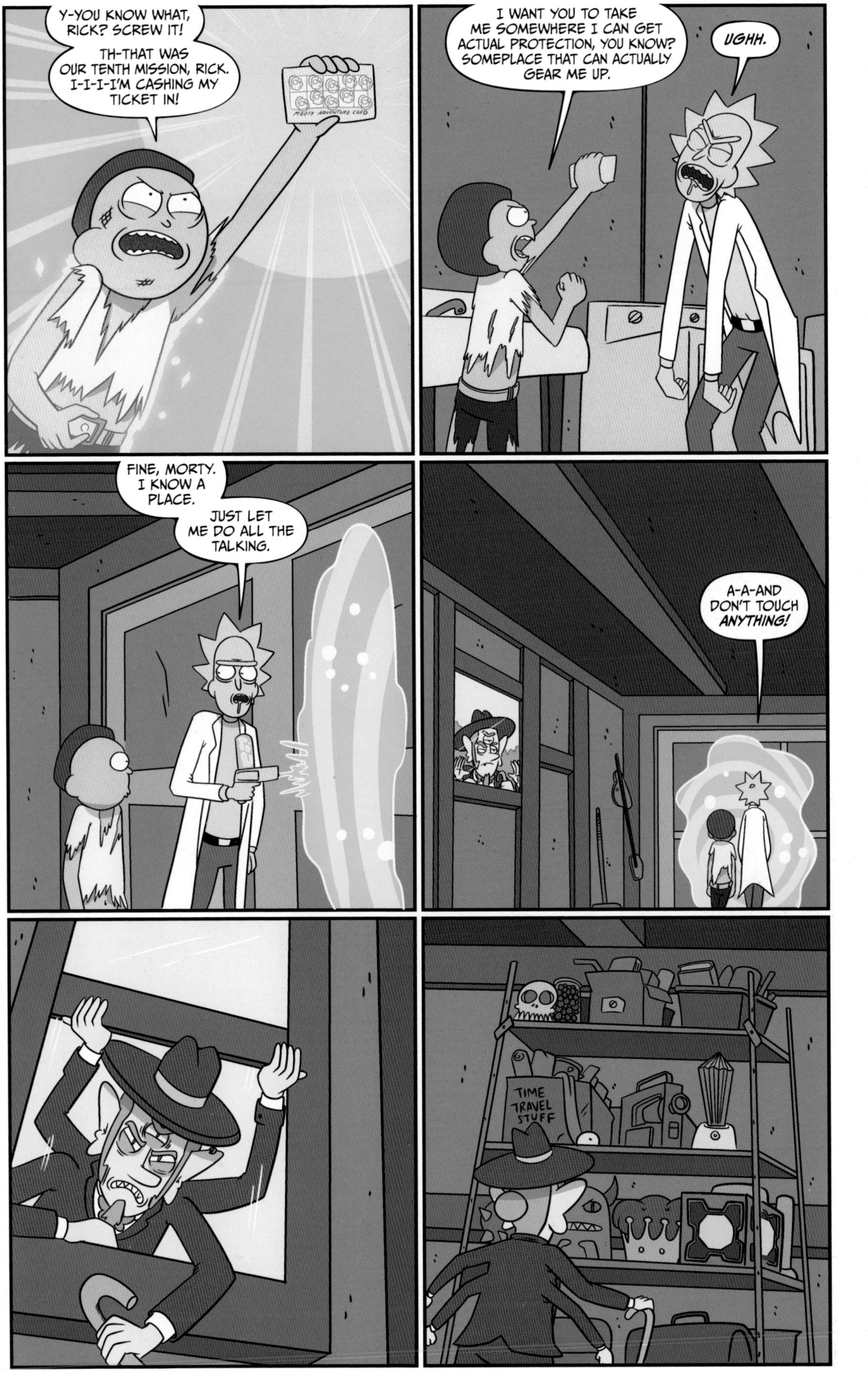
Y-YOU KNOW WHAT, RICK? SCREW IT!
TH-THAT WAS OUR TENTH MISSION, RICK. I-I-I-I'M CASHING MY TICKET IN!
MORTY ADVENTURE CARD
I WANT YOU TO TAKE ME SOMEWHERE I CAN GET ACTUAL PROTECTION, YOU KNOW? SOMEPLACE THAT CAN ACTUALLY GEAR ME UP.
UGHH.
FINE, MORTY. I KNOW A PLACE.
JUST LET ME DO ALL THE TALKING.
A-A-AND DON'T TOUCH ANYTHING!
TIME TRAVEL STUFF

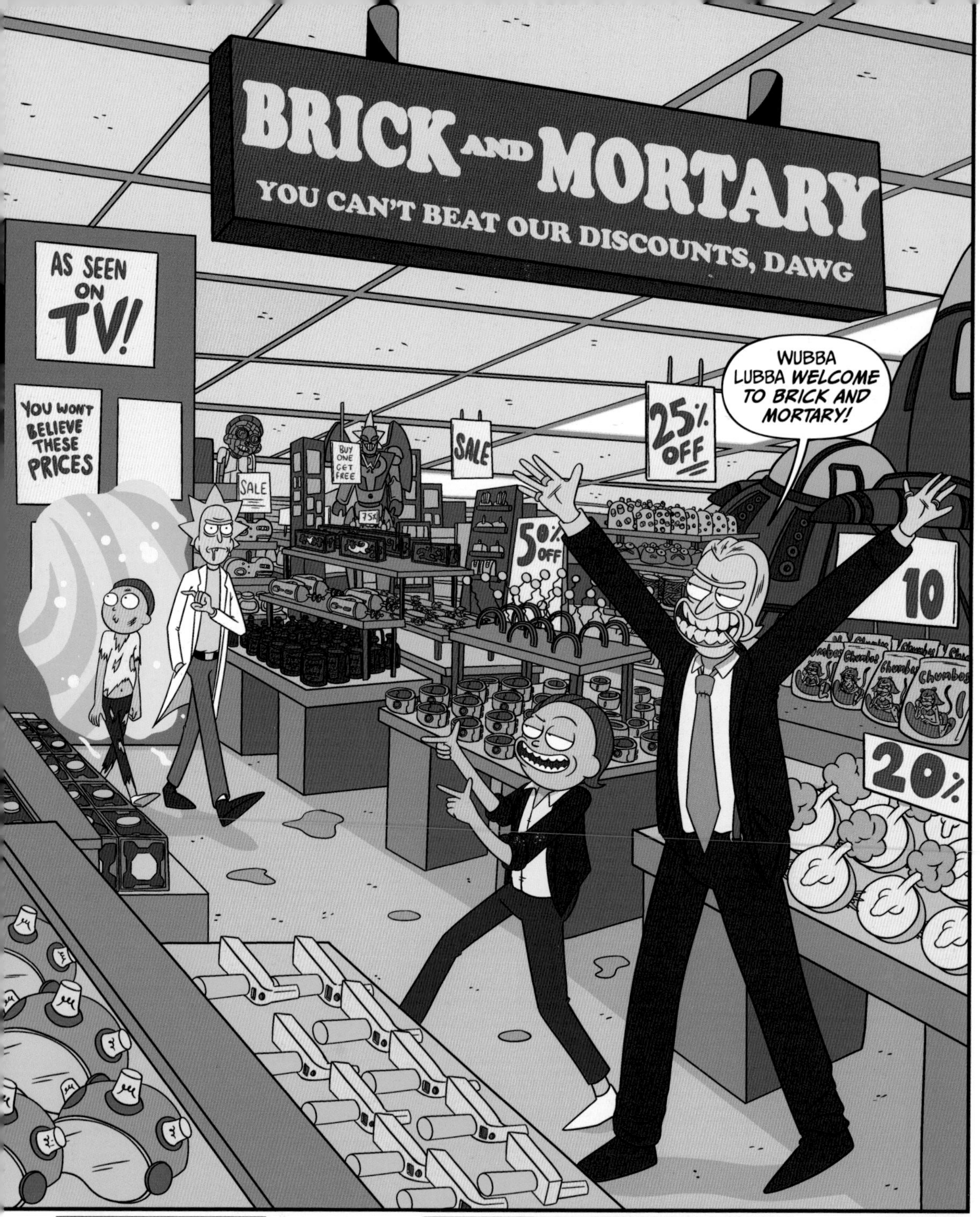
BRICK AND MORTARY
YOU CAN'T BEAT OUR DISCOUNTS, DAWG
AS SEEN ON TV!
YOU WON'T BELIEVE THESE PRICES
SALE
BUY ONE GET FREE
SALE
25% OFF
50% OFF
10
20%
WUBBA LUBBA *WELCOME TO BRICK AND MORTARY!*

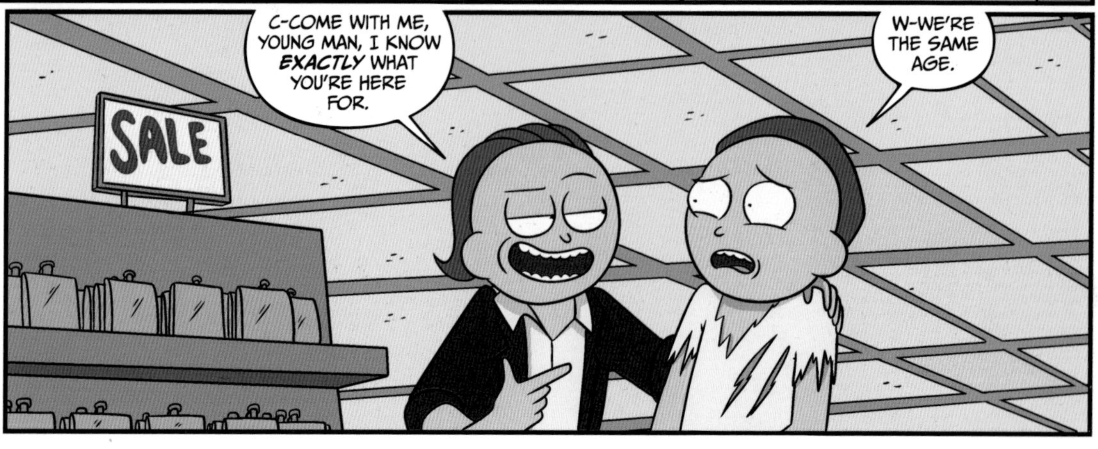
SALE
C-COME WITH ME, YOUNG MAN, I KNOW *EXACTLY* WHAT YOU'RE HERE FOR.
W-WE'RE THE SAME AGE.

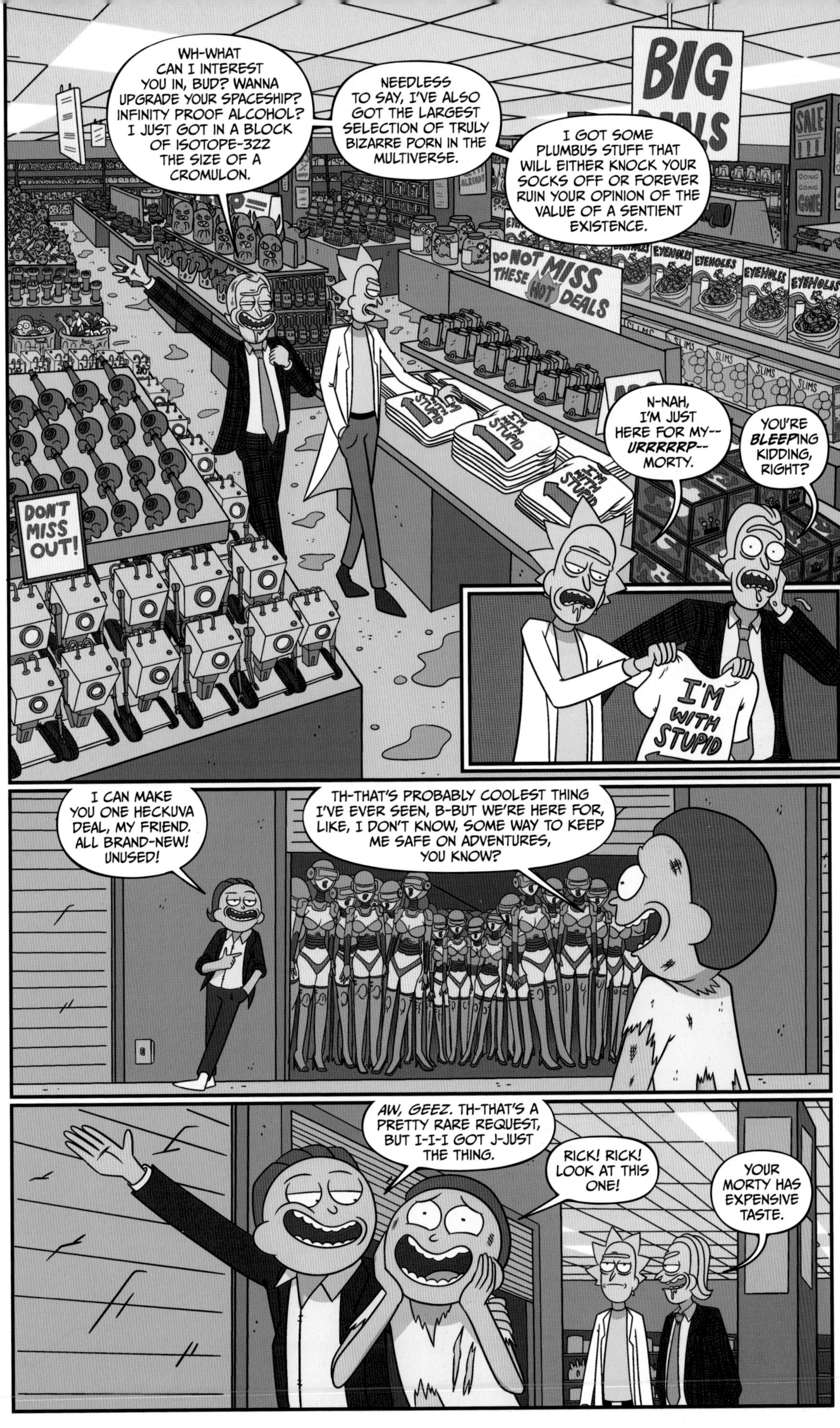
WH-WHAT CAN I INTEREST YOU IN, BUD? WANNA UPGRADE YOUR SPACESHIP? INFINITY PROOF ALCOHOL? I JUST GOT IN A BLOCK OF ISOTOPE-322 THE SIZE OF A CROMULON.
NEEDLESS TO SAY, I'VE ALSO GOT THE LARGEST SELECTION OF TRULY BIZARRE PORN IN THE MULTIVERSE.
I GOT SOME PLUMBUS STUFF THAT WILL EITHER KNOCK YOUR SOCKS OFF OR FOREVER RUIN YOUR OPINION OF THE VALUE OF A SENTIENT EXISTENCE.
BIG
DO NOT MISS THESE HOT DEALS
EYEHOLES
DON'T MISS OUT!
I'M WITH STUPID
N-NAH, I'M JUST HERE FOR MY-- *URRRRRP*-- MORTY.
YOU'RE *BLEEP*ING KIDDING, RIGHT?
I'M WITH STUPID
I CAN MAKE YOU ONE HECKUVA DEAL, MY FRIEND. ALL BRAND-NEW! UNUSED!
TH-THAT'S PROBABLY COOLEST THING I'VE EVER SEEN, B-BUT WE'RE HERE FOR, LIKE, I DON'T KNOW, SOME WAY TO KEEP ME SAFE ON ADVENTURES, YOU KNOW?
*AW, GEEZ.* TH-THAT'S A PRETTY RARE REQUEST, BUT I-I-I GOT J-JUST THE THING.
RICK! RICK! LOOK AT THIS ONE!
YOUR MORTY HAS EXPENSIVE TASTE.

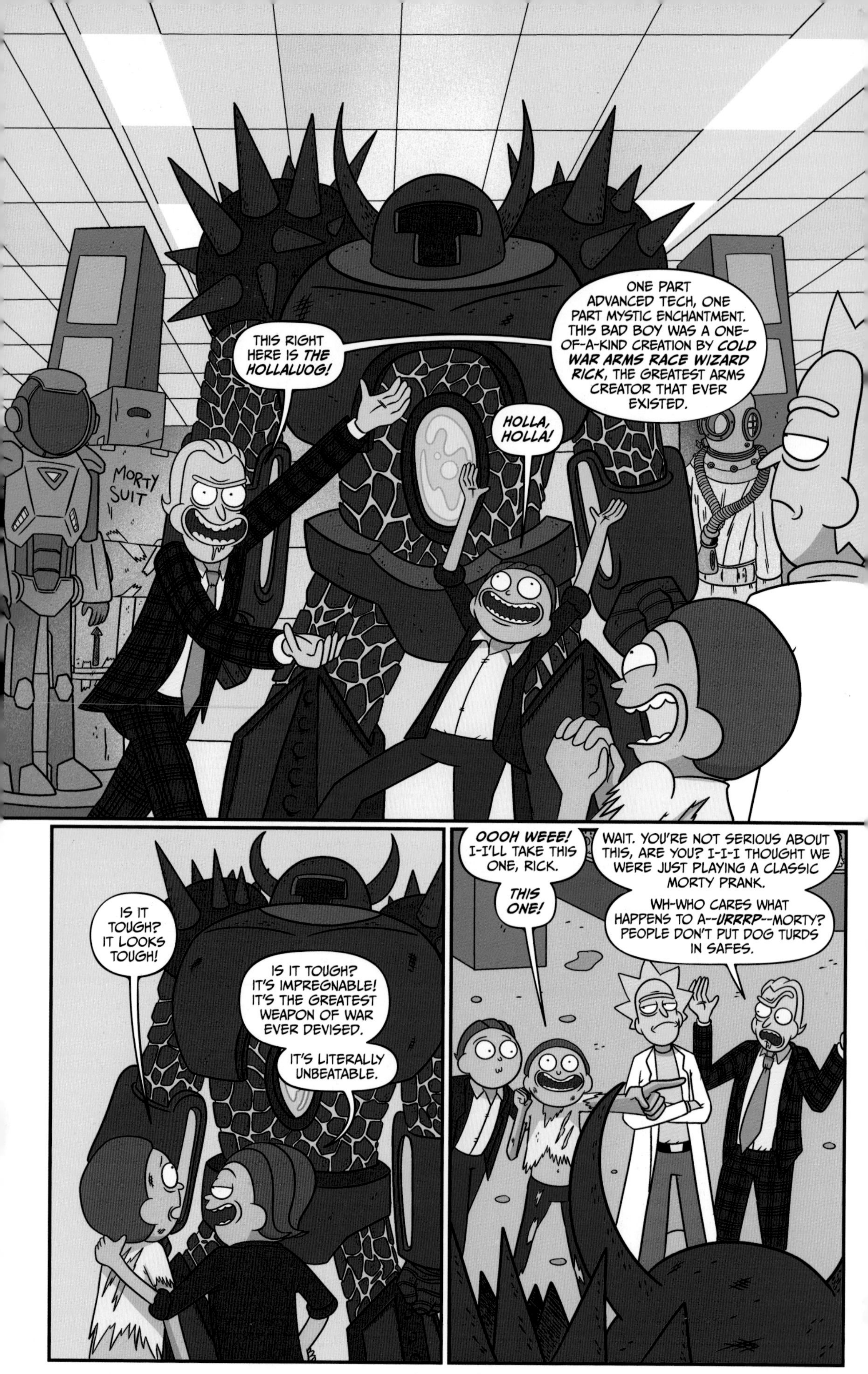
THIS RIGHT HERE IS *THE HOLLALUOG!*
ONE PART ADVANCED TECH, ONE PART MYSTIC ENCHANTMENT. THIS BAD BOY WAS A ONE-OF-A-KIND CREATION BY ***COLD WAR ARMS RACE WIZARD RICK***, THE GREATEST ARMS CREATOR THAT EVER EXISTED.
*HOLLA, HOLLA!*
MORTY SUIT
IS IT TOUGH? IT LOOKS TOUGH!
IS IT TOUGH? IT'S IMPREGNABLE! IT'S THE GREATEST WEAPON OF WAR EVER DEVISED.
IT'S LITERALLY UNBEATABLE.
***OOOH WEEE!*** I-I'LL TAKE THIS ONE, RICK.
*THIS ONE!*
WAIT. YOU'RE NOT SERIOUS ABOUT THIS, ARE YOU? I-I-I THOUGHT WE WERE JUST PLAYING A CLASSIC MORTY PRANK.
WH-WHO CARES WHAT HAPPENS TO A--***URRRP***--MORTY? PEOPLE DON'T PUT DOG TURDS IN SAFES.

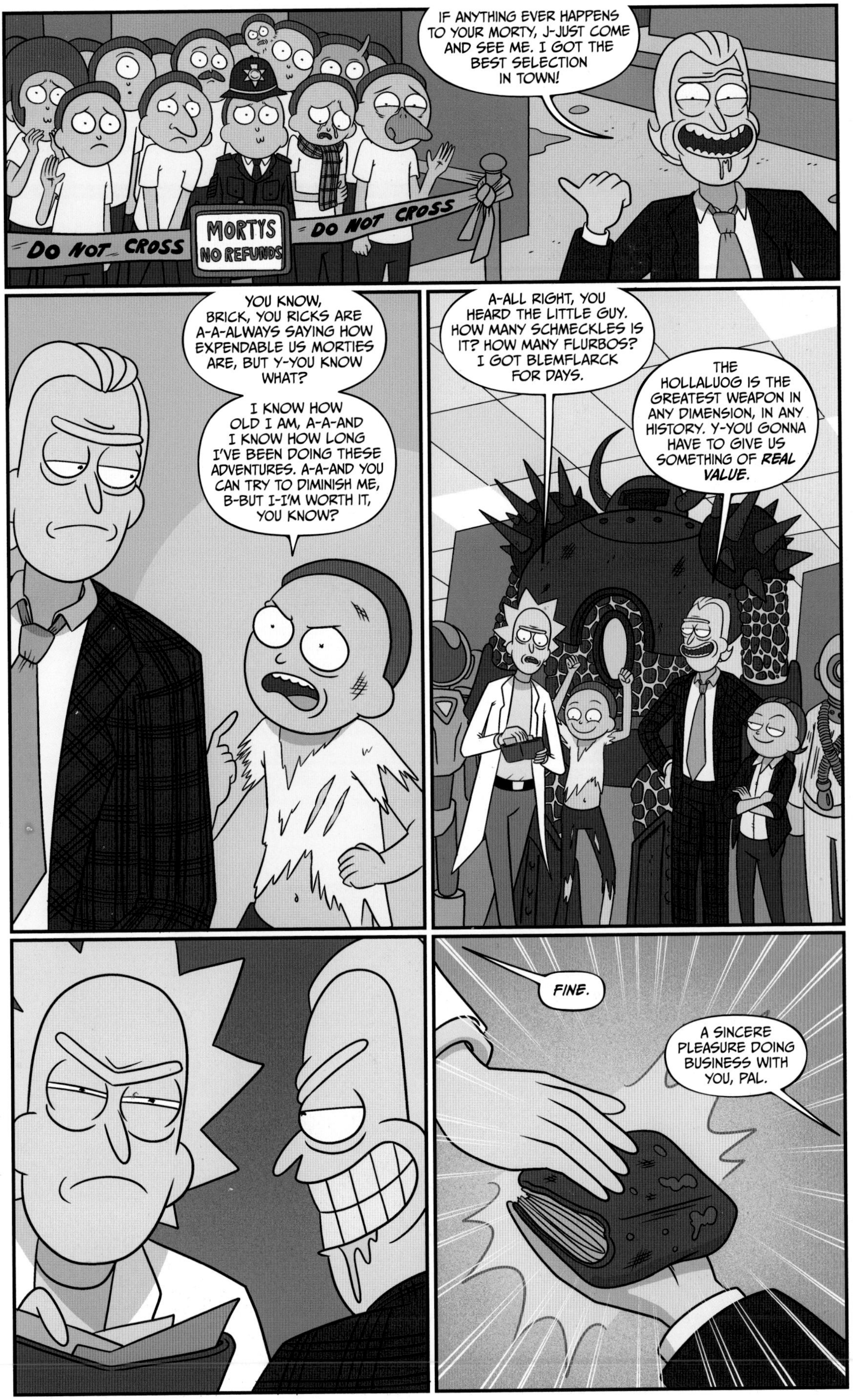
MORTYS NO REFUNDS
DO NOT CROSS
DO NOT CROSS
IF ANYTHING EVER HAPPENS TO YOUR MORTY, J-JUST COME AND SEE ME. I GOT THE BEST SELECTION IN TOWN!
YOU KNOW, BRICK, YOU RICKS ARE A-A-ALWAYS SAYING HOW EXPENDABLE US MORTIES ARE, BUT Y-YOU KNOW WHAT?
I KNOW HOW OLD I AM, A-A-AND I KNOW HOW LONG I'VE BEEN DOING THESE ADVENTURES. A-A-AND YOU CAN TRY TO DIMINISH ME, B-BUT I-I'M WORTH IT, YOU KNOW?
A-ALL RIGHT, YOU HEARD THE LITTLE GUY. HOW MANY SCHMECKLES IS IT? HOW MANY FLURBOS? I GOT BLEMFLARCK FOR DAYS.
THE HOLLALUOG IS THE GREATEST WEAPON IN ANY DIMENSION, IN ANY HISTORY. Y-YOU GONNA HAVE TO GIVE US SOMETHING OF *REAL VALUE*.
*FINE.*
A SINCERE PLEASURE DOING BUSINESS WITH YOU, PAL.

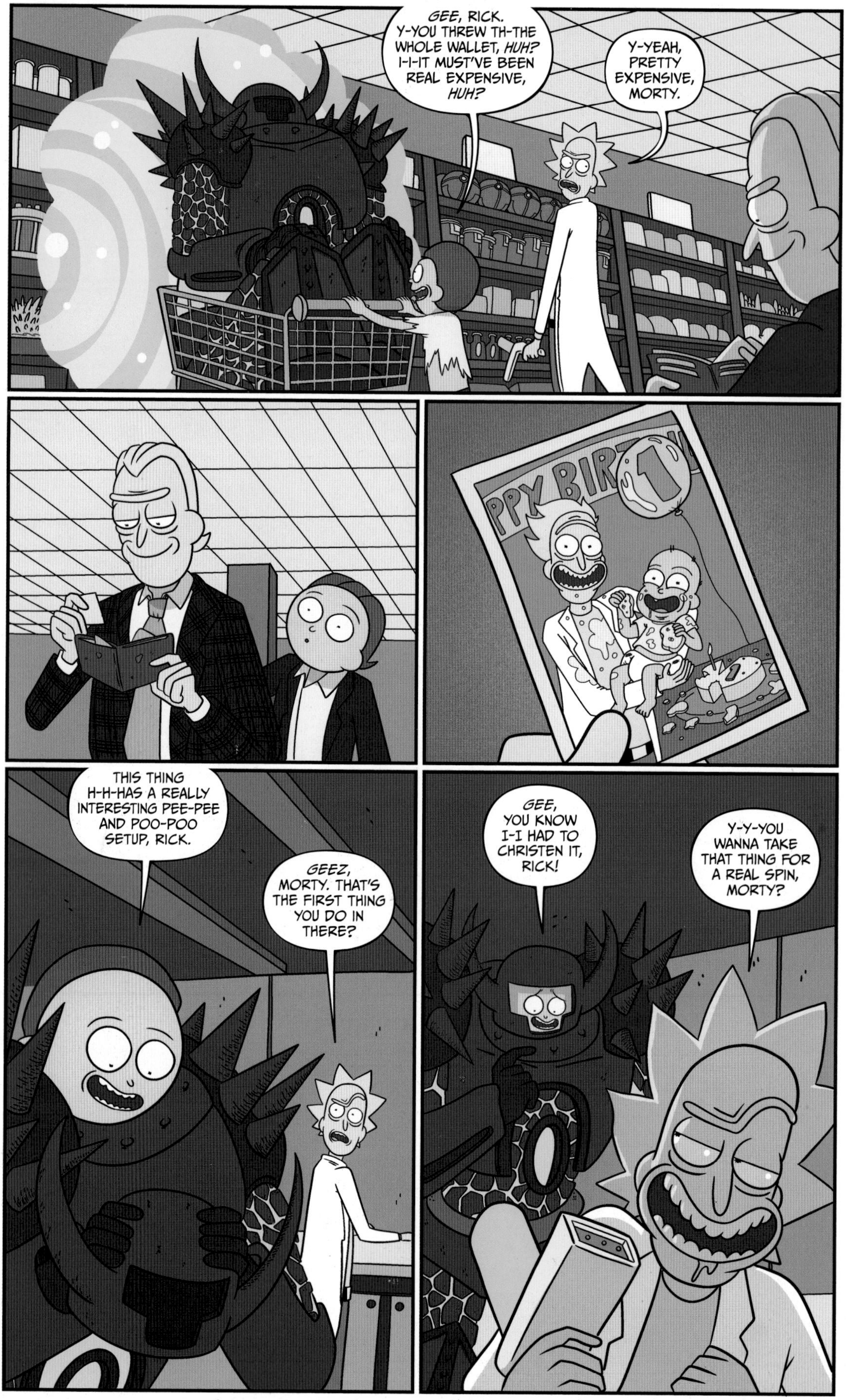
GEE, RICK. Y-YOU THREW TH-THE WHOLE WALLET, HUH? I-I-IT MUST'VE BEEN REAL EXPENSIVE, HUH?
Y-YEAH, PRETTY EXPENSIVE, MORTY.
THIS THING H-H-HAS A REALLY INTERESTING PEE-PEE AND POO-POO SETUP, RICK.
GEEZ, MORTY. THAT'S THE FIRST THING YOU DO IN THERE?
GEE, YOU KNOW I-I HAD TO CHRISTEN IT, RICK!
Y-Y-YOU WANNA TAKE THAT THING FOR A REAL SPIN, MORTY?

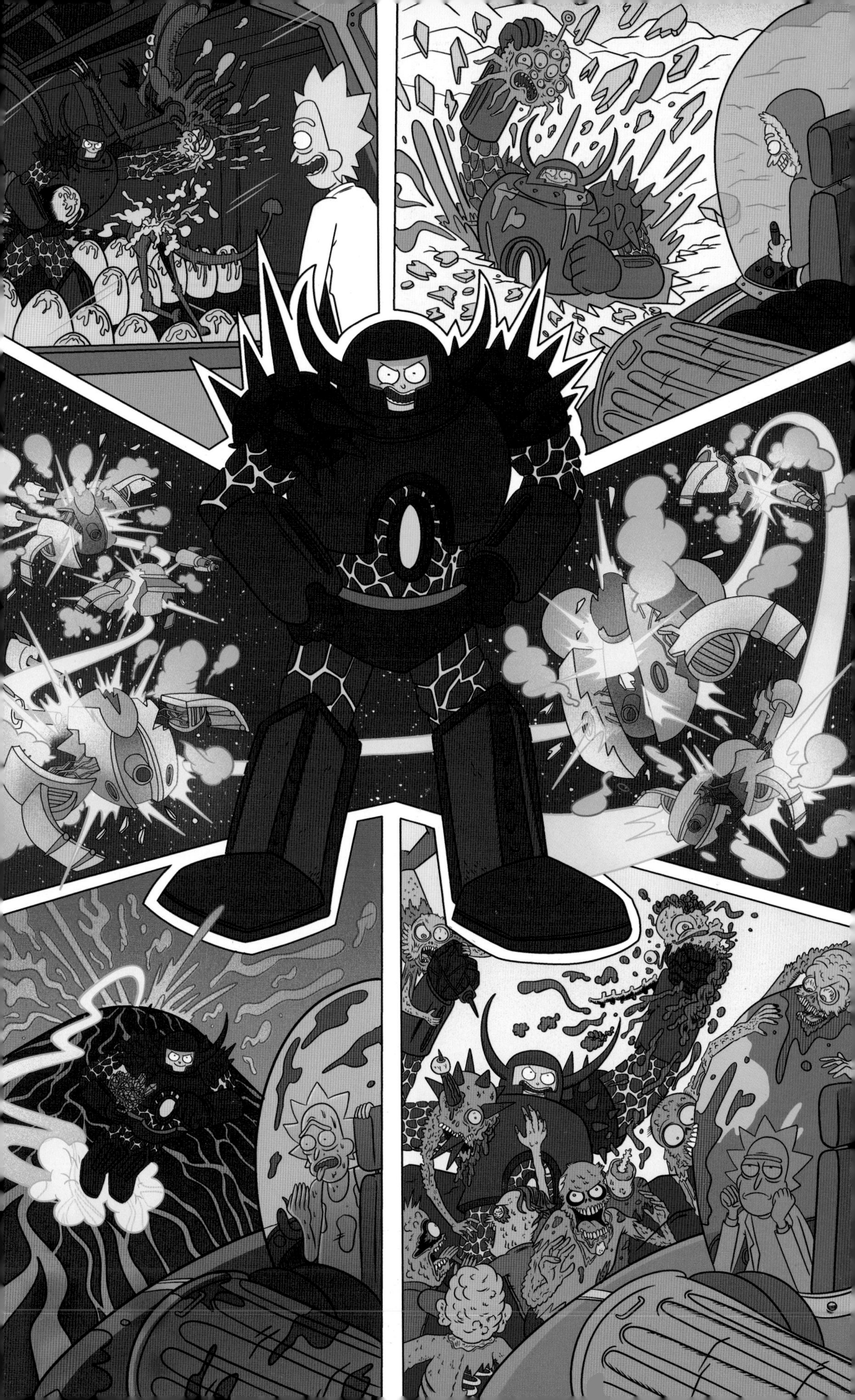

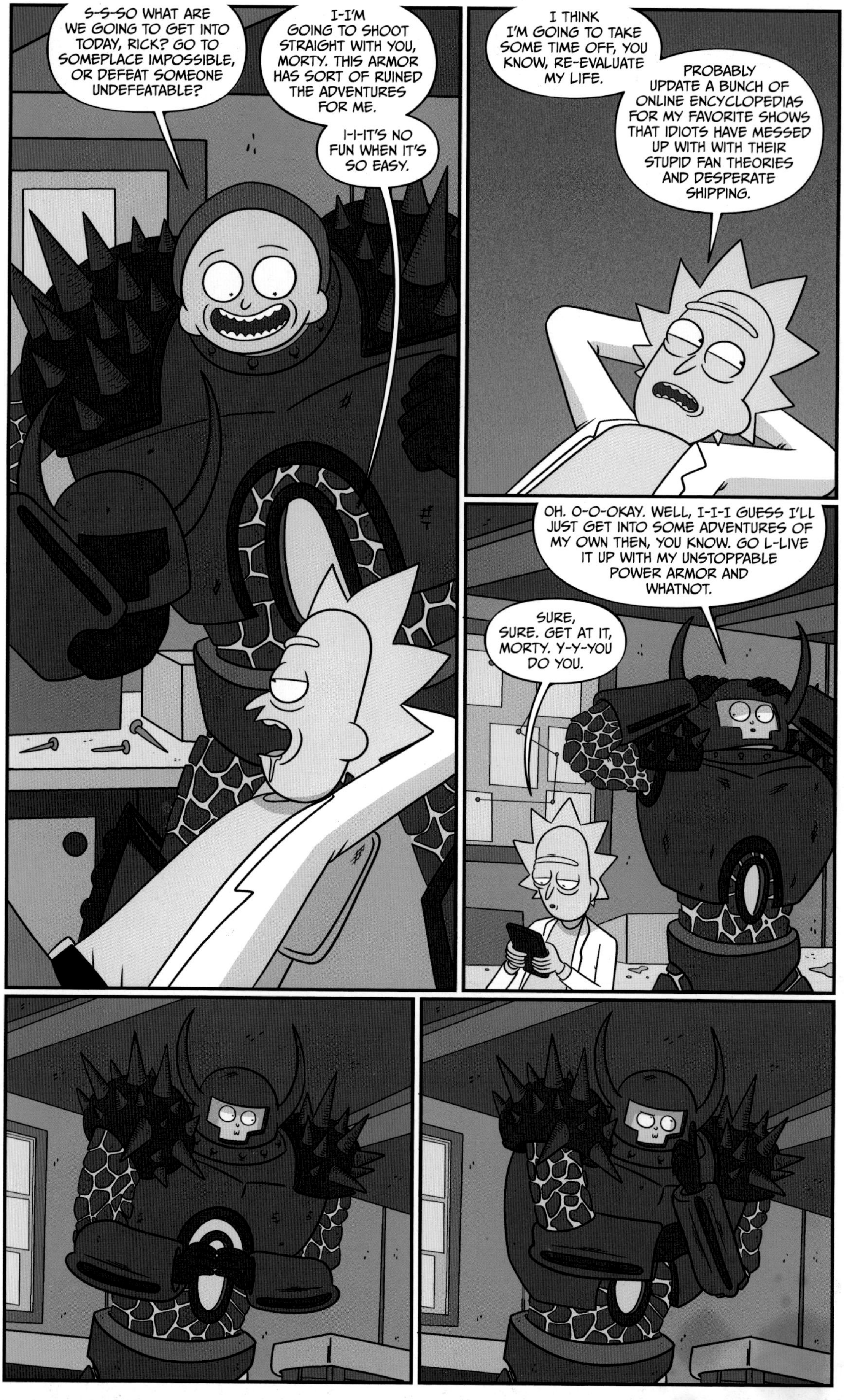
S-S-SO WHAT ARE WE GOING TO GET INTO TODAY, RICK? GO TO SOMEPLACE IMPOSSIBLE, OR DEFEAT SOMEONE UNDEFEATABLE?
I-I'M GOING TO SHOOT STRAIGHT WITH YOU, MORTY. THIS ARMOR HAS SORT OF RUINED THE ADVENTURES FOR ME.
I-I-IT'S NO FUN WHEN IT'S SO EASY.
I THINK I'M GOING TO TAKE SOME TIME OFF, YOU KNOW, RE-EVALUATE MY LIFE.
PROBABLY UPDATE A BUNCH OF ONLINE ENCYCLOPEDIAS FOR MY FAVORITE SHOWS THAT IDIOTS HAVE MESSED UP WITH WITH THEIR STUPID FAN THEORIES AND DESPERATE SHIPPING.
OH. O-O-OKAY. WELL, I-I-I GUESS I'LL JUST GET INTO SOME ADVENTURES OF MY OWN THEN, YOU KNOW. GO L-LIVE IT UP WITH MY UNSTOPPABLE POWER ARMOR AND WHATNOT.
SURE, SURE. GET AT IT, MORTY. Y-Y-YOU DO YOU.

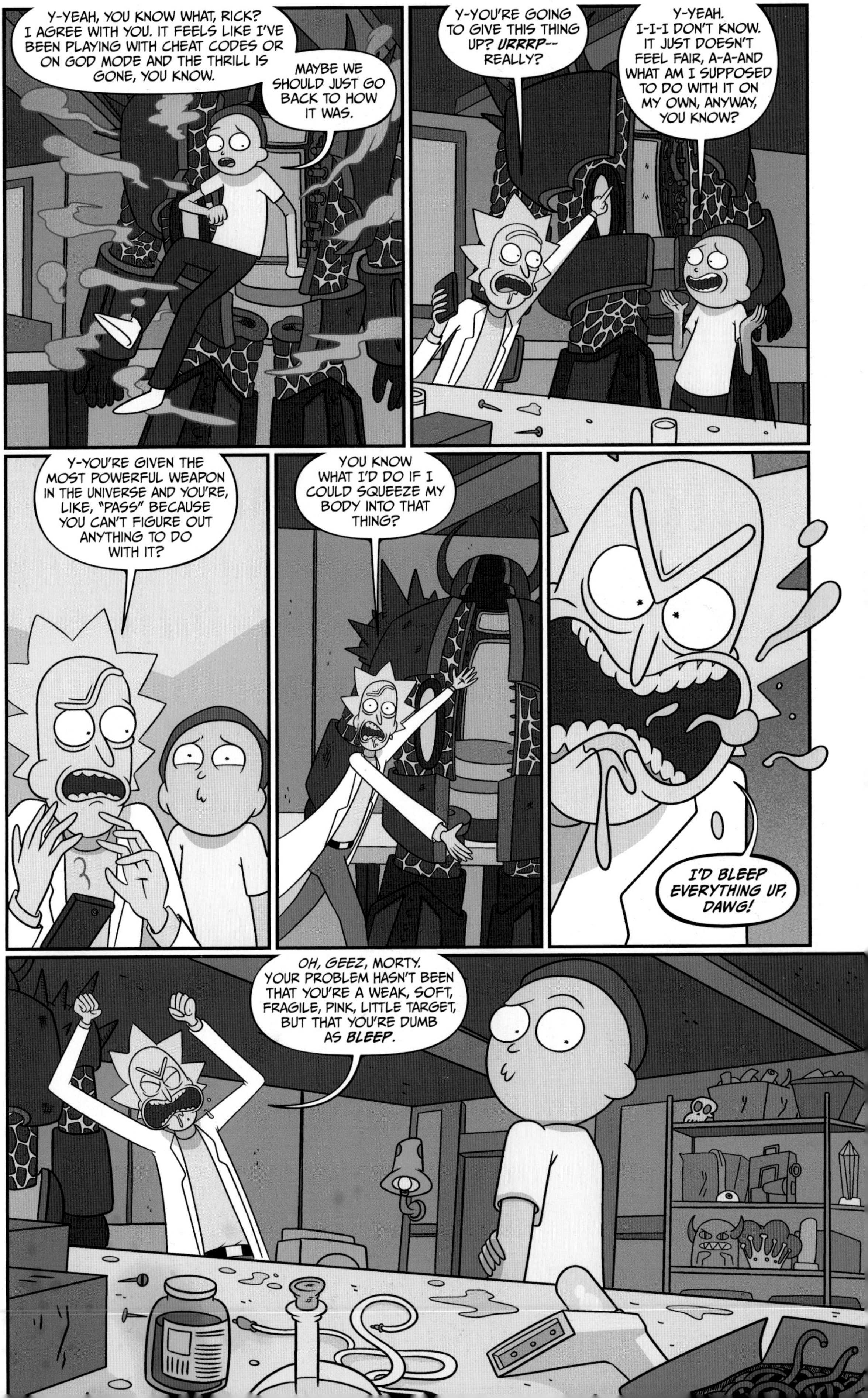
Y-YEAH, YOU KNOW WHAT, RICK? I AGREE WITH YOU. IT FEELS LIKE I'VE BEEN PLAYING WITH CHEAT CODES OR ON GOD MODE AND THE THRILL IS GONE, YOU KNOW.
MAYBE WE SHOULD JUST GO BACK TO HOW IT WAS.
Y-YOU'RE GOING TO GIVE THIS THING UP? URRRP-- REALLY?
Y-YEAH. I-I-I DON'T KNOW. IT JUST DOESN'T FEEL FAIR, A-A-AND WHAT AM I SUPPOSED TO DO WITH IT ON MY OWN, ANYWAY, YOU KNOW?
Y-YOU'RE GIVEN THE MOST POWERFUL WEAPON IN THE UNIVERSE AND YOU'RE, LIKE, "PASS" BECAUSE YOU CAN'T FIGURE OUT ANYTHING TO DO WITH IT?
YOU KNOW WHAT I'D DO IF I COULD SQUEEZE MY BODY INTO THAT THING?
I'D BLEEP EVERYTHING UP, DAWG!
OH, GEEZ, MORTY. YOUR PROBLEM HASN'T BEEN THAT YOU'RE A WEAK, SOFT, FRAGILE, PINK, LITTLE TARGET, BUT THAT YOU'RE DUMB AS BLEEP.

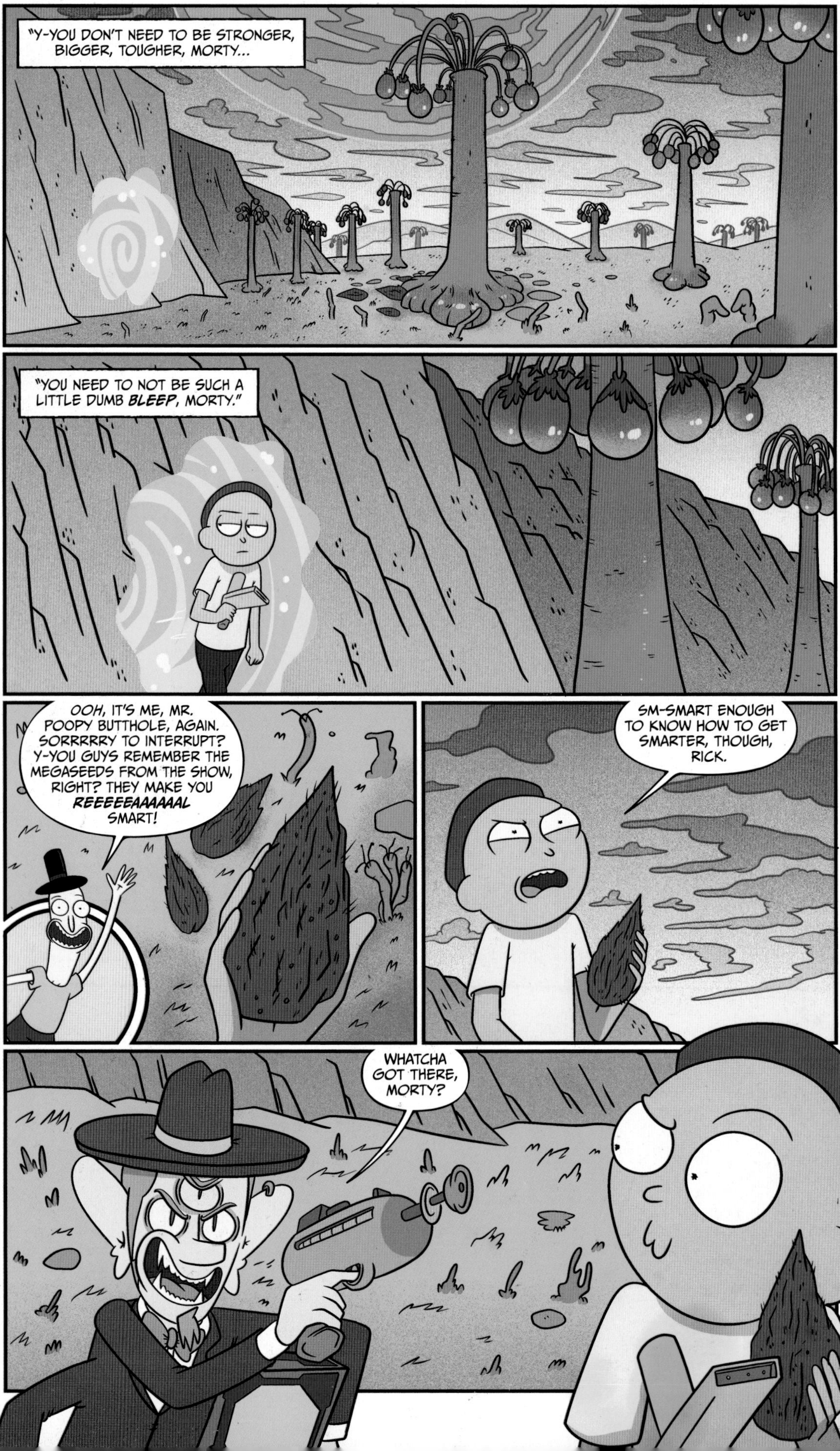
"Y-YOU DON'T NEED TO BE STRONGER, BIGGER, TOUGHER, MORTY...
"YOU NEED TO NOT BE SUCH A LITTLE DUMB *BLEEP*, MORTY."
*OOH*, IT'S ME, MR. POOPY BUTTHOLE, AGAIN. SORRRRRY TO INTERRUPT? Y-YOU GUYS REMEMBER THE MEGASEEDS FROM THE SHOW, RIGHT? THEY MAKE YOU ***REEEEEAAAAAAL*** SMART!
SM-SMART ENOUGH TO KNOW HOW TO GET SMARTER, THOUGH, RICK.
WHATCHA GOT THERE, MORTY?

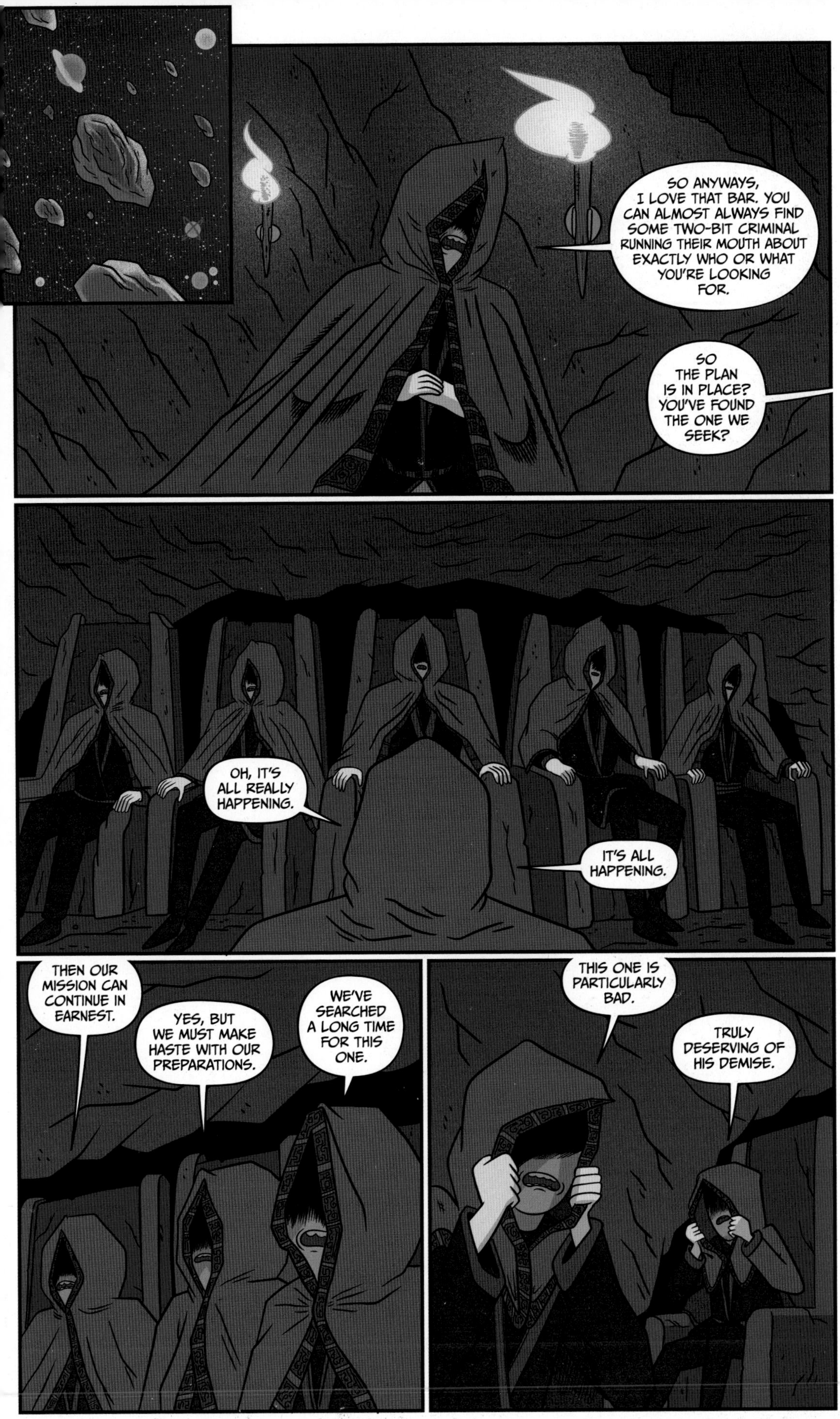
SO ANYWAYS, I LOVE THAT BAR. YOU CAN ALMOST ALWAYS FIND SOME TWO-BIT CRIMINAL RUNNING THEIR MOUTH ABOUT EXACTLY WHO OR WHAT YOU'RE LOOKING FOR.
SO THE PLAN IS IN PLACE? YOU'VE FOUND THE ONE WE SEEK?
OH, IT'S ALL REALLY HAPPENING.
IT'S ALL HAPPENING.
THEN OUR MISSION CAN CONTINUE IN EARNEST.
YES, BUT WE MUST MAKE HASTE WITH OUR PREPARATIONS.
WE'VE SEARCHED A LONG TIME FOR THIS ONE.
THIS ONE IS PARTICULARLY BAD.
TRULY DESERVING OF HIS DEMISE.

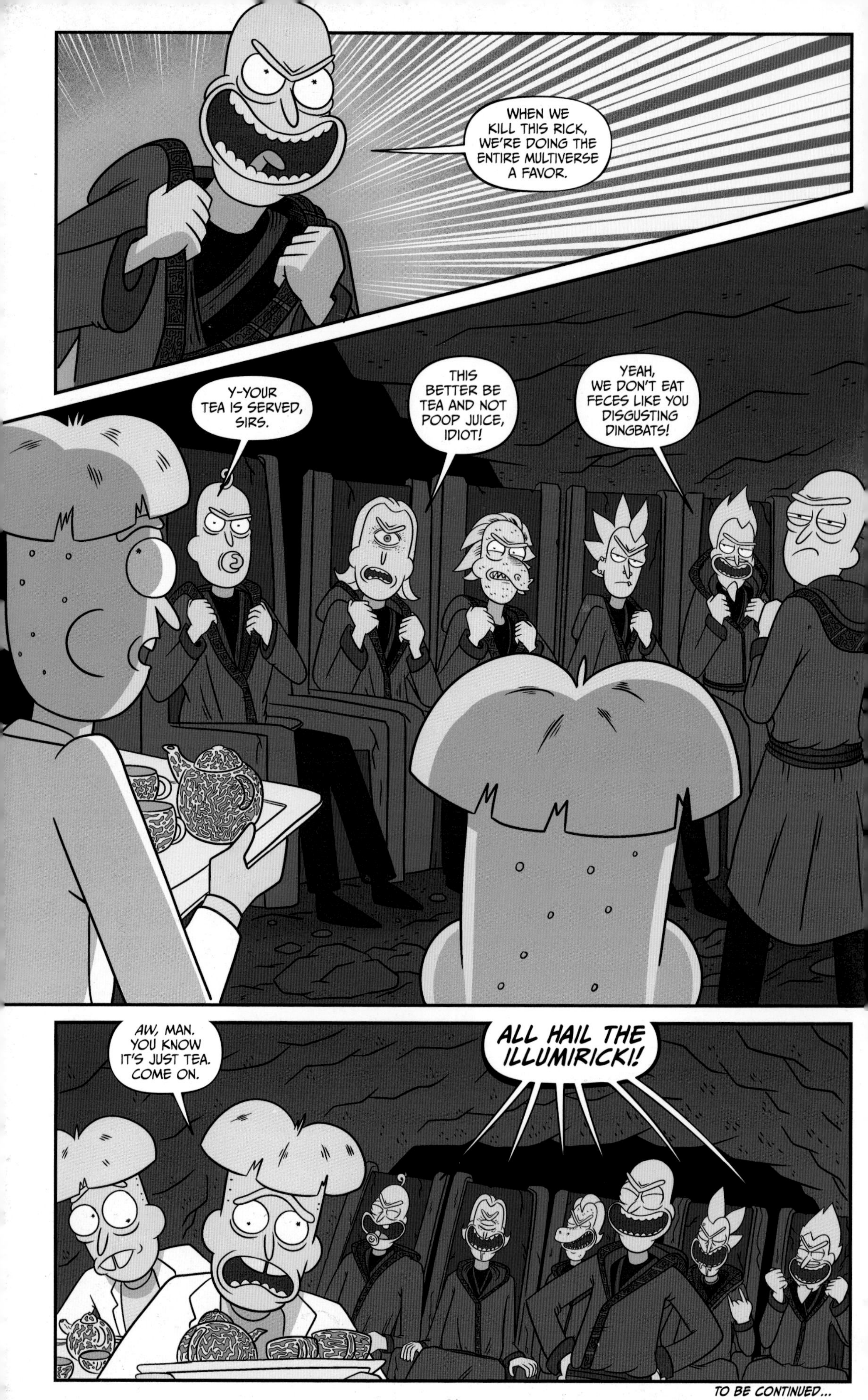
WHEN WE KILL THIS RICK, WE'RE DOING THE ENTIRE MULTIVERSE A FAVOR.
Y-YOUR TEA IS SERVED, SIRS.
THIS BETTER BE TEA AND NOT POOP JUICE, IDIOT!
YEAH, WE DON'T EAT FECES LIKE YOU DISGUSTING DINGBATS!
AW, MAN. YOU KNOW IT'S JUST TEA. COME ON.
ALL HAIL THE ILLUMIRICK!!

TO BE CONTINUED...

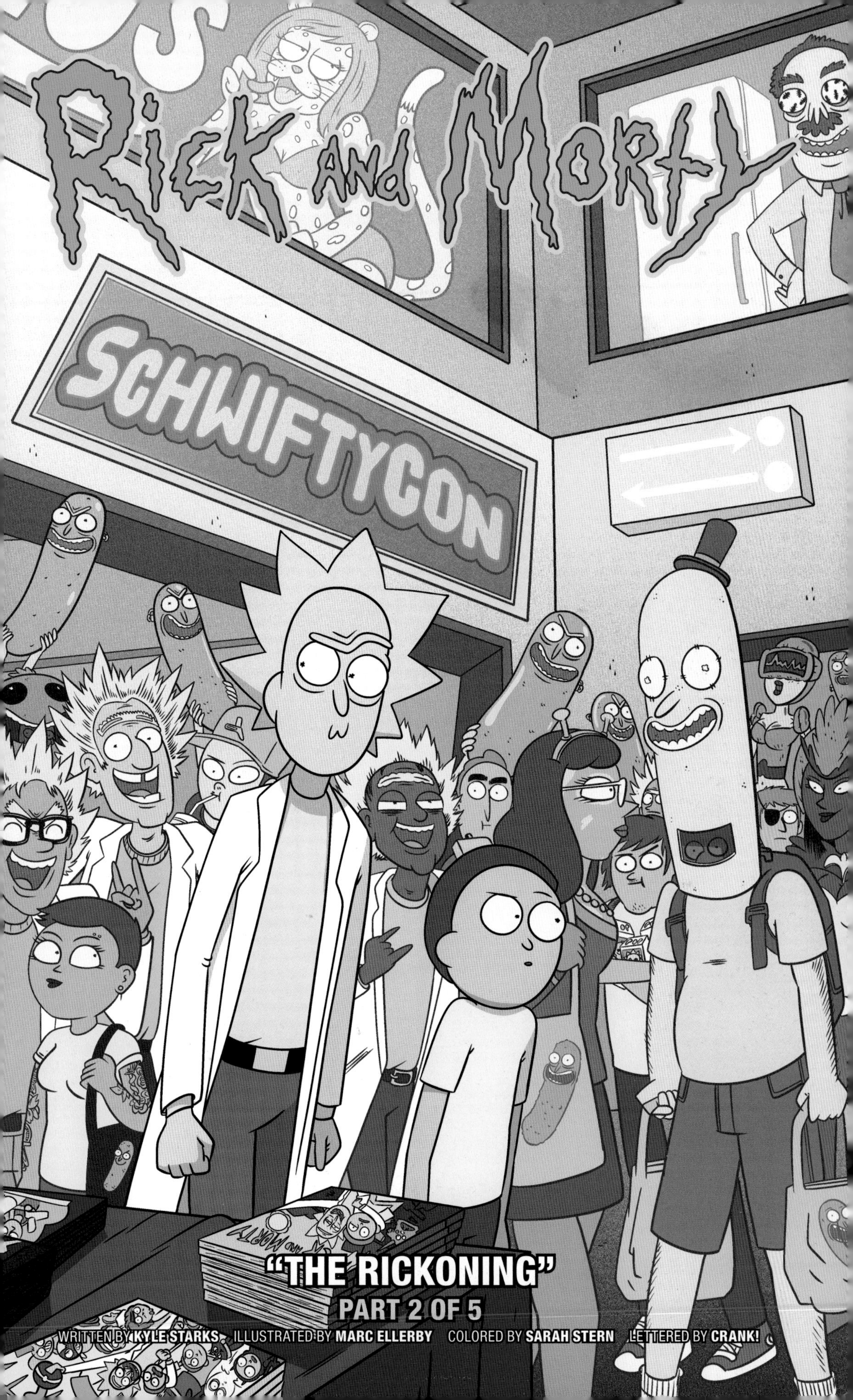
Rick and Morty
SCHWIFTYCON
"THE RICKONING"
PART 2 OF 5
WRITTEN BY KYLE STARKS ILLUSTRATED BY MARC ELLERBY COLORED BY SARAH STERN LETTERED BY CRANK!

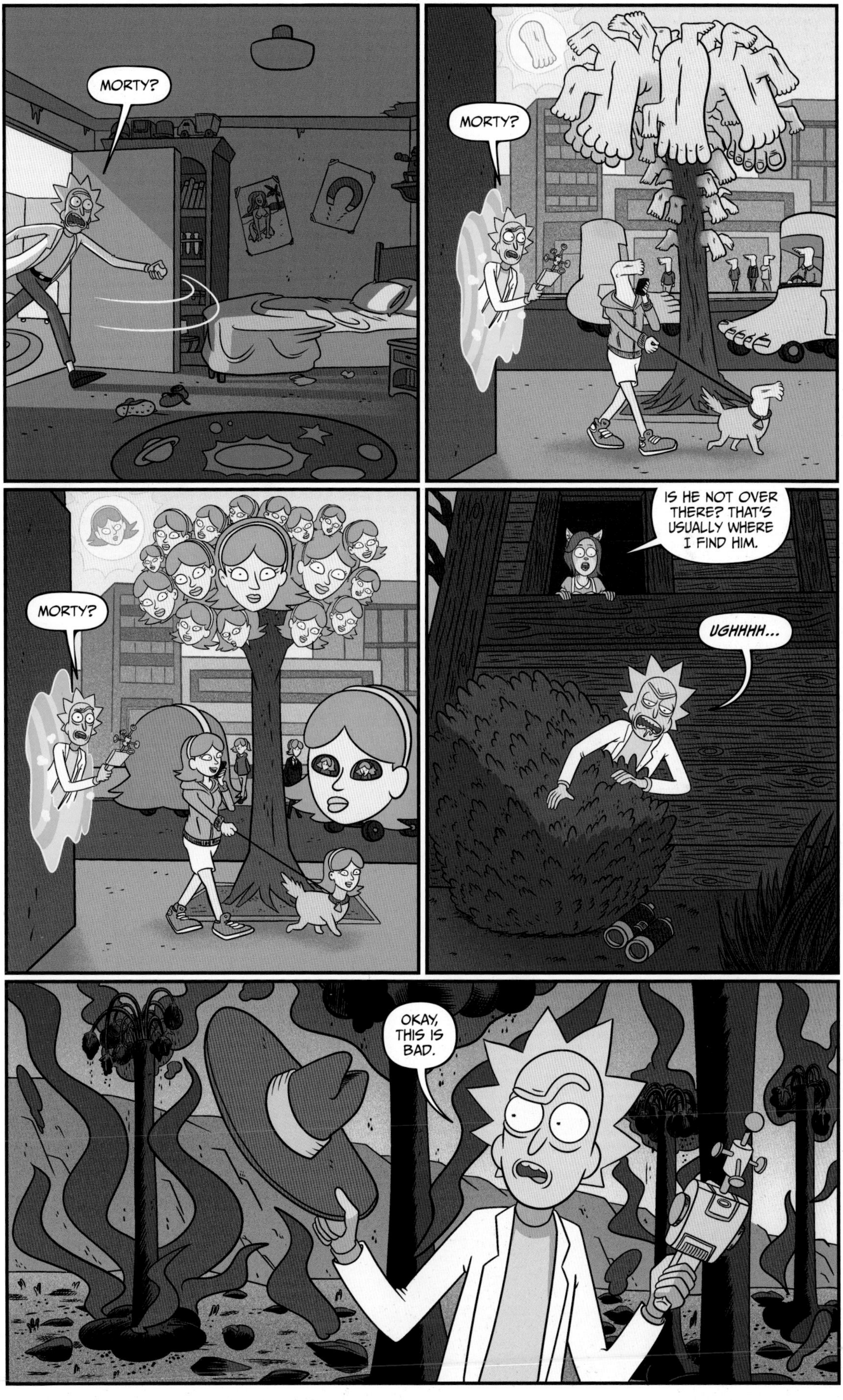
MORTY?
MORTY?
MORTY?
IS HE NOT OVER THERE? THAT'S USUALLY WHERE I FIND HIM.
UGHHHH...
OKAY, THIS IS BAD.

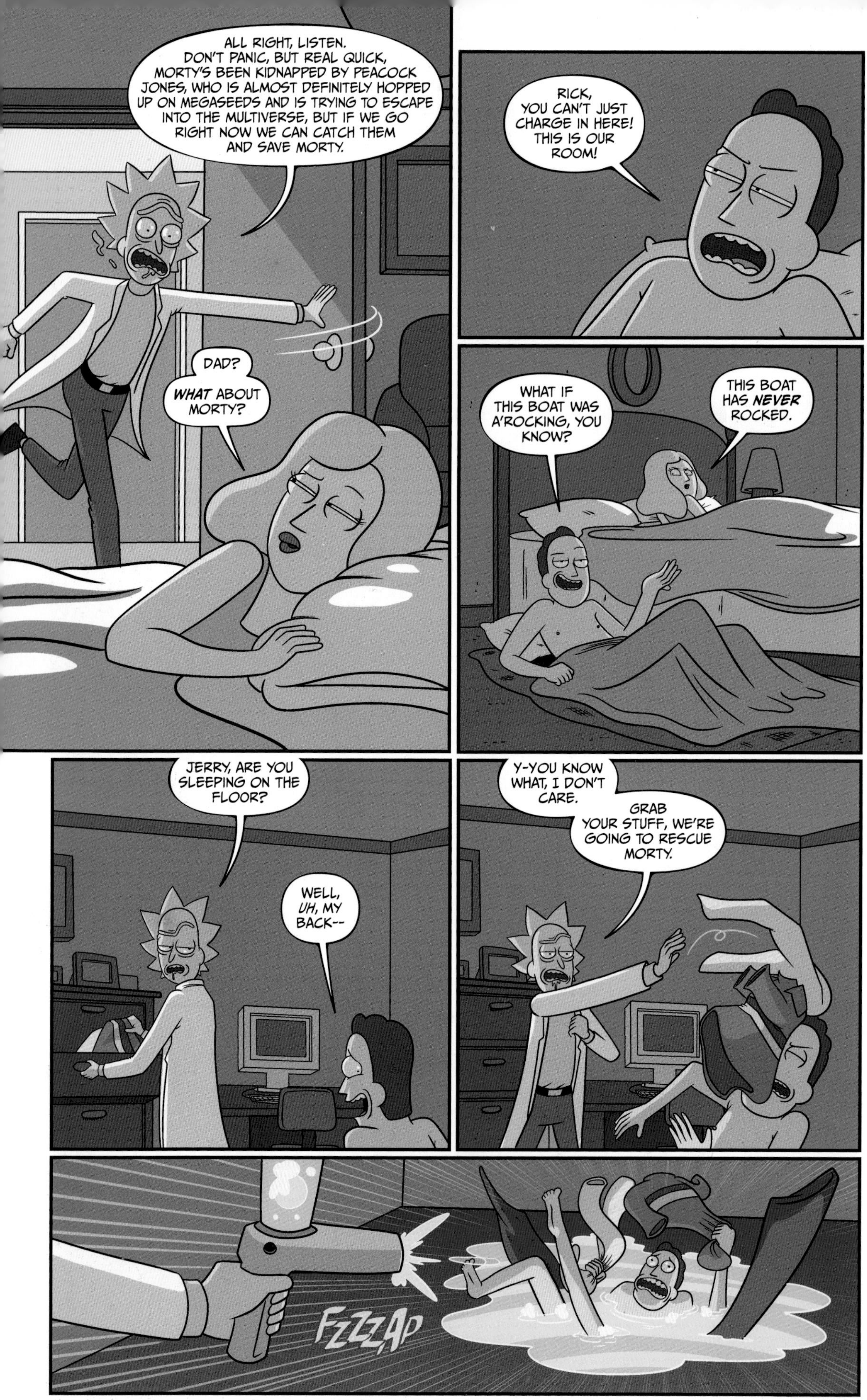
ALL RIGHT, LISTEN. DON'T PANIC, BUT REAL QUICK, MORTY'S BEEN KIDNAPPED BY PEACOCK JONES, WHO IS ALMOST DEFINITELY HOPPED UP ON MEGASEEDS AND IS TRYING TO ESCAPE INTO THE MULTIVERSE, BUT IF WE GO RIGHT NOW WE CAN CATCH THEM AND SAVE MORTY.
DAD? *WHAT* ABOUT MORTY?
RICK, YOU CAN'T JUST CHARGE IN HERE! THIS IS OUR ROOM!
WHAT IF THIS BOAT WAS A'ROCKING, YOU KNOW?
THIS BOAT HAS ***NEVER*** ROCKED.
JERRY, ARE YOU SLEEPING ON THE FLOOR?
WELL, *UH*, MY BACK--
Y-YOU KNOW WHAT, I DON'T CARE.
GRAB YOUR STUFF, WE'RE GOING TO RESCUE MORTY.
FZZZAP

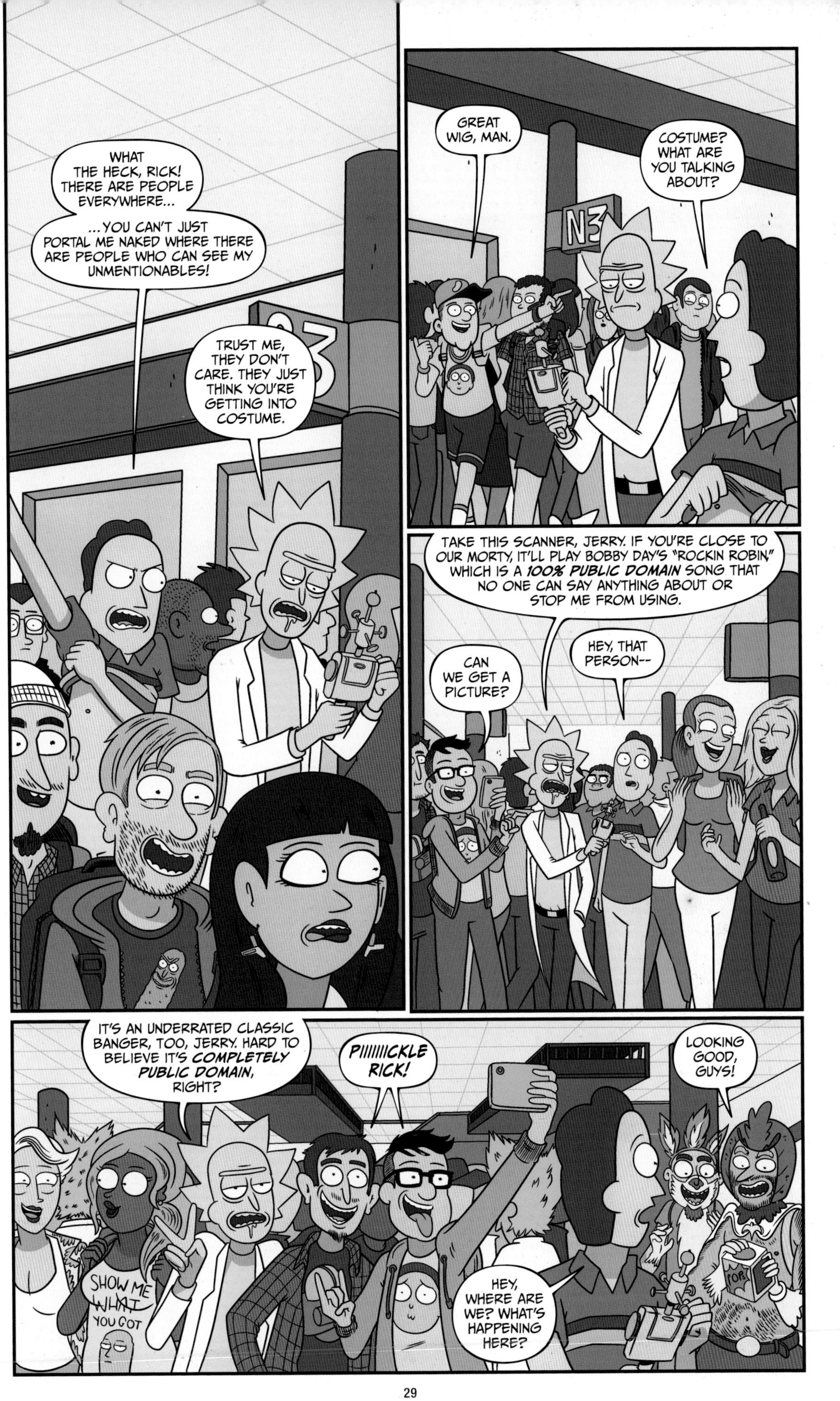
WHAT THE HECK, RICK! THERE ARE PEOPLE EVERYWHERE...
...YOU CAN'T JUST PORTAL ME NAKED WHERE THERE ARE PEOPLE WHO CAN SEE MY UNMENTIONABLES!
TRUST ME, THEY DON'T CARE. THEY JUST THINK YOU'RE GETTING INTO COSTUME.
GREAT WIG, MAN.
N3
COSTUME? WHAT ARE YOU TALKING ABOUT?
TAKE THIS SCANNER, JERRY. IF YOU'RE CLOSE TO OUR MORTY, IT'LL PLAY BOBBY DAY'S "ROCKIN ROBIN," WHICH IS A *100% PUBLIC DOMAIN* SONG THAT NO ONE CAN SAY ANYTHING ABOUT OR STOP ME FROM USING.
CAN WE GET A PICTURE?
HEY, THAT PERSON--
IT'S AN UNDERRATED CLASSIC BANGER, TOO, JERRY. HARD TO BELIEVE IT'S *COMPLETELY PUBLIC DOMAIN*, RIGHT?
PIIIIIICKLE RICK!
LOOKING GOOD, GUYS!
SHOW ME WHAT YOU GOT
HEY, WHERE ARE WE? WHAT'S HAPPENING HERE?

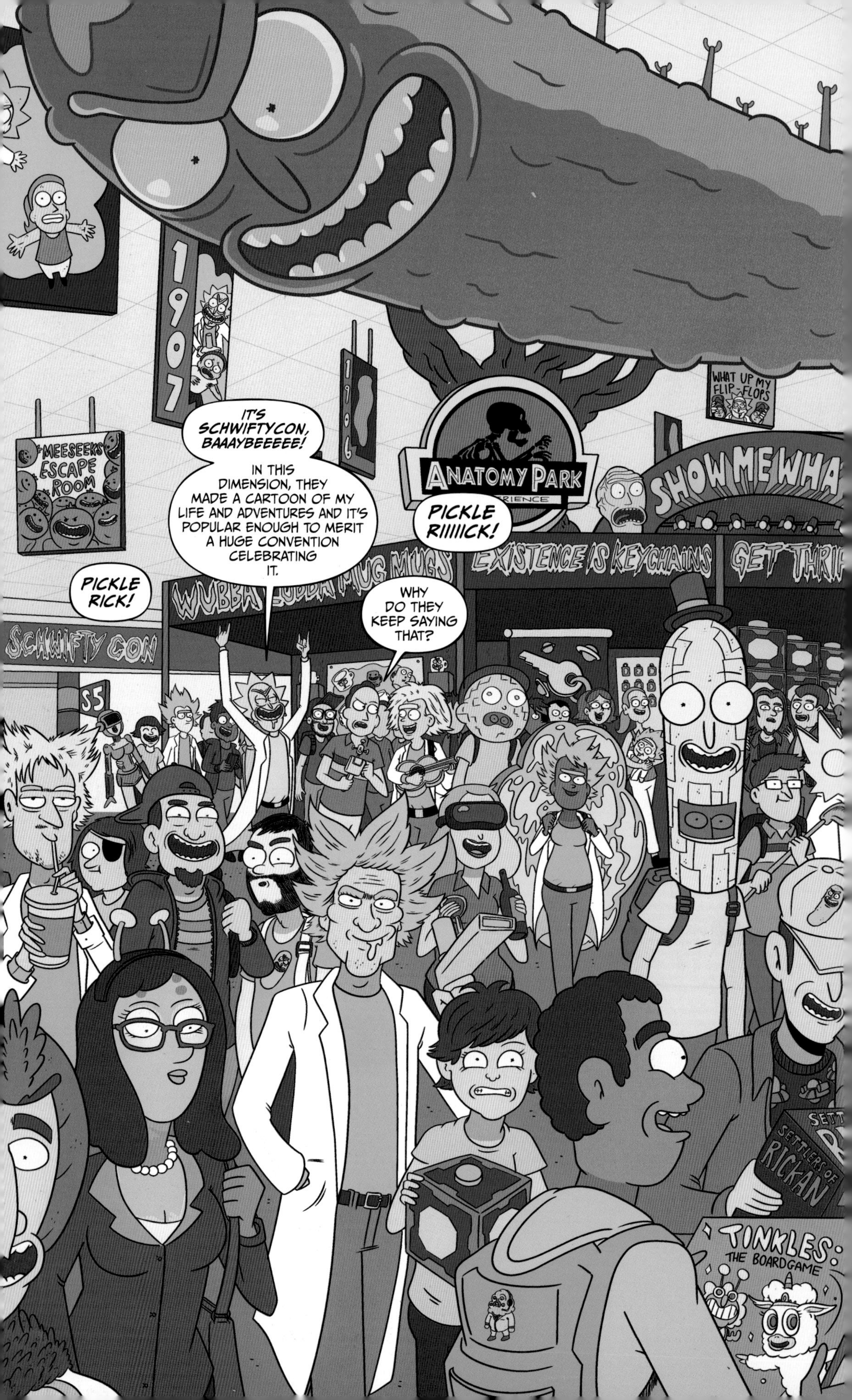

IT'S SCHWIFTYCON, BAAAYBEEEEE!
IN THIS DIMENSION, THEY MADE A CARTOON OF MY LIFE AND ADVENTURES AND IT'S POPULAR ENOUGH TO MERIT A HUGE CONVENTION CELEBRATING IT.
PICKLE RIIIIICK!
PICKLE RICK!
WHY DO THEY KEEP SAYING THAT?
1907
MEESEEKS ESCAPE ROOM
ANATOMY PARK
WHAT UP MY FLIP-FLOPS
EXISTENCE IS KEYCHAINS
SCHWIFTY CON
S5
SETTLERS OF RICKAN
TINKLES: THE BOARDGAME

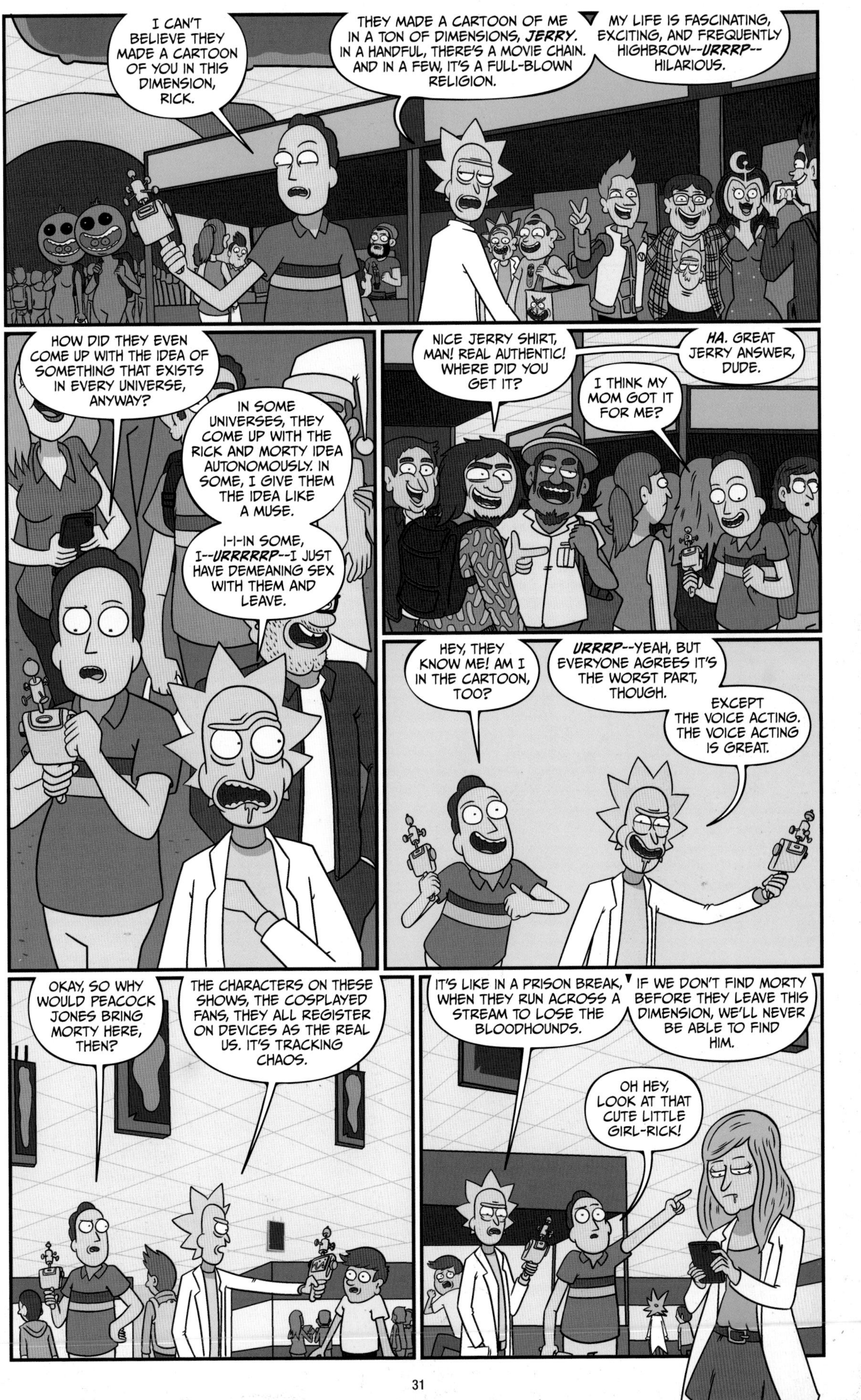
I CAN'T BELIEVE THEY MADE A CARTOON OF YOU IN THIS DIMENSION, RICK.
THEY MADE A CARTOON OF ME IN A TON OF DIMENSIONS, *JERRY*. IN A HANDFUL, THERE'S A MOVIE CHAIN. AND IN A FEW, IT'S A FULL-BLOWN RELIGION.
MY LIFE IS FASCINATING, EXCITING, AND FREQUENTLY HIGHBROW--*URRRP*--HILARIOUS.
HOW DID THEY EVEN COME UP WITH THE IDEA OF SOMETHING THAT EXISTS IN EVERY UNIVERSE, ANYWAY?
IN SOME UNIVERSES, THEY COME UP WITH THE RICK AND MORTY IDEA AUTONOMOUSLY. IN SOME, I GIVE THEM THE IDEA LIKE A MUSE.
I-I-IN SOME, I--*URRRRRP*--I JUST HAVE DEMEANING SEX WITH THEM AND LEAVE.
NICE JERRY SHIRT, MAN! REAL AUTHENTIC! WHERE DID YOU GET IT?
I THINK MY MOM GOT IT FOR ME?
*HA.* GREAT JERRY ANSWER, DUDE.
HEY, THEY KNOW ME! AM I IN THE CARTOON, TOO?
*URRRP*--YEAH, BUT EVERYONE AGREES IT'S THE WORST PART, THOUGH.
EXCEPT THE VOICE ACTING. THE VOICE ACTING IS GREAT.
OKAY, SO WHY WOULD PEACOCK JONES BRING MORTY HERE, THEN?
THE CHARACTERS ON THESE SHOWS, THE COSPLAYED FANS, THEY ALL REGISTER ON DEVICES AS THE REAL US. IT'S TRACKING CHAOS.
IT'S LIKE IN A PRISON BREAK, WHEN THEY RUN ACROSS A STREAM TO LOSE THE BLOODHOUNDS.
IF WE DON'T FIND MORTY BEFORE THEY LEAVE THIS DIMENSION, WE'LL NEVER BE ABLE TO FIND HIM.
OH HEY, LOOK AT THAT CUTE LITTLE GIRL-RICK!

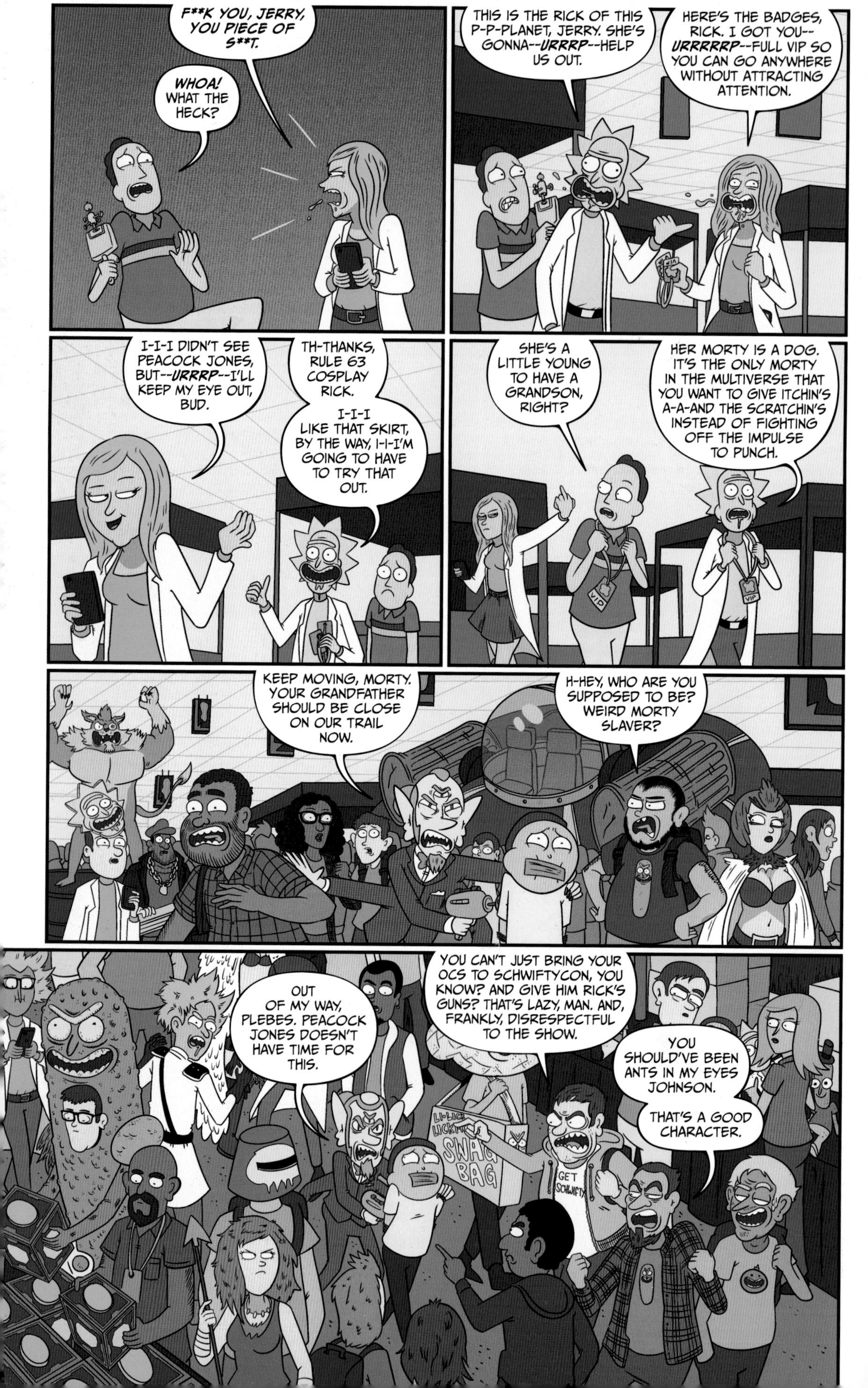
F**K YOU, JERRY, YOU PIECE OF S**T.
WHOA! WHAT THE HECK?
THIS IS THE RICK OF THIS P-P-PLANET, JERRY. SHE'S GONNA--URRRP--HELP US OUT.
HERE'S THE BADGES, RICK. I GOT YOU--URRRRRP--FULL VIP SO YOU CAN GO ANYWHERE WITHOUT ATTRACTING ATTENTION.
I-I-I DIDN'T SEE PEACOCK JONES, BUT--URRRP--I'LL KEEP MY EYE OUT, BUD.
TH-THANKS, RULE 63 COSPLAY RICK.
I-I-I LIKE THAT SKIRT, BY THE WAY, I-I-I'M GOING TO HAVE TO TRY THAT OUT.
SHE'S A LITTLE YOUNG TO HAVE A GRANDSON, RIGHT?
HER MORTY IS A DOG. IT'S THE ONLY MORTY IN THE MULTIVERSE THAT YOU WANT TO GIVE ITCHIN'S A-A-AND THE SCRATCHIN'S INSTEAD OF FIGHTING OFF THE IMPULSE TO PUNCH.
VIP
VIP
KEEP MOVING, MORTY. YOUR GRANDFATHER SHOULD BE CLOSE ON OUR TRAIL NOW.
H-HEY, WHO ARE YOU SUPPOSED TO BE? WEIRD MORTY SLAVER?
OUT OF MY WAY, PLEBES. PEACOCK JONES DOESN'T HAVE TIME FOR THIS.
YOU CAN'T JUST BRING YOUR OCS TO SCHWIFTYCON, YOU KNOW? AND GIVE HIM RICK'S GUNS? THAT'S LAZY, MAN. AND, FRANKLY, DISRESPECTFUL TO THE SHOW.
YOU SHOULD'VE BEEN ANTS IN MY EYES JOHNSON.
THAT'S A GOOD CHARACTER.
SWAG BAG
GET SCHWIFTY

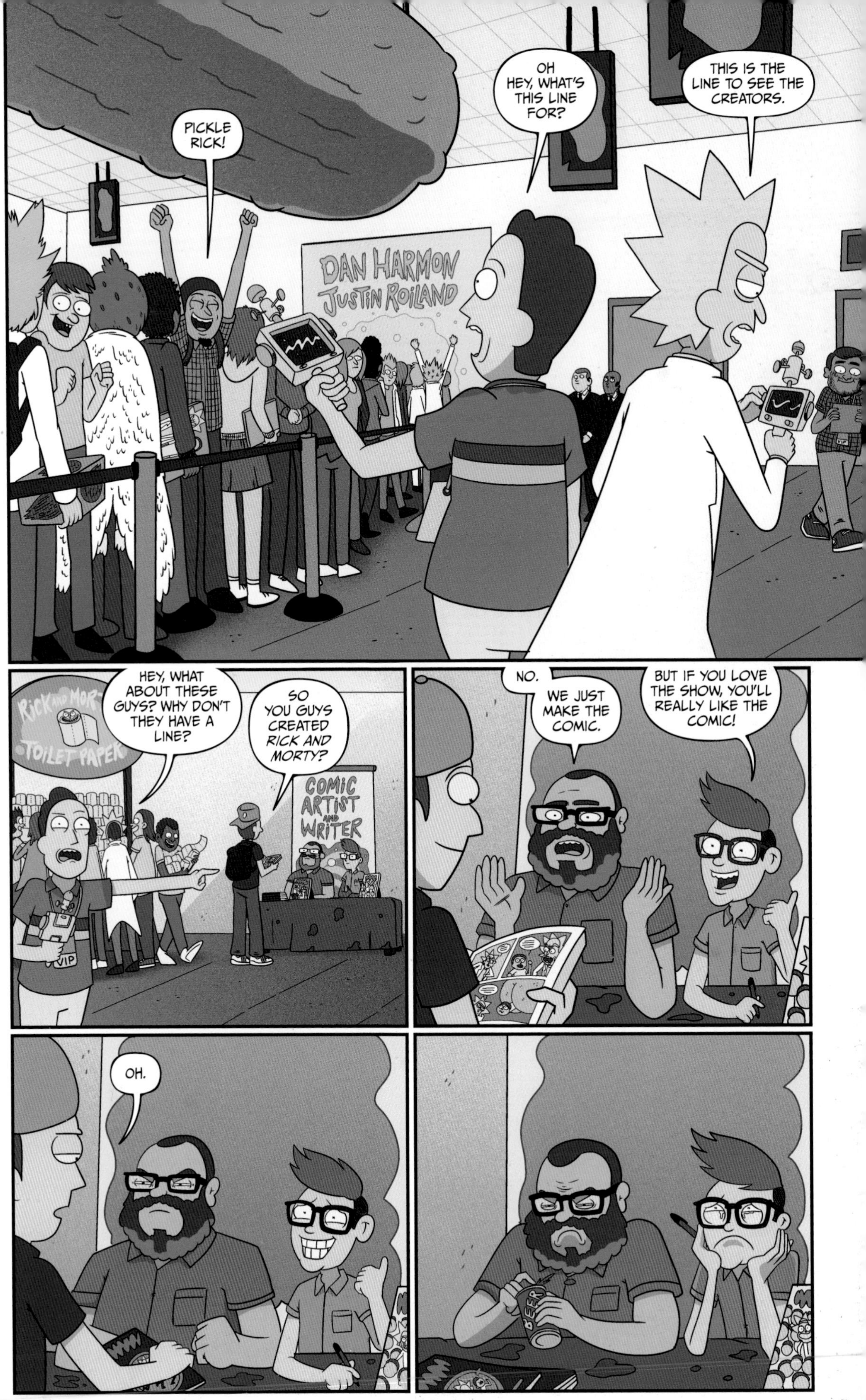
PICKLE RICK!
OH HEY, WHAT'S THIS LINE FOR?
THIS IS THE LINE TO SEE THE CREATORS.
DAN HARMON
JUSTIN ROILAND
RICK AND MORTY TOILET PAPER
HEY, WHAT ABOUT THESE GUYS? WHY DON'T THEY HAVE A LINE?
SO YOU GUYS CREATED *RICK AND MORTY*?
COMIC ARTIST AND WRITER
VIP
NO.
WE JUST MAKE THE COMIC.
BUT IF YOU LOVE THE SHOW, YOU'LL REALLY LIKE THE COMIC!
OH.
BEER

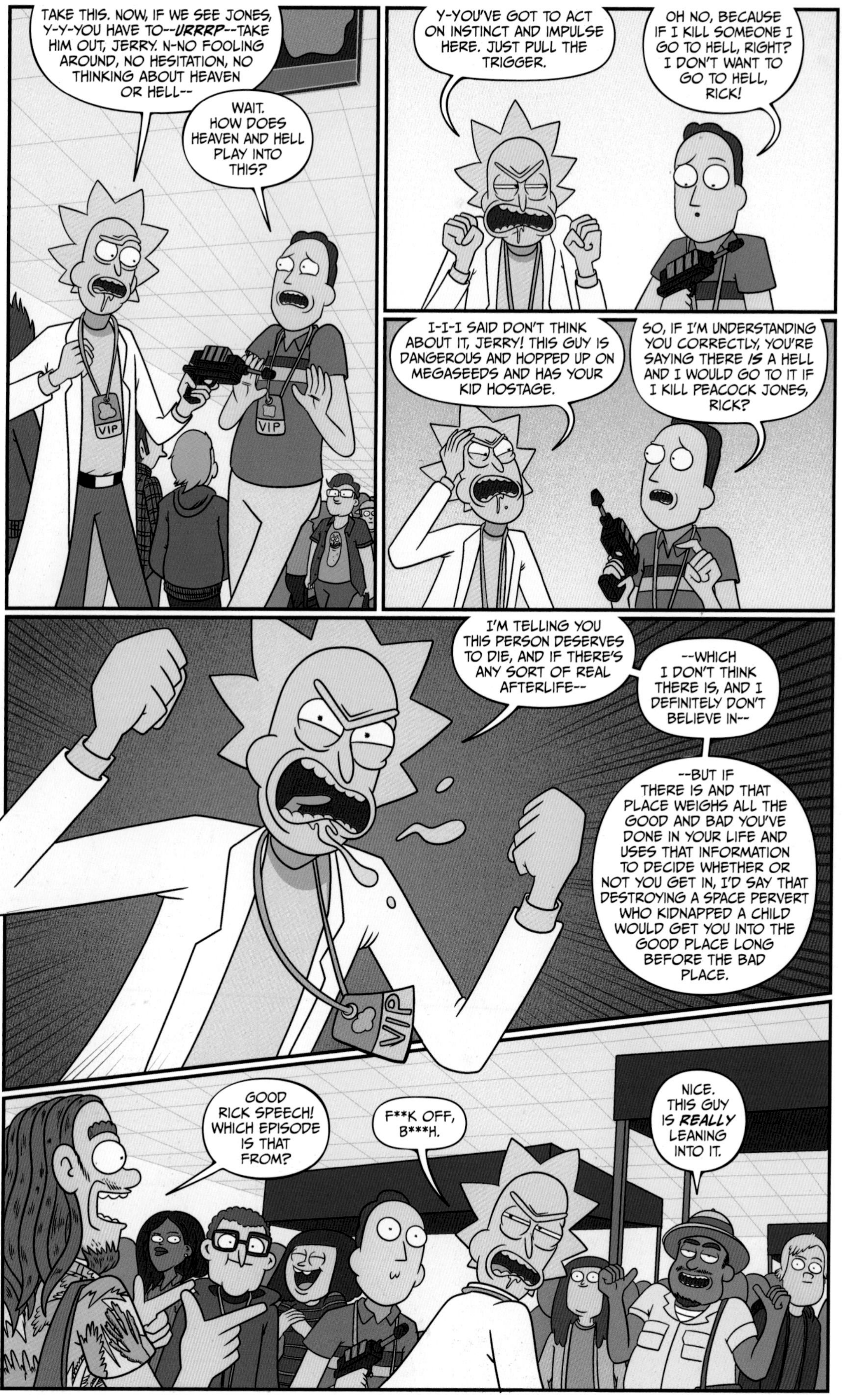
TAKE THIS. NOW, IF WE SEE JONES, Y-Y-YOU HAVE TO--*URRRP*--TAKE HIM OUT, JERRY. N-NO FOOLING AROUND, NO HESITATION, NO THINKING ABOUT HEAVEN OR HELL--
WAIT. HOW DOES HEAVEN AND HELL PLAY INTO THIS?
VIP
VIP
Y-YOU'VE GOT TO ACT ON INSTINCT AND IMPULSE HERE. JUST PULL THE TRIGGER.
OH NO, BECAUSE IF I KILL SOMEONE I GO TO HELL, RIGHT? I DON'T WANT TO GO TO HELL, RICK!
I-I-I SAID DON'T THINK ABOUT IT, JERRY! THIS GUY IS DANGEROUS AND HOPPED UP ON MEGASEEDS AND HAS YOUR KID HOSTAGE.
SO, IF I'M UNDERSTANDING YOU CORRECTLY, YOU'RE SAYING THERE *IS* A HELL AND I WOULD GO TO IT IF I KILL PEACOCK JONES, RICK?
I'M TELLING YOU THIS PERSON DESERVES TO DIE, AND IF THERE'S ANY SORT OF REAL AFTERLIFE--
--WHICH I DON'T THINK THERE IS, AND I DEFINITELY DON'T BELIEVE IN--
--BUT IF THERE IS AND THAT PLACE WEIGHS ALL THE GOOD AND BAD YOU'VE DONE IN YOUR LIFE AND USES THAT INFORMATION TO DECIDE WHETHER OR NOT YOU GET IN, I'D SAY THAT DESTROYING A SPACE PERVERT WHO KIDNAPPED A CHILD WOULD GET YOU INTO THE GOOD PLACE LONG BEFORE THE BAD PLACE.
VIP
GOOD RICK SPEECH! WHICH EPISODE IS THAT FROM?
F**K OFF, B***H.
NICE. THIS GUY IS ***REALLY*** LEANING INTO IT.

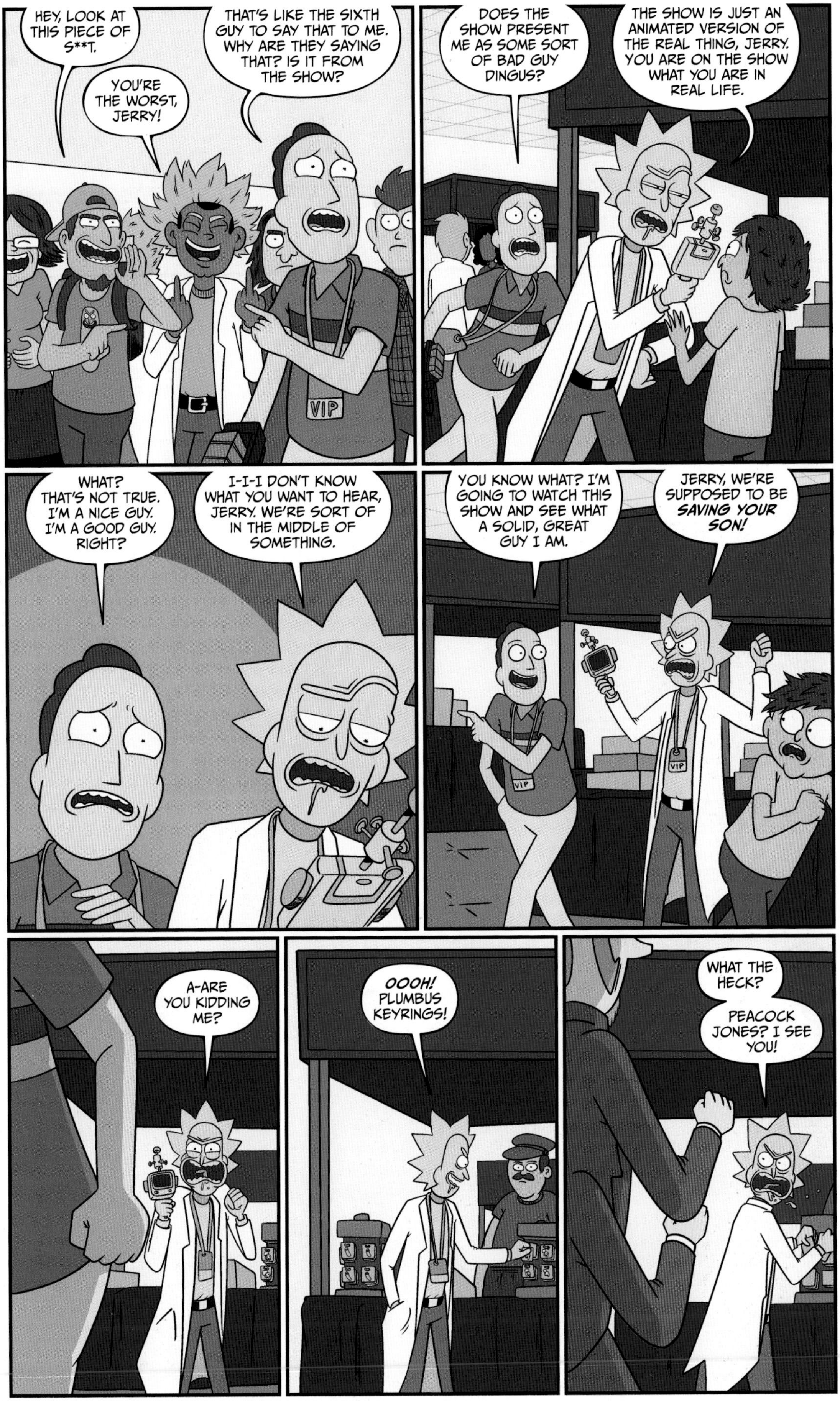
HEY, LOOK AT THIS PIECE OF S**T.
YOU'RE THE WORST, JERRY!
THAT'S LIKE THE SIXTH GUY TO SAY THAT TO ME. WHY ARE THEY SAYING THAT? IS IT FROM THE SHOW?
DOES THE SHOW PRESENT ME AS SOME SORT OF BAD GUY DINGUS?
THE SHOW IS JUST AN ANIMATED VERSION OF THE REAL THING, JERRY. YOU ARE ON THE SHOW WHAT YOU ARE IN REAL LIFE.
VIP
WHAT? THAT'S NOT TRUE. I'M A NICE GUY. I'M A GOOD GUY. RIGHT?
I-I-I DON'T KNOW WHAT YOU WANT TO HEAR, JERRY. WE'RE SORT OF IN THE MIDDLE OF SOMETHING.
YOU KNOW WHAT? I'M GOING TO WATCH THIS SHOW AND SEE WHAT A SOLID, GREAT GUY I AM.
JERRY, WE'RE SUPPOSED TO BE ***SAVING YOUR SON!***
VIP
VIP
A-ARE YOU KIDDING ME?
***OOOH!*** PLUMBUS KEYRINGS!
WHAT THE HECK?
PEACOCK JONES? I SEE YOU!

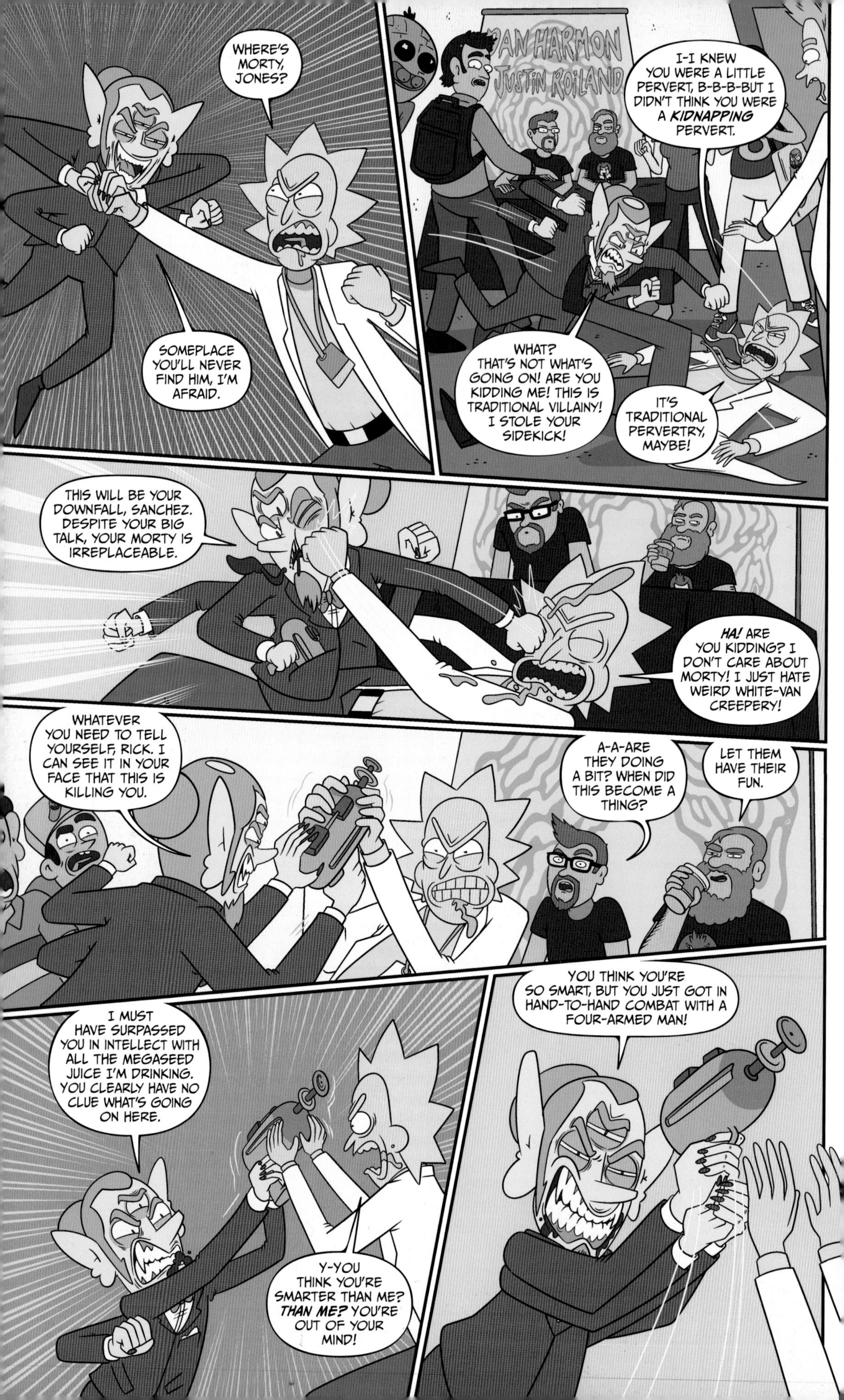
WHERE'S MORTY, JONES?
SOMEPLACE YOU'LL NEVER FIND HIM, I'M AFRAID.
DAN HARMON
JUSTIN ROILAND
I-I KNEW YOU WERE A LITTLE PERVERT, B-B-B-BUT I DIDN'T THINK YOU WERE A KIDNAPPING PERVERT.
WHAT? THAT'S NOT WHAT'S GOING ON! ARE YOU KIDDING ME! THIS IS TRADITIONAL VILLAINY! I STOLE YOUR SIDEKICK!
IT'S TRADITIONAL PERVERTRY, MAYBE!
THIS WILL BE YOUR DOWNFALL, SANCHEZ. DESPITE YOUR BIG TALK, YOUR MORTY IS IRREPLACEABLE.
HA! ARE YOU KIDDING? I DON'T CARE ABOUT MORTY! I JUST HATE WEIRD WHITE-VAN CREEPERY!
WHATEVER YOU NEED TO TELL YOURSELF, RICK. I CAN SEE IT IN YOUR FACE THAT THIS IS KILLING YOU.
A-A-ARE THEY DOING A BIT? WHEN DID THIS BECOME A THING?
LET THEM HAVE THEIR FUN.
I MUST HAVE SURPASSED YOU IN INTELLECT WITH ALL THE MEGASEED JUICE I'M DRINKING. YOU CLEARLY HAVE NO CLUE WHAT'S GOING ON HERE.
Y-YOU THINK YOU'RE SMARTER THAN ME? THAN ME? YOU'RE OUT OF YOUR MIND!
YOU THINK YOU'RE SO SMART, BUT YOU JUST GOT IN HAND-TO-HAND COMBAT WITH A FOUR-ARMED MAN!

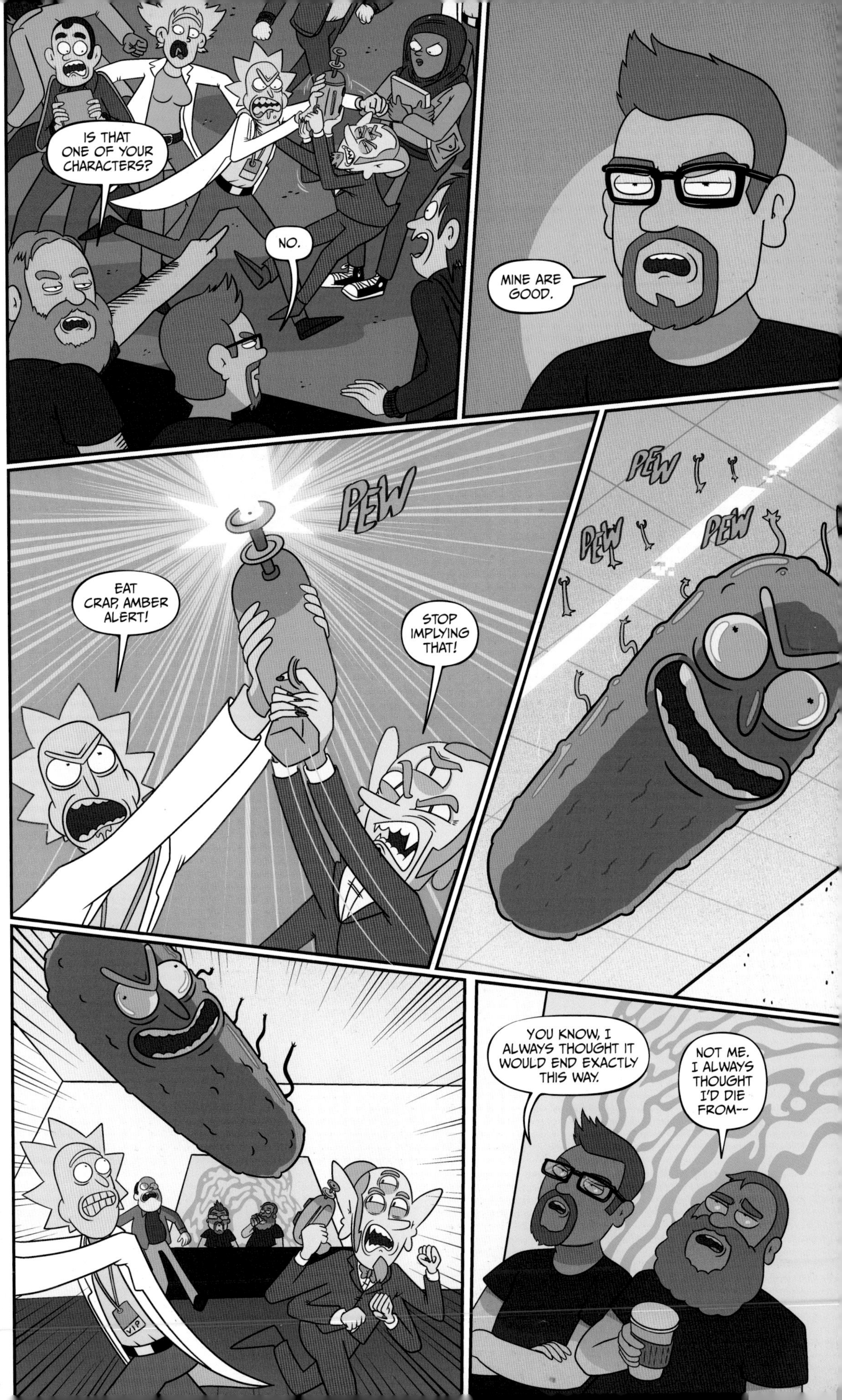
IS THAT ONE OF YOUR CHARACTERS?
NO.
MINE ARE GOOD.
EAT CRAP, AMBER ALERT!
PEW
STOP IMPLYING THAT!
PEW
PEW
PEW
YOU KNOW, I ALWAYS THOUGHT IT WOULD END EXACTLY THIS WAY.
NOT ME. I ALWAYS THOUGHT I'D DIE FROM--

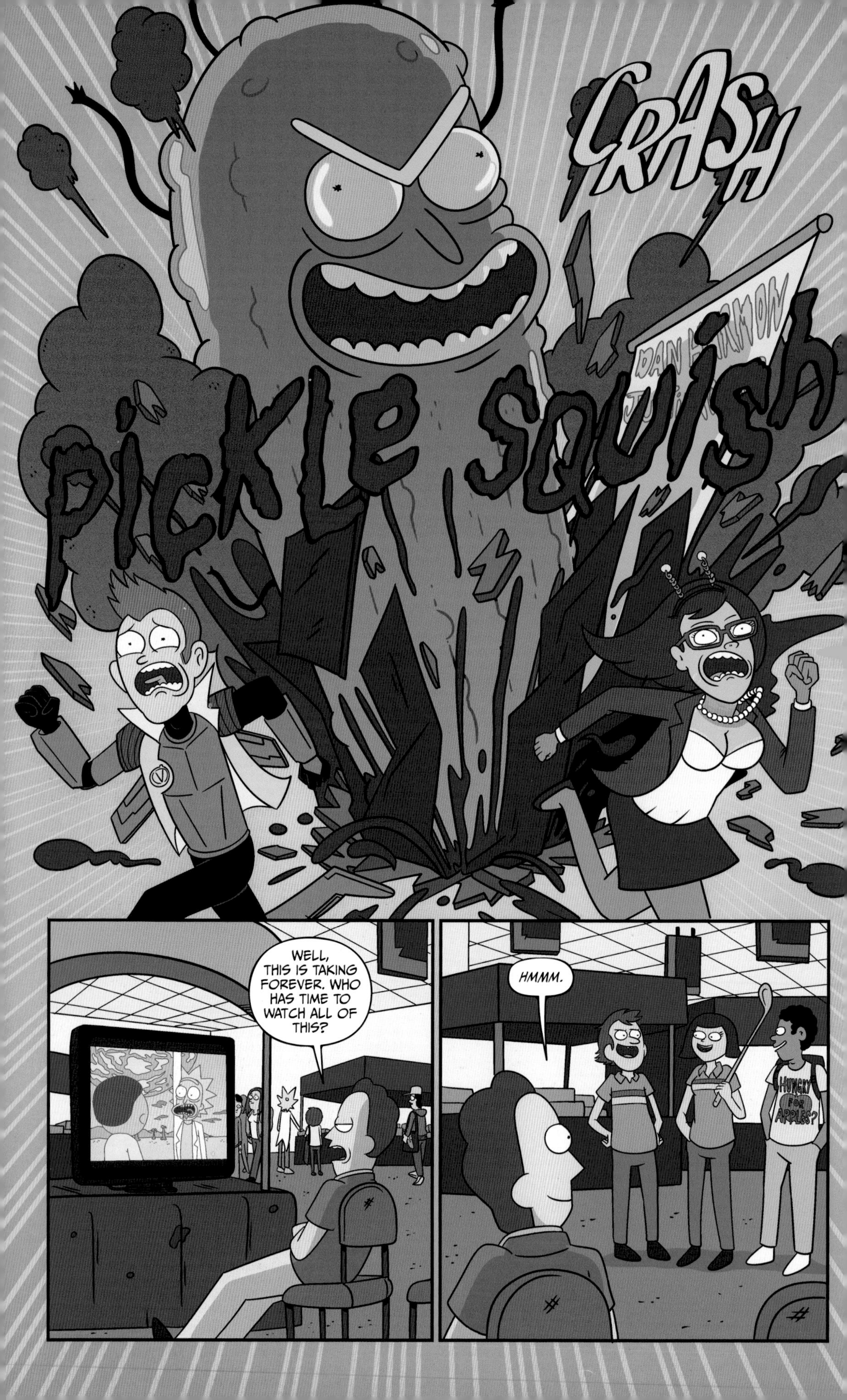
CRASH
PICKLE SQUISH
WELL, THIS IS TAKING FOREVER. WHO HAS TIME TO WATCH ALL OF THIS?
HMMM.
HUNGRY FOR APPLES?

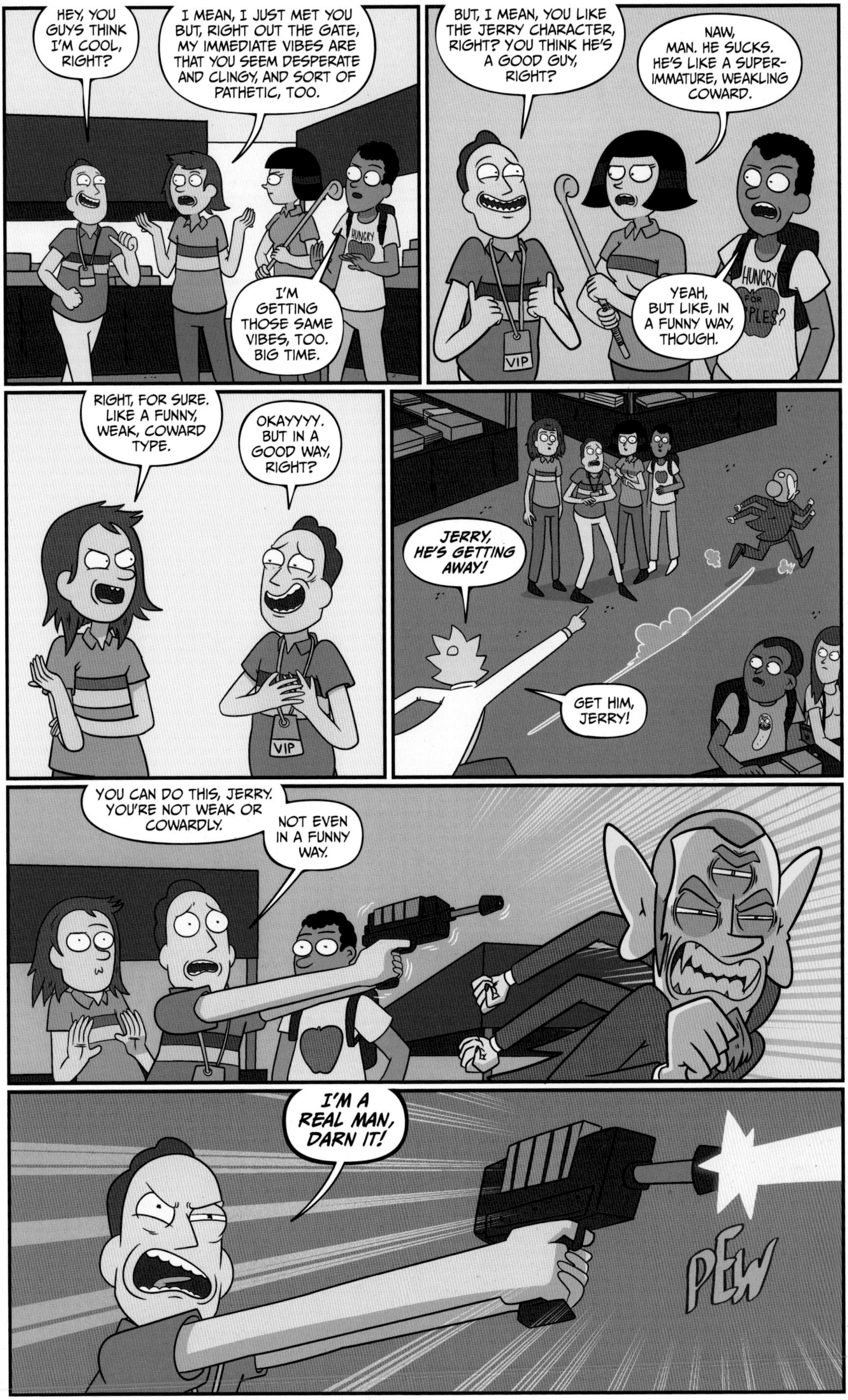
HEY, YOU GUYS THINK I'M COOL, RIGHT?
I MEAN, I JUST MET YOU BUT, RIGHT OUT THE GATE, MY IMMEDIATE VIBES ARE THAT YOU SEEM DESPERATE AND CLINGY, AND SORT OF PATHETIC, TOO.
HUNGRY
I'M GETTING THOSE SAME VIBES, TOO. BIG TIME.
BUT, I MEAN, YOU LIKE THE JERRY CHARACTER, RIGHT? YOU THINK HE'S A GOOD GUY, RIGHT?
NAW, MAN. HE SUCKS. HE'S LIKE A SUPER-IMMATURE, WEAKLING COWARD.
VIP
YEAH, BUT LIKE, IN A FUNNY WAY, THOUGH.
RIGHT, FOR SURE. LIKE A FUNNY, WEAK, COWARD TYPE.
OKAYYYY. BUT IN A GOOD WAY, RIGHT?
VIP
JERRY, HE'S GETTING AWAY!
GET HIM, JERRY!
YOU CAN DO THIS, JERRY. YOU'RE NOT WEAK OR COWARDLY.
NOT EVEN IN A FUNNY WAY.
I'M A REAL MAN, DARN IT!
PEW

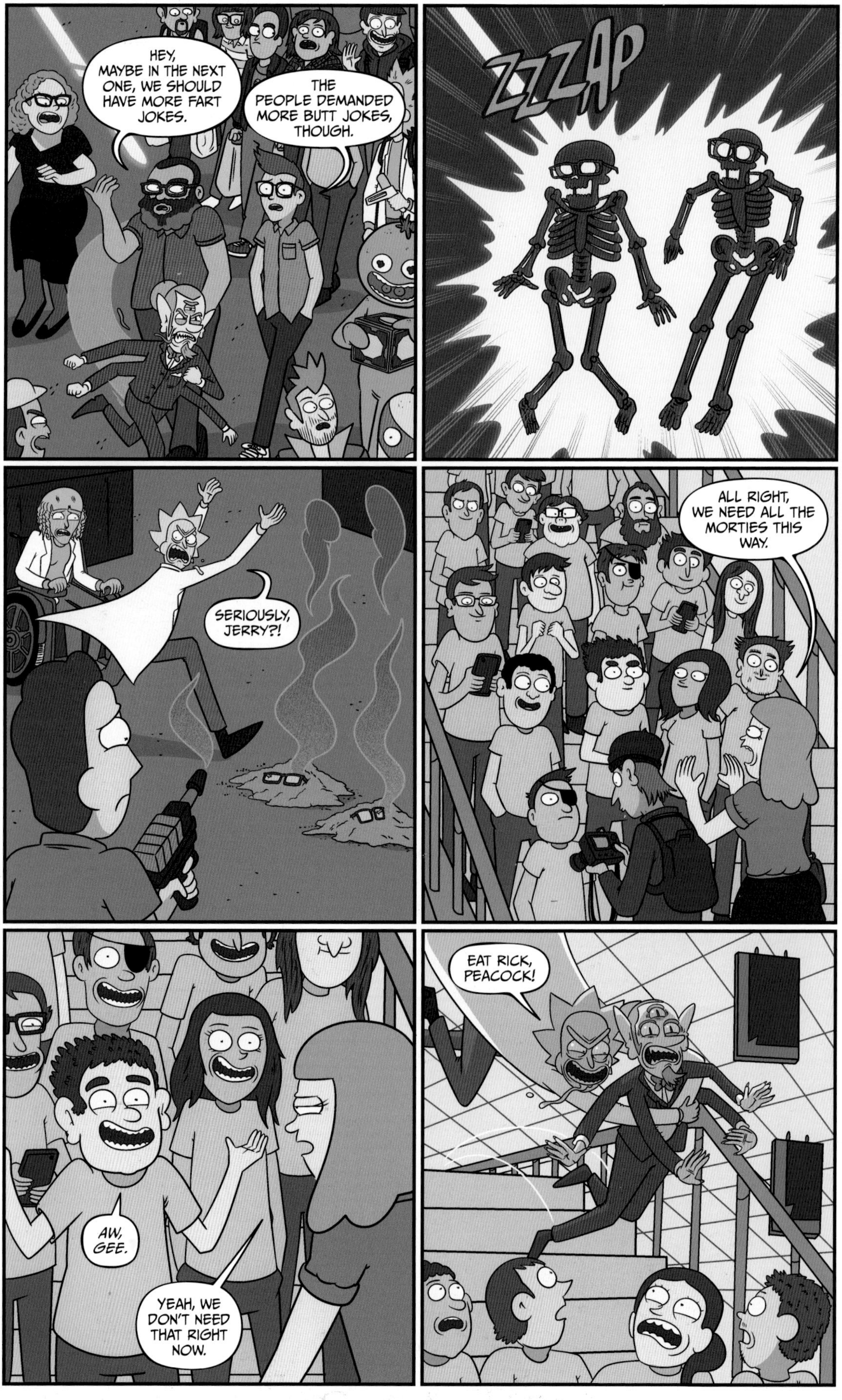
HEY, MAYBE IN THE NEXT ONE, WE SHOULD HAVE MORE FART JOKES.
THE PEOPLE DEMANDED MORE BUTT JOKES, THOUGH.
ZZZAP
SERIOUSLY, JERRY?!
ALL RIGHT, WE NEED ALL THE MORTIES THIS WAY.
AW, GEE.
YEAH, WE DON'T NEED THAT RIGHT NOW.
EAT RICK, PEACOCK!

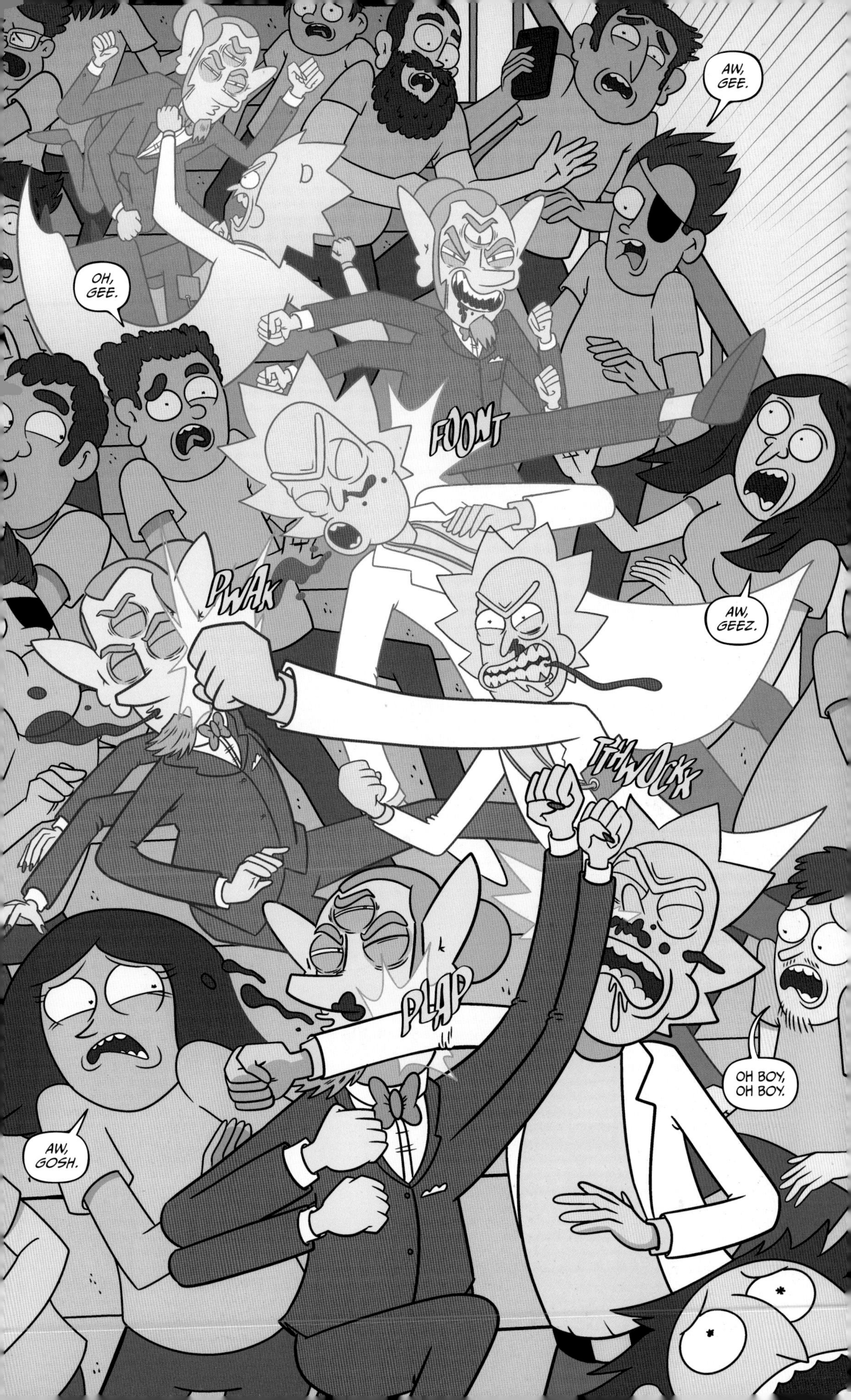
AW, GEE.
OH, GEE.
FOONT
PWAK
AW, GEEZ.
THWOCK
PLAP
OH BOY, OH BOY.
AW, GOSH.

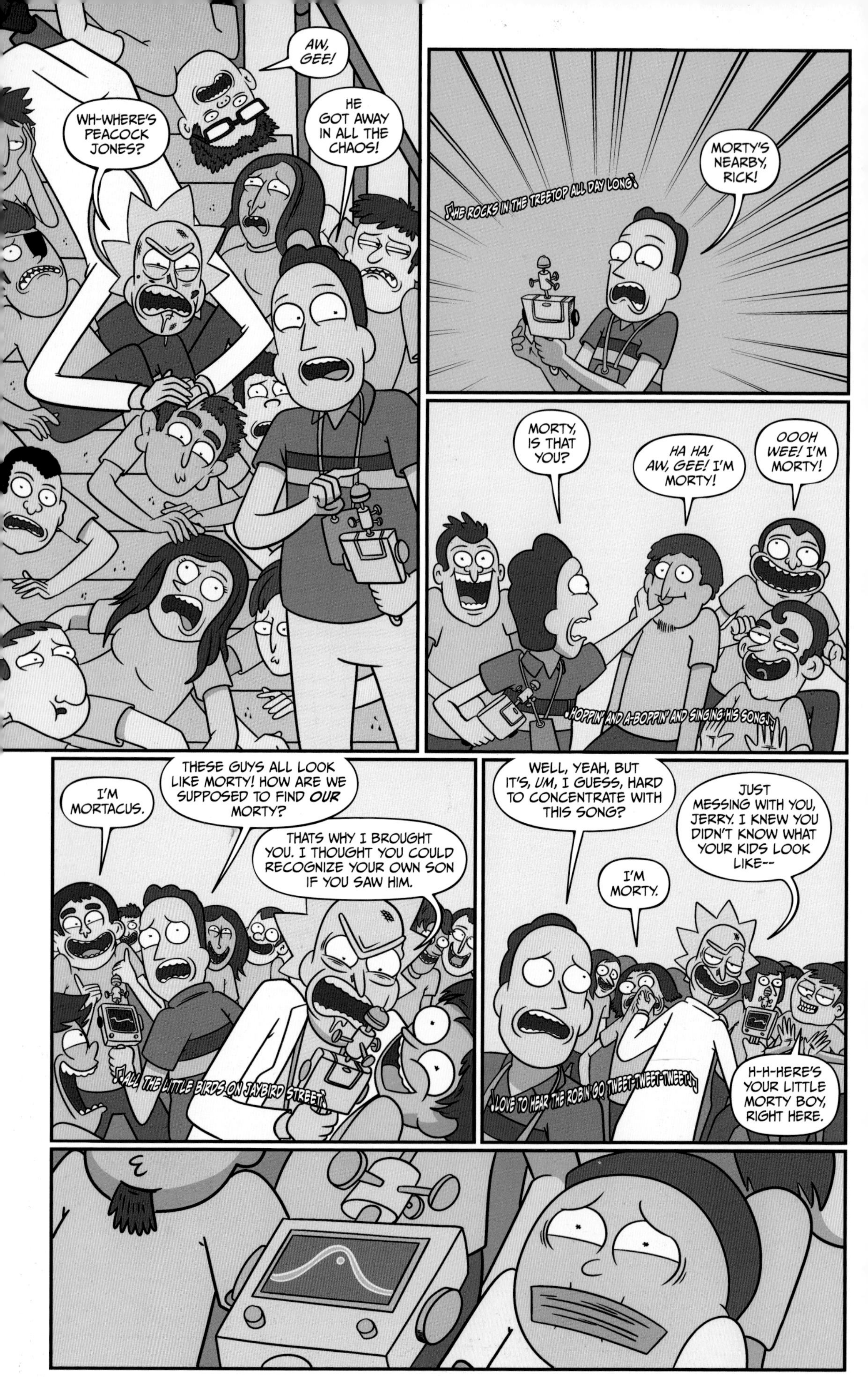
AW, GEE!
WH-WHERE'S PEACOCK JONES?
HE GOT AWAY IN ALL THE CHAOS!
HE ROCKS IN THE TREETOP ALL DAY LONG
MORTY'S NEARBY, RICK!
MORTY, IS THAT YOU?
HA HA! AW, GEE! I'M MORTY!
OOOH WEE! I'M MORTY!
HOPPIN' AND A-BOPPIN' AND SINGING HIS SONG
I'M MORTACUS.
THESE GUYS ALL LOOK LIKE MORTY! HOW ARE WE SUPPOSED TO FIND *OUR* MORTY?
THATS WHY I BROUGHT YOU. I THOUGHT YOU COULD RECOGNIZE YOUR OWN SON IF YOU SAW HIM.
ALL THE LITTLE BIRDS ON JAYBIRD STREET
WELL, YEAH, BUT IT'S, *UM*, I GUESS, HARD TO CONCENTRATE WITH THIS SONG?
I'M MORTY.
JUST MESSING WITH YOU, JERRY. I KNEW YOU DIDN'T KNOW WHAT YOUR KIDS LOOK LIKE--
LOVE TO HEAR THE ROBIN GO TWEET-TWEET-TWEET
H-H-HERE'S YOUR LITTLE MORTY BOY, RIGHT HERE.

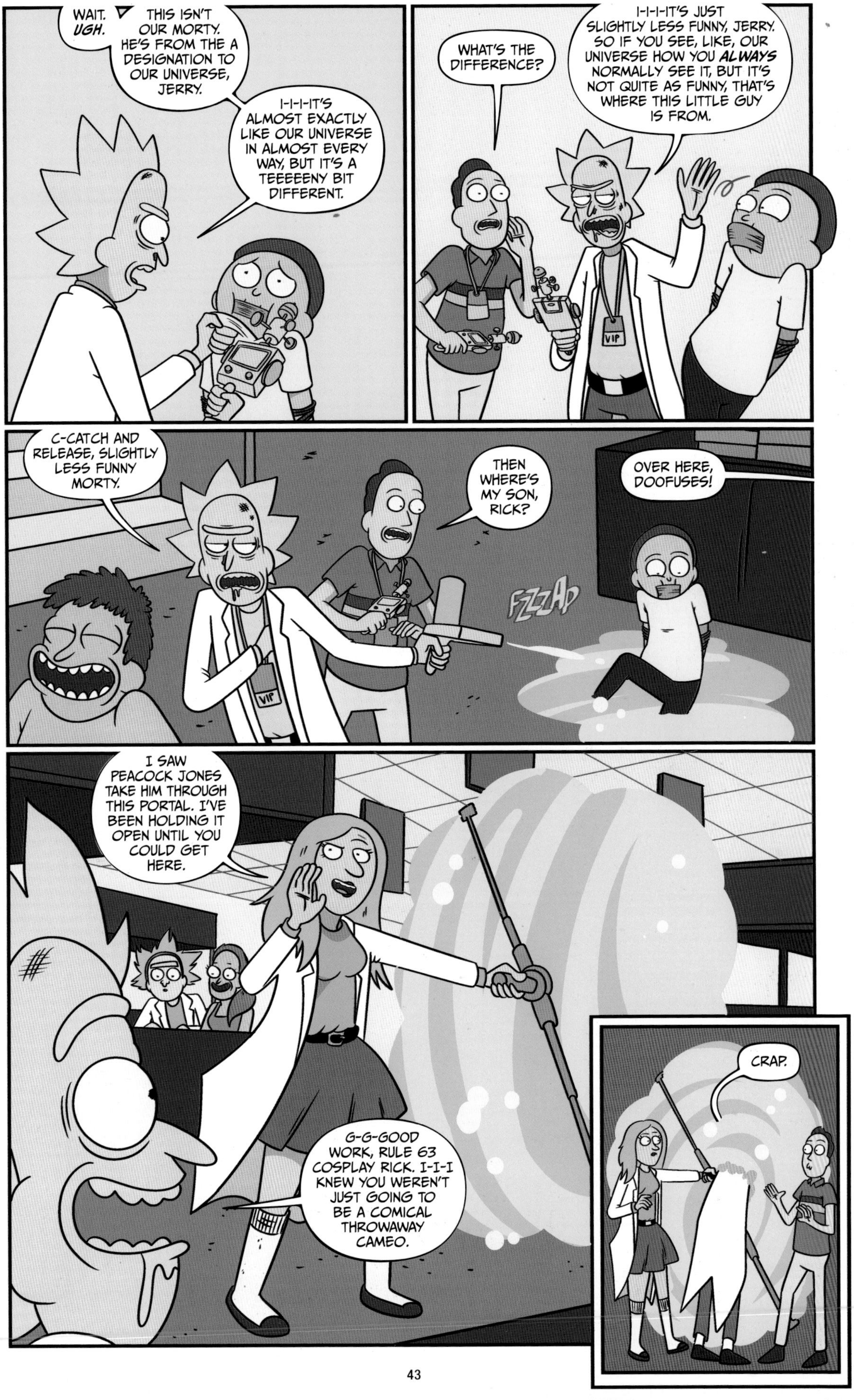
WAIT. UGH.
THIS ISN'T OUR MORTY. HE'S FROM THE A DESIGNATION TO OUR UNIVERSE, JERRY.
I-I-I-IT'S ALMOST EXACTLY LIKE OUR UNIVERSE IN ALMOST EVERY WAY, BUT IT'S A TEEEEENY BIT DIFFERENT.
WHAT'S THE DIFFERENCE?
I-I-I-IT'S JUST SLIGHTLY LESS FUNNY, JERRY. SO IF YOU SEE, LIKE, OUR UNIVERSE HOW YOU ALWAYS NORMALLY SEE IT, BUT IT'S NOT QUITE AS FUNNY, THAT'S WHERE THIS LITTLE GUY IS FROM.
VIP
C-CATCH AND RELEASE, SLIGHTLY LESS FUNNY MORTY.
THEN WHERE'S MY SON, RICK?
OVER HERE, DOOFUSES!
FZZZAP
VIP
I SAW PEACOCK JONES TAKE HIM THROUGH THIS PORTAL. I'VE BEEN HOLDING IT OPEN UNTIL YOU COULD GET HERE.
G-G-GOOD WORK, RULE 63 COSPLAY RICK. I-I-I KNEW YOU WEREN'T JUST GOING TO BE A COMICAL THROWAWAY CAMEO.
CRAP.

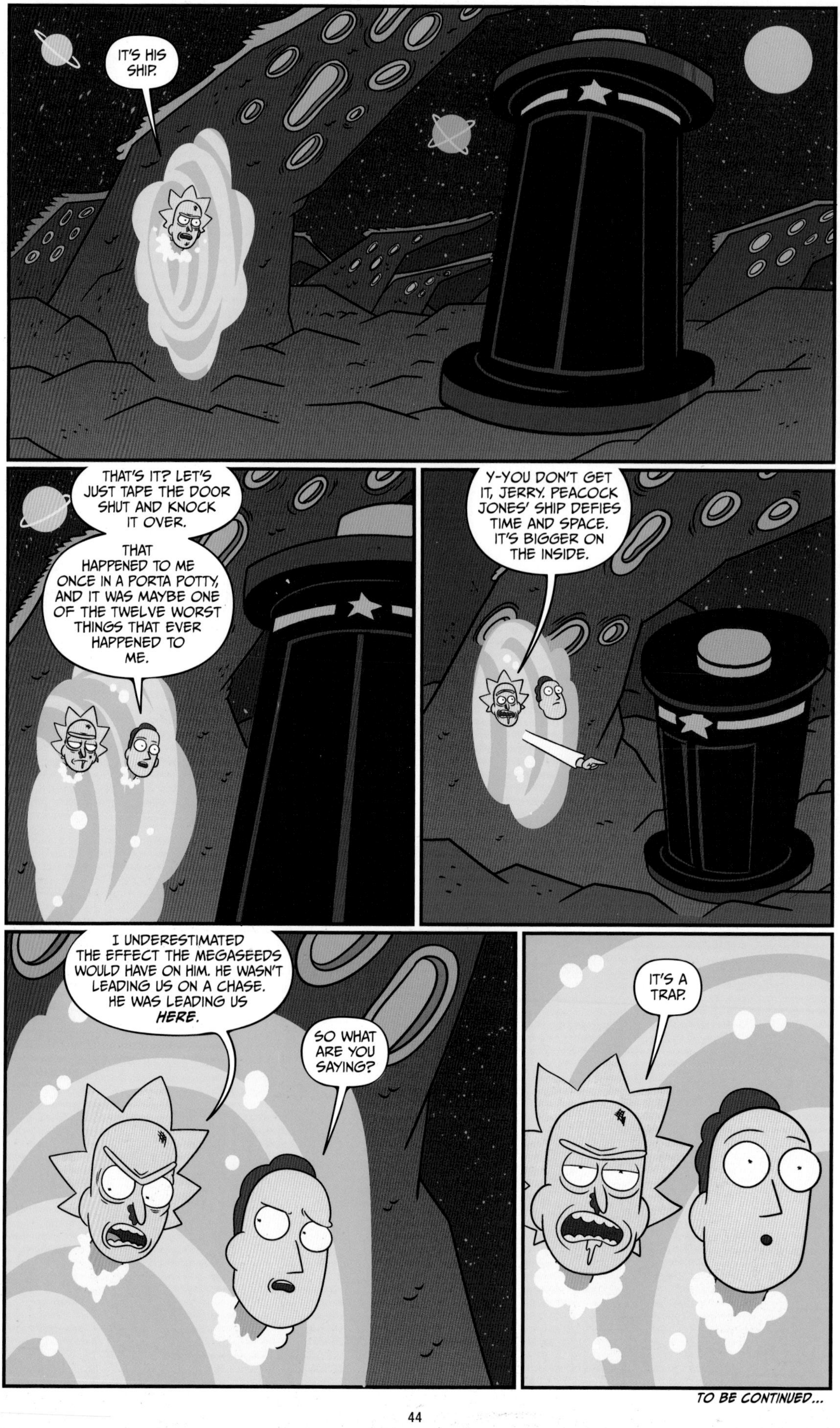
IT'S HIS SHIP.
THAT'S IT? LET'S JUST TAPE THE DOOR SHUT AND KNOCK IT OVER.
THAT HAPPENED TO ME ONCE IN A PORTA POTTY, AND IT WAS MAYBE ONE OF THE TWELVE WORST THINGS THAT EVER HAPPENED TO ME.
Y-YOU DON'T GET IT, JERRY. PEACOCK JONES' SHIP DEFIES TIME AND SPACE. IT'S BIGGER ON THE INSIDE.
I UNDERESTIMATED THE EFFECT THE MEGASEEDS WOULD HAVE ON HIM. HE WASN'T LEADING US ON A CHASE. HE WAS LEADING US *HERE*.
SO WHAT ARE YOU SAYING?
IT'S A TRAP.

*TO BE CONTINUED...*

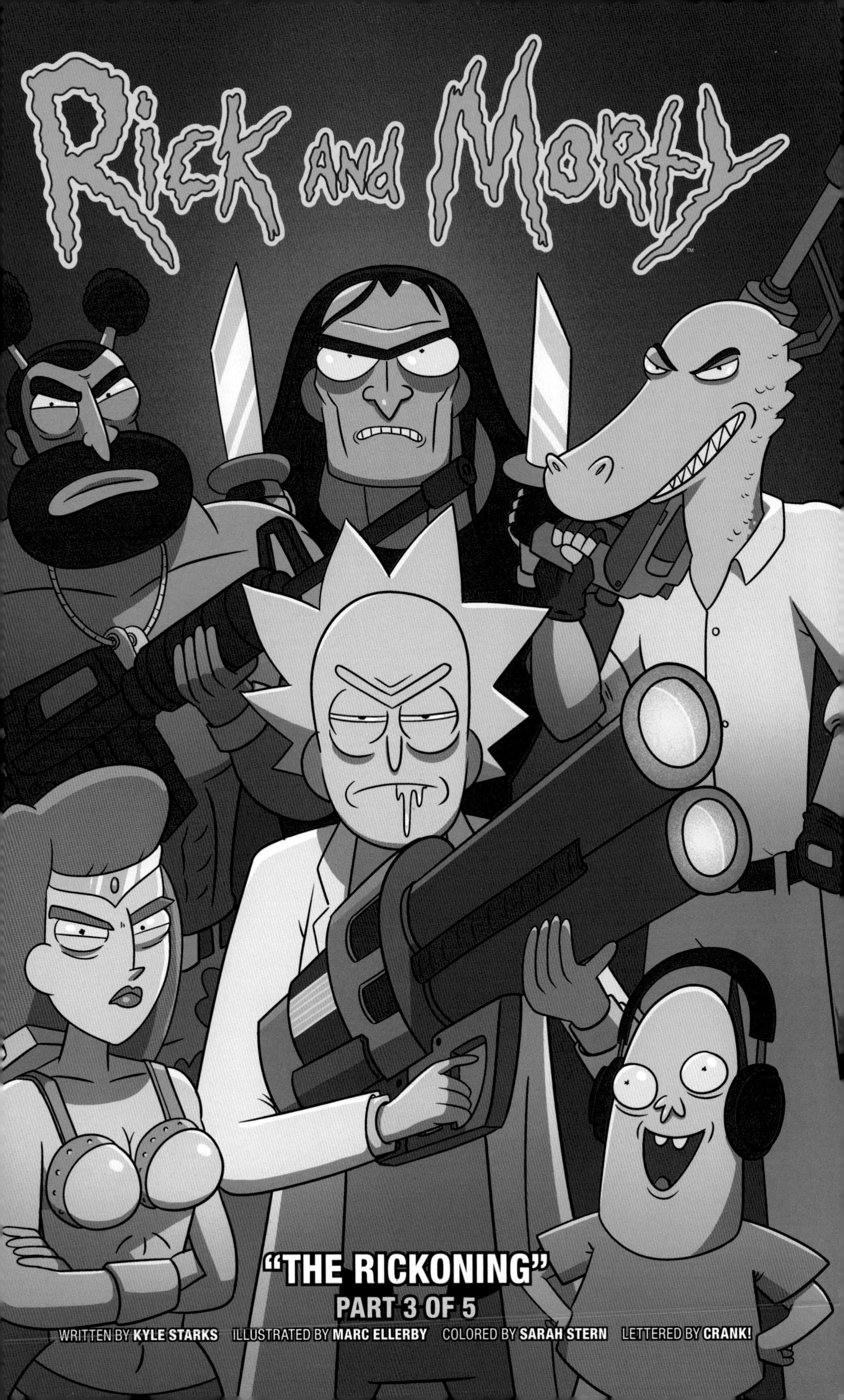
Rick and Morty™
"THE RICKONING"
PART 3 OF 5
WRITTEN BY KYLE STARKS ILLUSTRATED BY MARC ELLERBY COLORED BY SARAH STERN LETTERED BY CRANK!

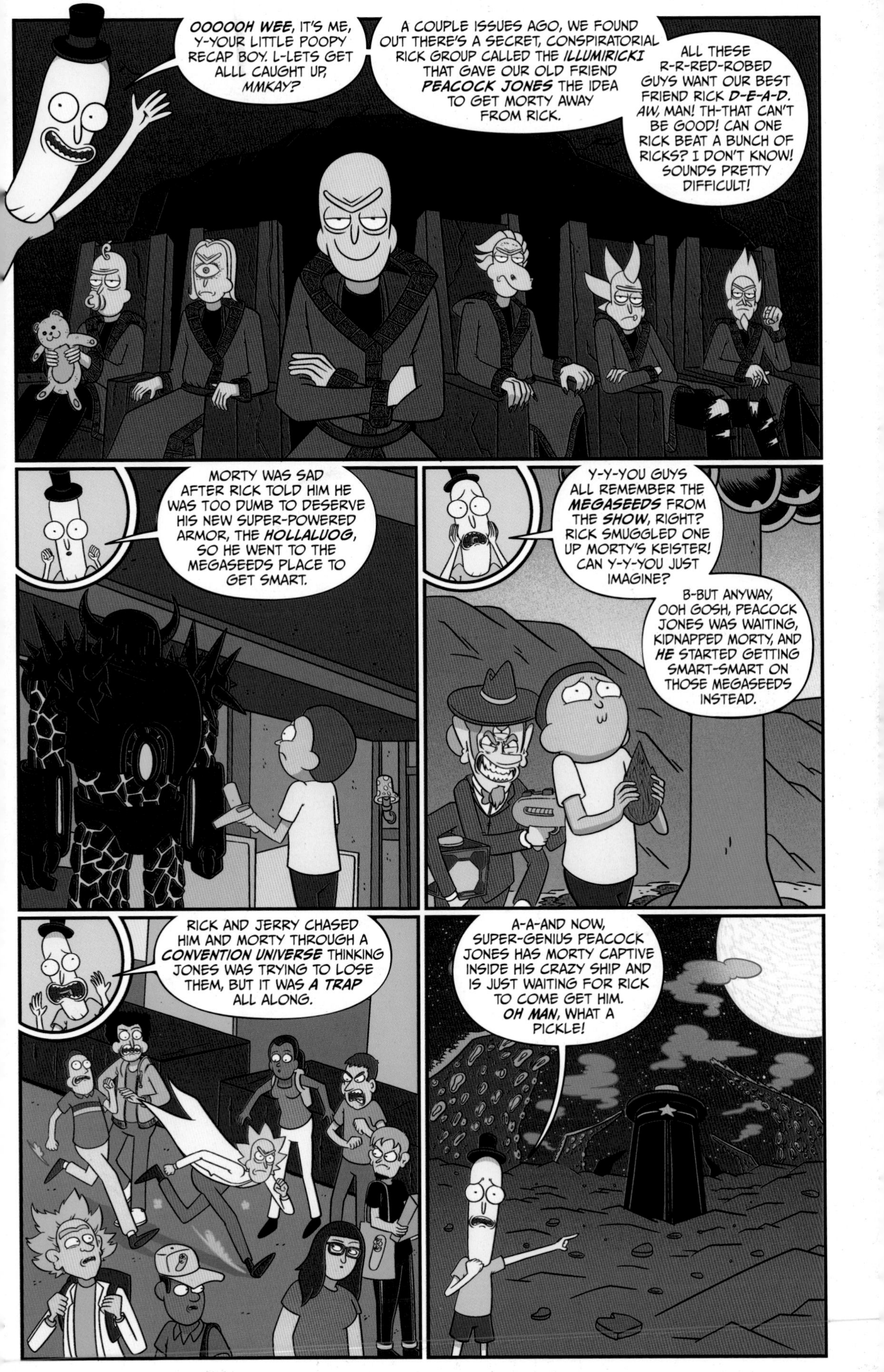
OOOOOH WEE, IT'S ME, Y-YOUR LITTLE POOPY RECAP BOY. L-LETS GET ALLL CAUGHT UP, MMKAY?
A COUPLE ISSUES AGO, WE FOUND OUT THERE'S A SECRET, CONSPIRATORIAL RICK GROUP CALLED THE ILLUMIRICKI THAT GAVE OUR OLD FRIEND PEACOCK JONES THE IDEA TO GET MORTY AWAY FROM RICK.
ALL THESE R-R-RED-ROBED GUYS WANT OUR BEST FRIEND RICK D-E-A-D. AW, MAN! TH-THAT CAN'T BE GOOD! CAN ONE RICK BEAT A BUNCH OF RICKS? I DON'T KNOW! SOUNDS PRETTY DIFFICULT!
MORTY WAS SAD AFTER RICK TOLD HIM HE WAS TOO DUMB TO DESERVE HIS NEW SUPER-POWERED ARMOR, THE HOLLALUOG, SO HE WENT TO THE MEGASEEDS PLACE TO GET SMART.
Y-Y-YOU GUYS ALL REMEMBER THE MEGASEEDS FROM THE SHOW, RIGHT? RICK SMUGGLED ONE UP MORTY'S KEISTER! CAN Y-Y-YOU JUST IMAGINE?
B-BUT ANYWAY, OOH GOSH, PEACOCK JONES WAS WAITING, KIDNAPPED MORTY, AND HE STARTED GETTING SMART-SMART ON THOSE MEGASEEDS INSTEAD.
RICK AND JERRY CHASED HIM AND MORTY THROUGH A CONVENTION UNIVERSE THINKING JONES WAS TRYING TO LOSE THEM, BUT IT WAS A TRAP ALL ALONG.
A-A-AND NOW, SUPER-GENIUS PEACOCK JONES HAS MORTY CAPTIVE INSIDE HIS CRAZY SHIP AND IS JUST WAITING FOR RICK TO COME GET HIM. OH MAN, WHAT A PICKLE!

KILL RICK SANCHEZ.

ALL RIGHT, SO WE KNOW THIS IS A TRAP, BUT WE NEED A PLAN.

SO WE HAVE TO GO IN THERE AND SAVE MORTY. BUT--

--AND THIS IS THE TRICKY PART--

WE HAVE TO DO IT AND NOT GET OURSELVES KILLED.

S-S-SOMETIMES I ASK MYSELF, "WHAT IF I GOT A SIDEKICK THAT WASN'T DUMB AS A TURNIP," BUT THEN I REMEMBER THAT TIME I WAS SHIPWRECKED ON TURNIP-45 AND THE TURNIP PEOPLE WERE SURPRISINGLY HELPFUL.

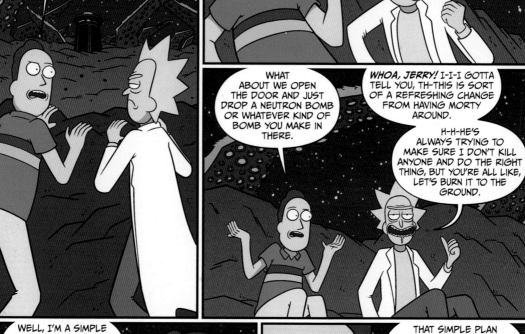

WHAT ABOUT WE OPEN THE DOOR AND JUST DROP A NEUTRON BOMB OR WHATEVER KIND OF BOMB YOU MAKE IN THERE.

WHOA, JERRY! I-I-I GOTTA TELL YOU, TH-THIS IS SORT OF A REFRESHING CHANGE FROM HAVING MORTY AROUND.

H-H-HE'S ALWAYS TRYING TO MAKE SURE I DON'T KILL ANYONE AND DO THE RIGHT THING, BUT YOU'RE ALL LIKE, LET'S BURN IT TO THE GROUND.

WELL, I'M A SIMPLE MAN, AND I ONLY SEE SIMPLE SOLUTIONS, AND I DON'T REALLY BOTHER TAKING THE TIME THINKING OUT PROS OR CONS OR REPERCUSSIONS.

THAT SIMPLE PLAN WOULD DEFINITELY TURN YOUR SON INTO A MORTY-SIZED PILE OF SMOKING ASH...SO IT'S STILL A DUMB PLAN, JERRY. NOT SURPRISINGLY.

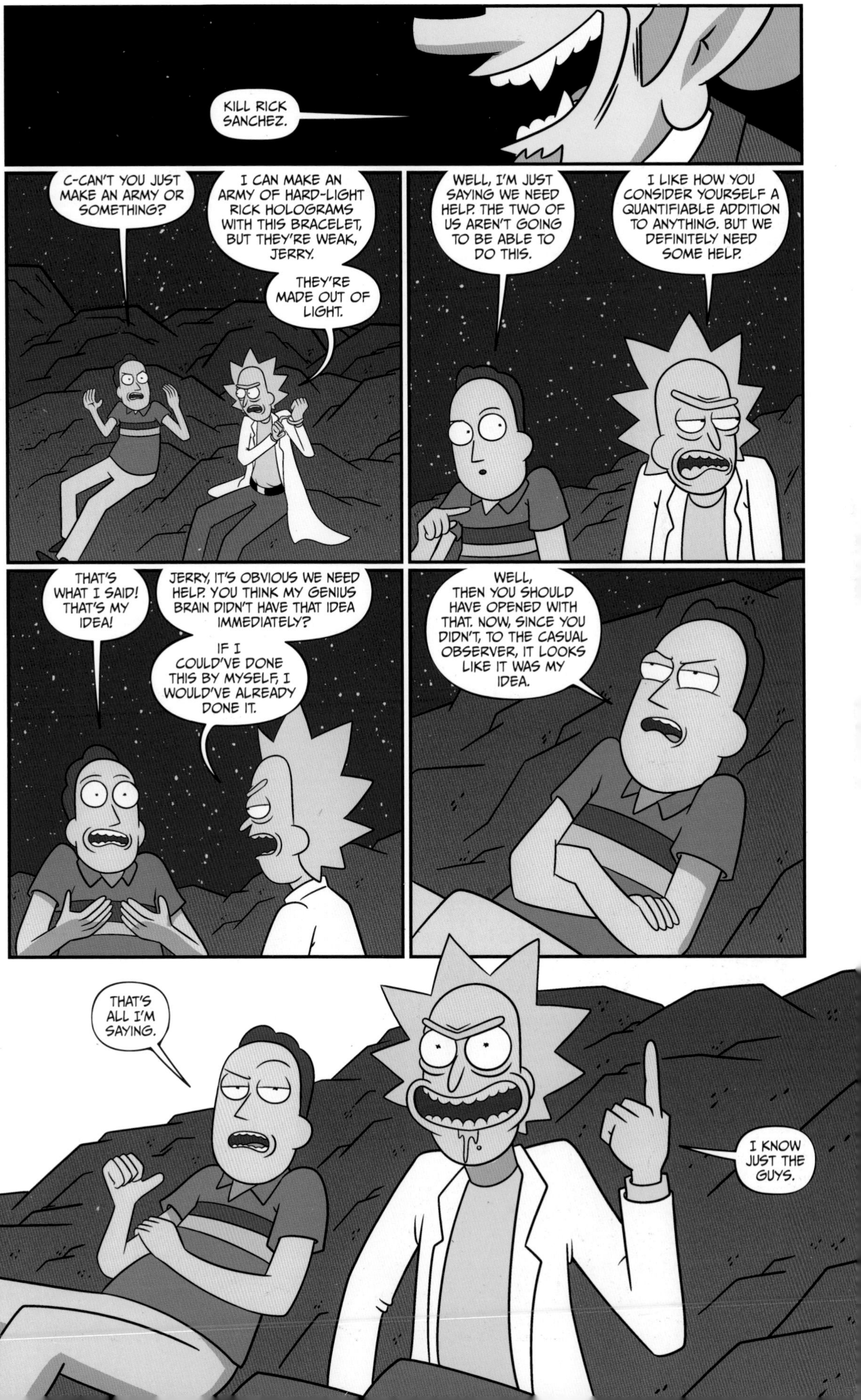
KILL RICK SANCHEZ.
C-CAN'T YOU JUST MAKE AN ARMY OR SOMETHING?
I CAN MAKE AN ARMY OF HARD-LIGHT RICK HOLOGRAMS WITH THIS BRACELET, BUT THEY'RE WEAK, JERRY.
THEY'RE MADE OUT OF LIGHT.
WELL, I'M JUST SAYING WE NEED HELP. THE TWO OF US AREN'T GOING TO BE ABLE TO DO THIS.
I LIKE HOW YOU CONSIDER YOURSELF A QUANTIFIABLE ADDITION TO ANYTHING. BUT WE DEFINITELY NEED SOME HELP.
THAT'S WHAT I SAID! THAT'S MY IDEA!
JERRY, IT'S OBVIOUS WE NEED HELP. YOU THINK MY GENIUS BRAIN DIDN'T HAVE THAT IDEA IMMEDIATELY?
IF I COULD'VE DONE THIS BY MYSELF, I WOULD'VE ALREADY DONE IT.
WELL, THEN YOU SHOULD HAVE OPENED WITH THAT. NOW, SINCE YOU DIDN'T, TO THE CASUAL OBSERVER, IT LOOKS LIKE IT WAS MY IDEA.
THAT'S ALL I'M SAYING.
I KNOW JUST THE GUYS.

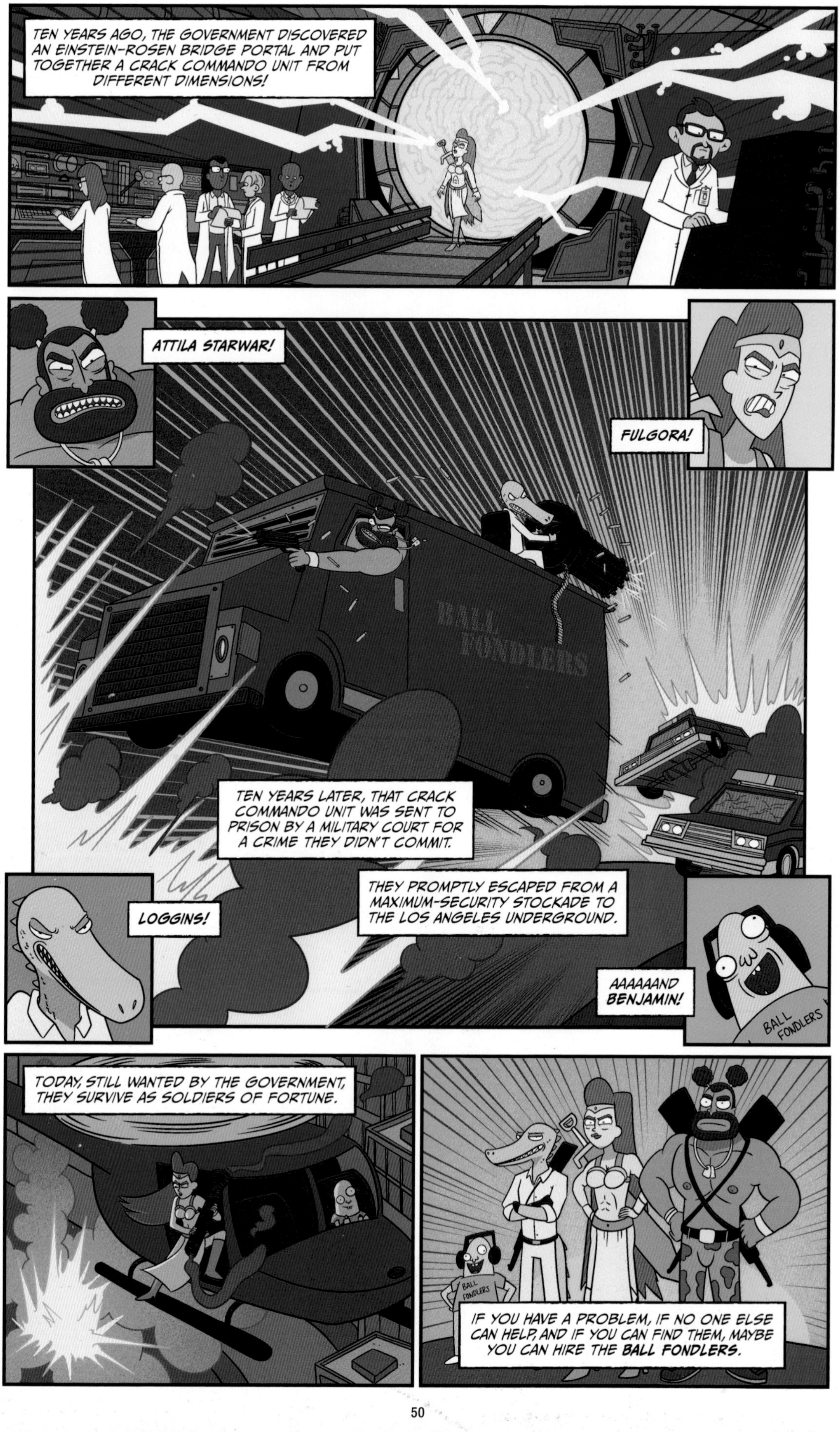
TEN YEARS AGO, THE GOVERNMENT DISCOVERED AN EINSTEIN-ROSEN BRIDGE PORTAL AND PUT TOGETHER A CRACK COMMANDO UNIT FROM DIFFERENT DIMENSIONS!
ATTILA STARWAR!
FULGORA!
BALL FONDLERS
TEN YEARS LATER, THAT CRACK COMMANDO UNIT WAS SENT TO PRISON BY A MILITARY COURT FOR A CRIME THEY DIDN'T COMMIT.
LOGGINS!
THEY PROMPTLY ESCAPED FROM A MAXIMUM-SECURITY STOCKADE TO THE LOS ANGELES UNDERGROUND.
AAAAAAND BENJAMIN!
BALL FONDLERS
TODAY, STILL WANTED BY THE GOVERNMENT, THEY SURVIVE AS SOLDIERS OF FORTUNE.
BALL FONDLERS
IF YOU HAVE A PROBLEM, IF NO ONE ELSE CAN HELP, AND IF YOU CAN FIND THEM, MAYBE YOU CAN HIRE THE BALL FONDLERS.

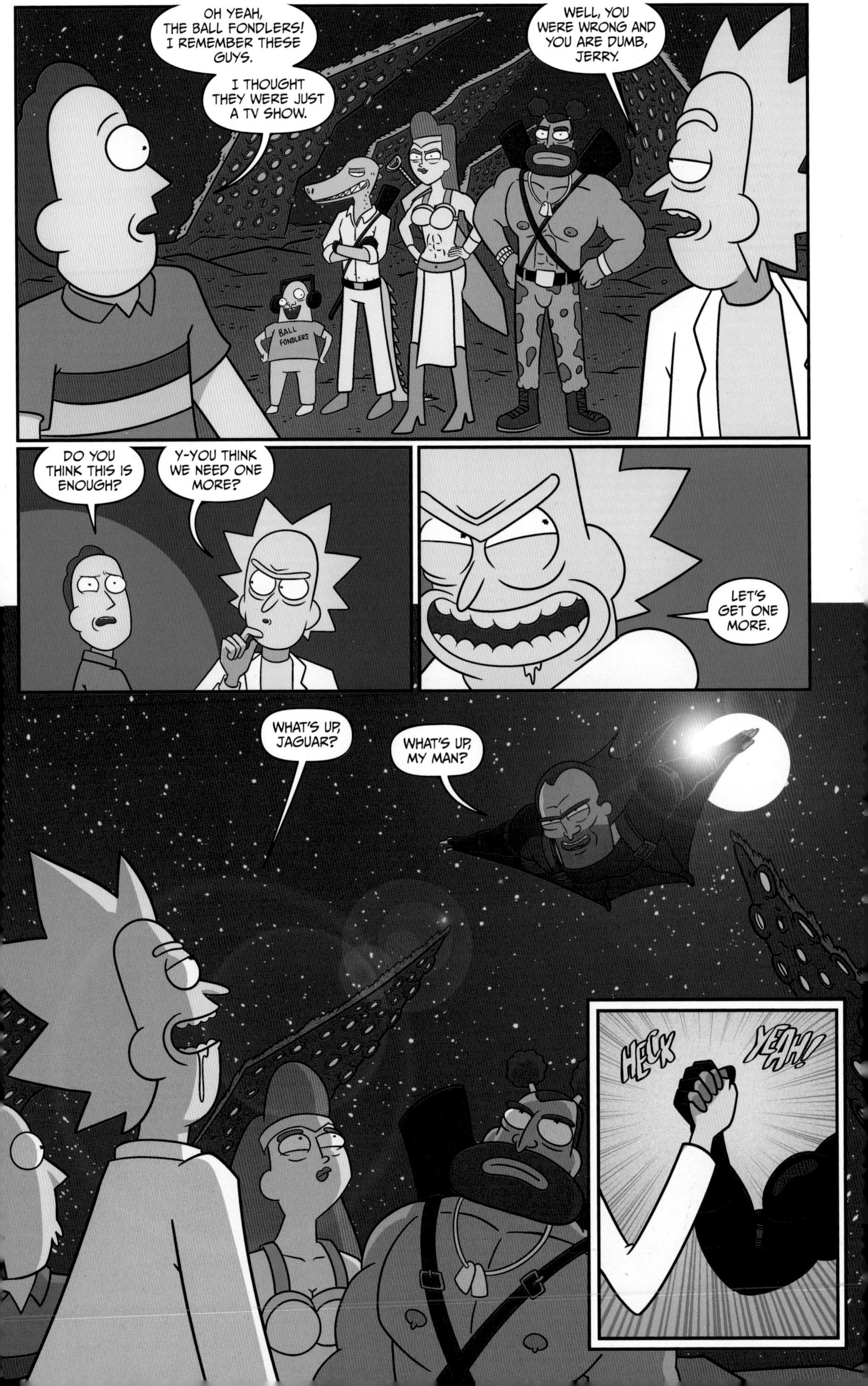
OH YEAH, THE BALL FONDLERS! I REMEMBER THESE GUYS.
I THOUGHT THEY WERE JUST A TV SHOW.
WELL, YOU WERE WRONG AND YOU ARE DUMB, JERRY.
BALL FONDLERS
DO YOU THINK THIS IS ENOUGH?
Y-YOU THINK WE NEED ONE MORE?
LET'S GET ONE MORE.
WHAT'S UP, JAGUAR?
WHAT'S UP, MY MAN?
HECK YEAH!

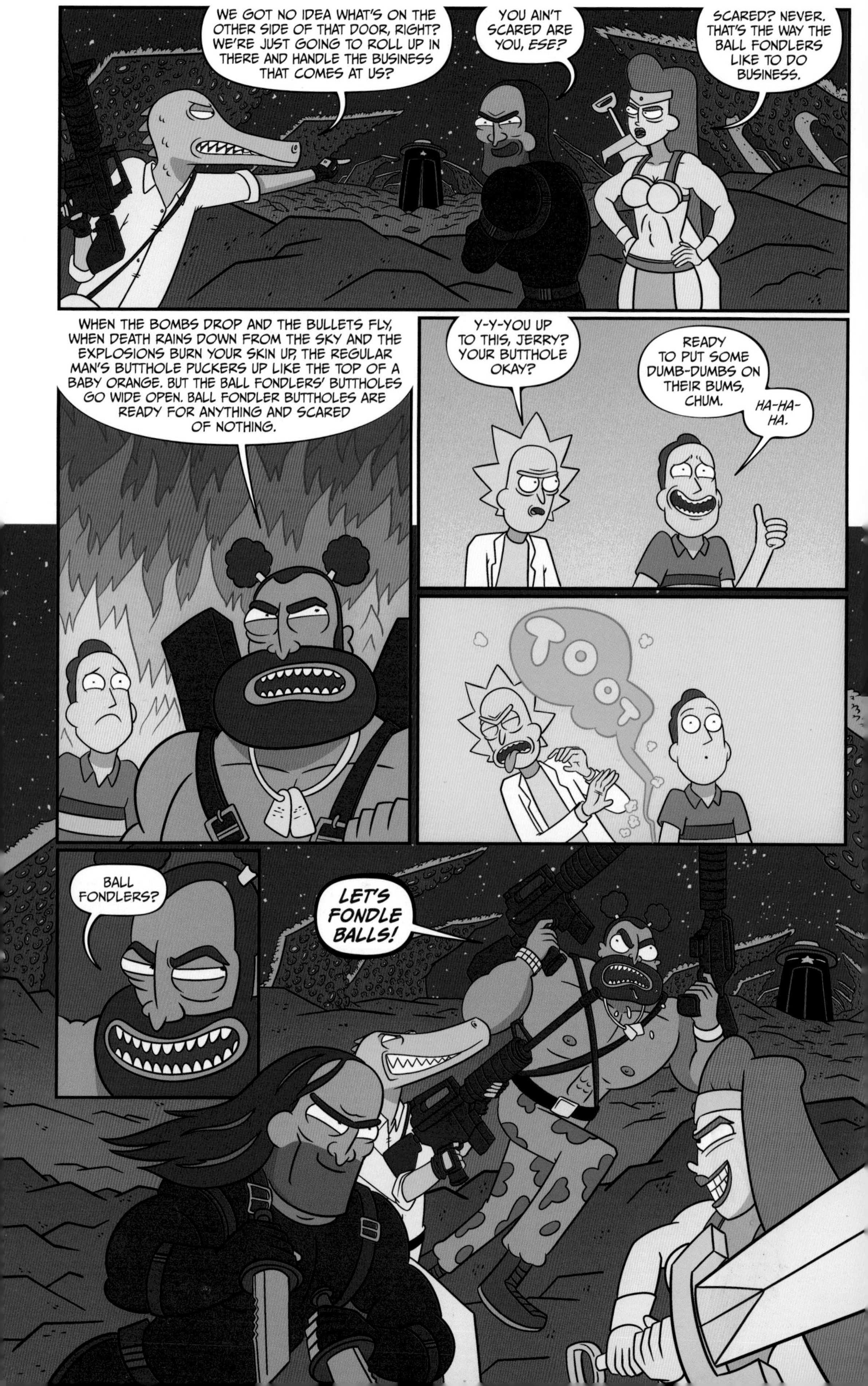
WE GOT NO IDEA WHAT'S ON THE OTHER SIDE OF THAT DOOR, RIGHT? WE'RE JUST GOING TO ROLL UP IN THERE AND HANDLE THE BUSINESS THAT COMES AT US?
YOU AIN'T SCARED ARE YOU, *ESE*?
SCARED? NEVER. THAT'S THE WAY THE BALL FONDLERS LIKE TO DO BUSINESS.
WHEN THE BOMBS DROP AND THE BULLETS FLY, WHEN DEATH RAINS DOWN FROM THE SKY AND THE EXPLOSIONS BURN YOUR SKIN UP, THE REGULAR MAN'S BUTTHOLE PUCKERS UP LIKE THE TOP OF A BABY ORANGE. BUT THE BALL FONDLERS' BUTTHOLES GO WIDE OPEN. BALL FONDLER BUTTHOLES ARE READY FOR ANYTHING AND SCARED OF NOTHING.
Y-Y-YOU UP TO THIS, JERRY? YOUR BUTTHOLE OKAY?
READY TO PUT SOME DUMB-DUMBS ON THEIR BUMS, CHUM.
HA-HA-HA.
TOOT
BALL FONDLERS?
LET'S FONDLE BALLS!

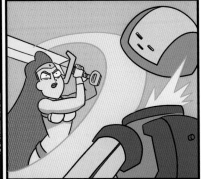

PEW! PEW!

PEW!

YOU DON'T HAVE TO MAKE THE GUN NOISES, JERRY!

I DON'T KNOW WHAT I'M DOING, AND THAT'S OKAY!

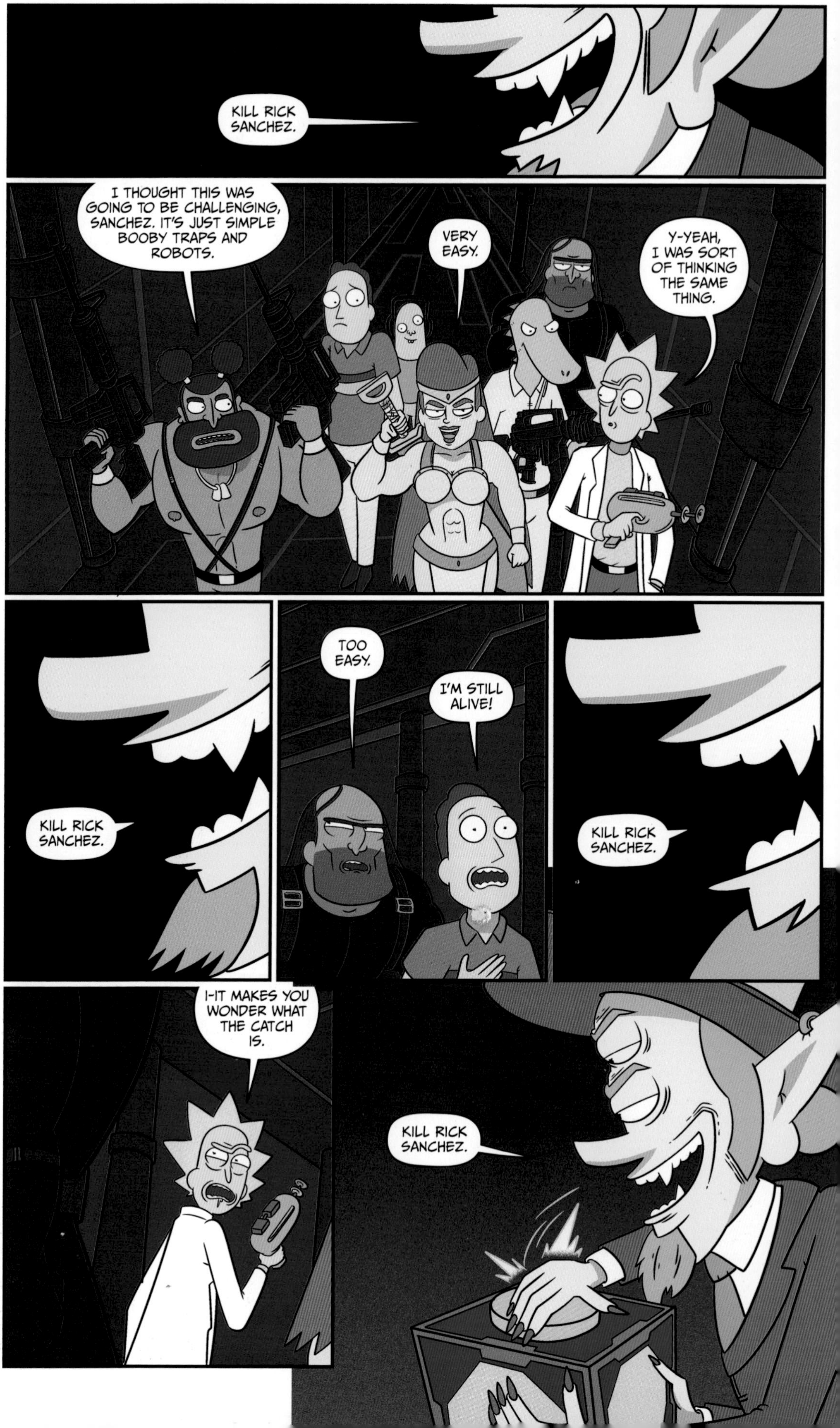
KILL RICK SANCHEZ.
I THOUGHT THIS WAS GOING TO BE CHALLENGING, SANCHEZ. IT'S JUST SIMPLE BOOBY TRAPS AND ROBOTS.
VERY EASY.
Y-YEAH, I WAS SORT OF THINKING THE SAME THING.
KILL RICK SANCHEZ.
TOO EASY.
I'M STILL ALIVE!
KILL RICK SANCHEZ.
I-IT MAKES YOU WONDER WHAT THE CATCH IS.
KILL RICK SANCHEZ.

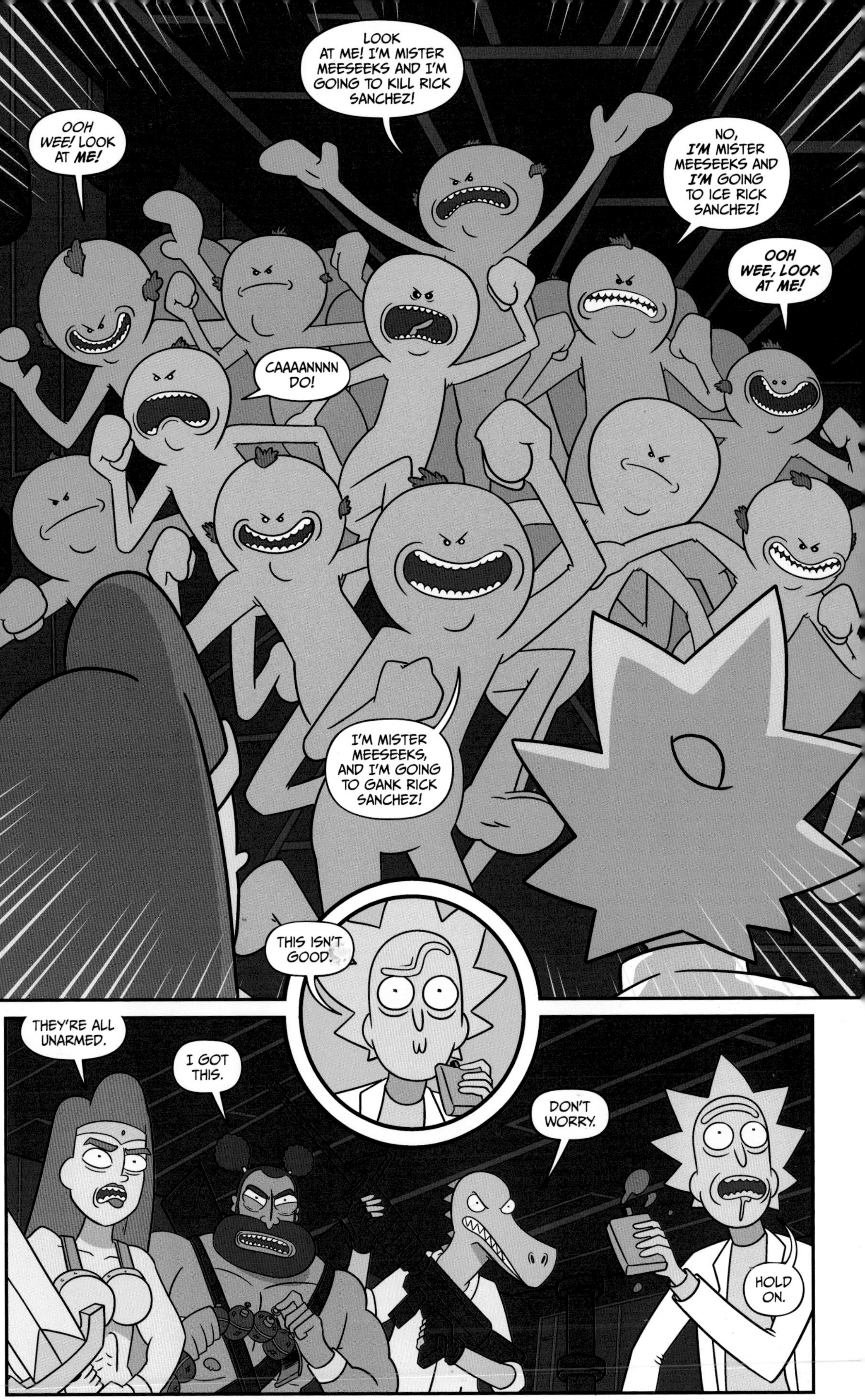
OOH WEE! LOOK AT *ME!*
LOOK AT ME! I'M MISTER MEESEEKS AND I'M GOING TO KILL RICK SANCHEZ!
NO, *I'M* MISTER MEESEEKS AND *I'M* GOING TO ICE RICK SANCHEZ!
OOH WEE, LOOK AT ME!
CAAAANNNN DO!
I'M MISTER MEESEEKS, AND I'M GOING TO GANK RICK SANCHEZ!
THIS ISN'T GOOD.
THEY'RE ALL UNARMED.
I GOT THIS.
DON'T WORRY.
HOLD ON.

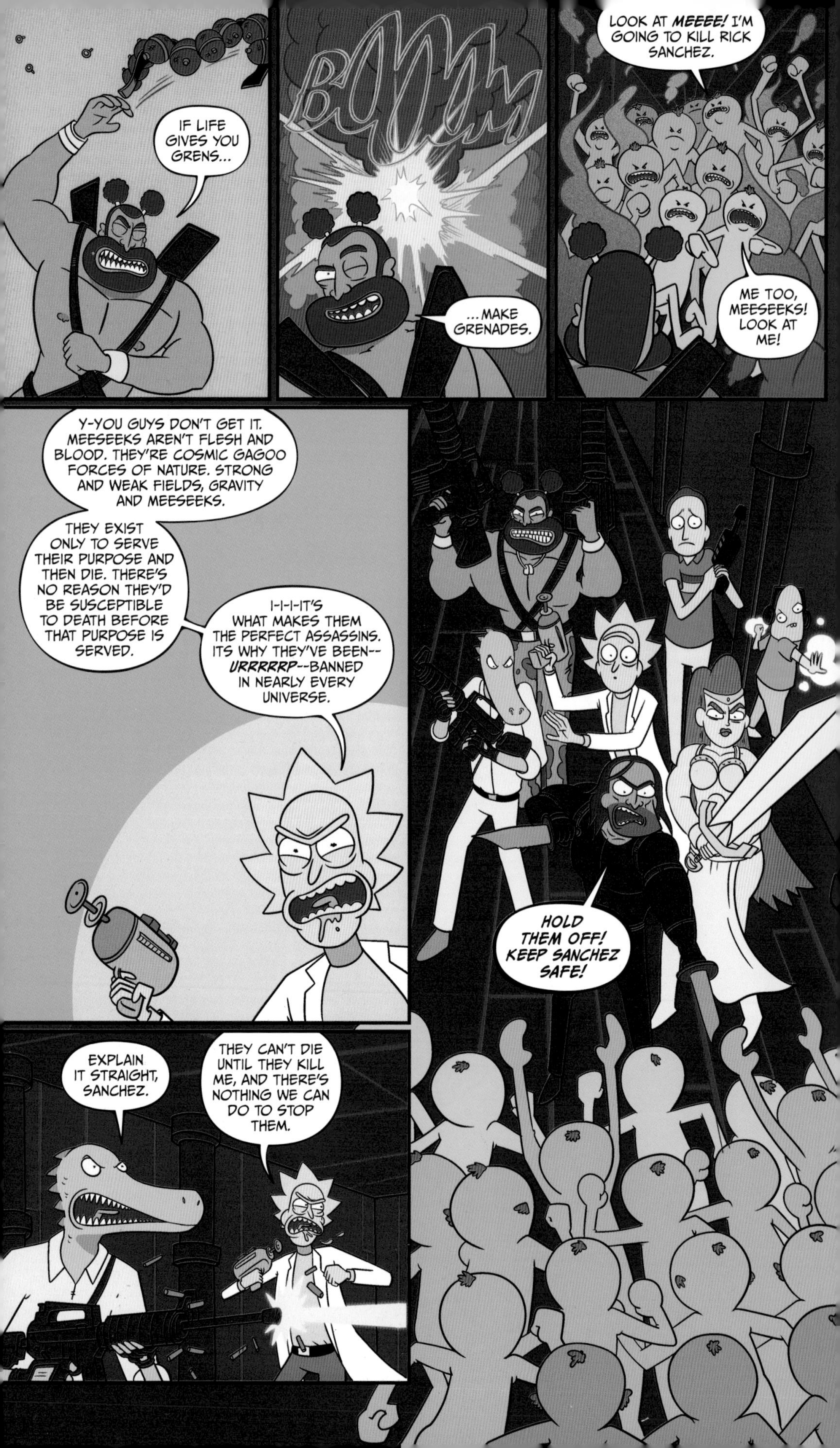
IF LIFE GIVES YOU GRENS...
BOOM
...MAKE GRENADES.
LOOK AT MEEEE! I'M GOING TO KILL RICK SANCHEZ.
ME TOO, MEESEEKS! LOOK AT ME!
Y-YOU GUYS DON'T GET IT. MEESEEKS AREN'T FLESH AND BLOOD. THEY'RE COSMIC GAGOO FORCES OF NATURE. STRONG AND WEAK FIELDS, GRAVITY AND MEESEEKS.
THEY EXIST ONLY TO SERVE THEIR PURPOSE AND THEN DIE. THERE'S NO REASON THEY'D BE SUSCEPTIBLE TO DEATH BEFORE THAT PURPOSE IS SERVED.
I-I-I-IT'S WHAT MAKES THEM THE PERFECT ASSASSINS. ITS WHY THEY'VE BEEN-- URRRRRP--BANNED IN NEARLY EVERY UNIVERSE.
HOLD THEM OFF! KEEP SANCHEZ SAFE!
EXPLAIN IT STRAIGHT, SANCHEZ.
THEY CAN'T DIE UNTIL THEY KILL ME, AND THERE'S NOTHING WE CAN DO TO STOP THEM.

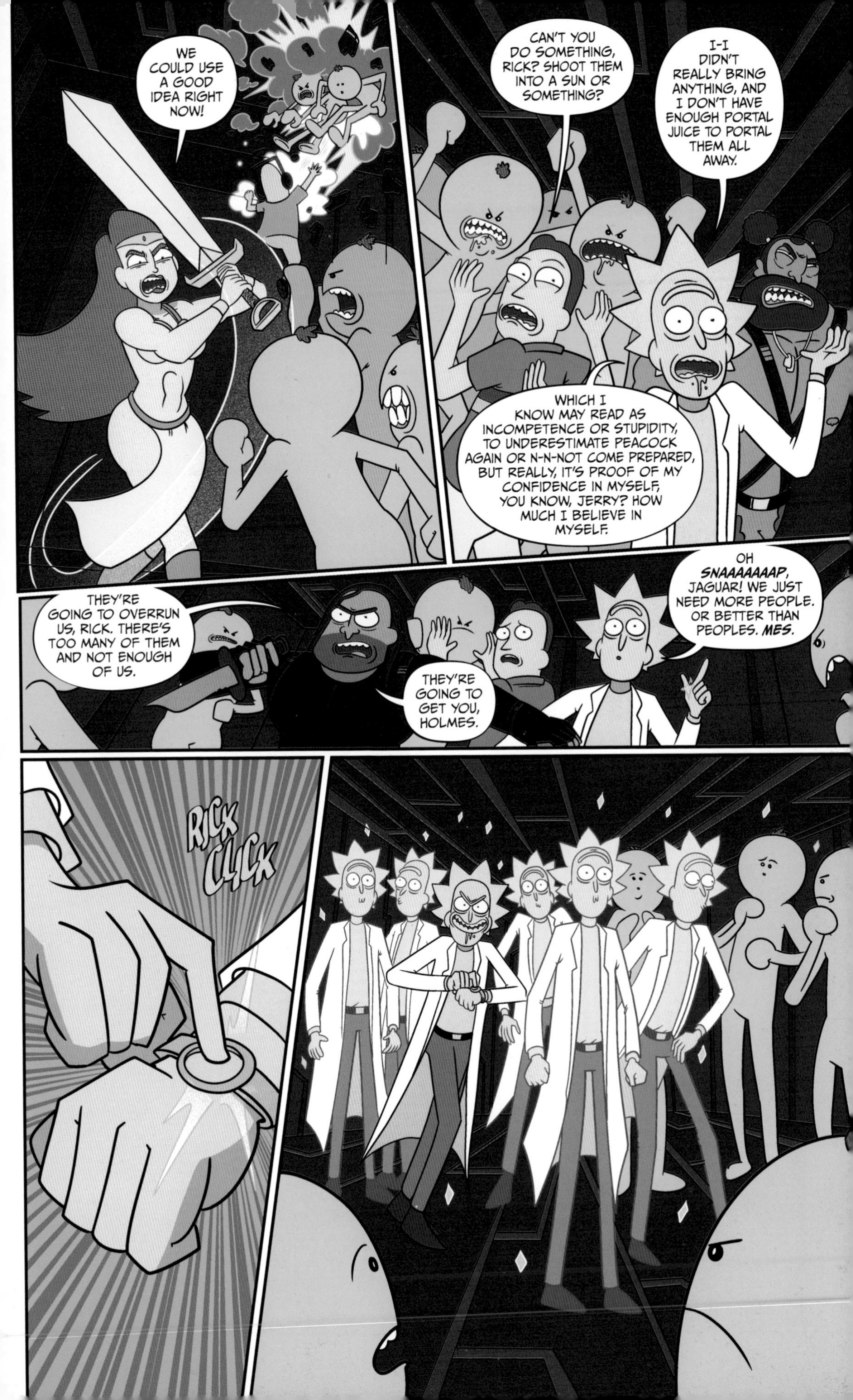
WE COULD USE A GOOD IDEA RIGHT NOW!
CAN'T YOU DO SOMETHING, RICK? SHOOT THEM INTO A SUN OR SOMETHING?
I-I DIDN'T REALLY BRING ANYTHING, AND I DON'T HAVE ENOUGH PORTAL JUICE TO PORTAL THEM ALL AWAY.
WHICH I KNOW MAY READ AS INCOMPETENCE OR STUPIDITY, TO UNDERESTIMATE PEACOCK AGAIN OR N-N-NOT COME PREPARED, BUT REALLY, IT'S PROOF OF MY CONFIDENCE IN MYSELF, YOU KNOW, JERRY? HOW MUCH I BELIEVE IN MYSELF.
THEY'RE GOING TO OVERRUN US, RICK. THERE'S TOO MANY OF THEM AND NOT ENOUGH OF US.
THEY'RE GOING TO GET YOU, HOLMES.
OH SNAAAAAAAP, JAGUAR! WE JUST NEED MORE PEOPLE. OR BETTER THAN PEOPLES. MES.
RICK CLICK

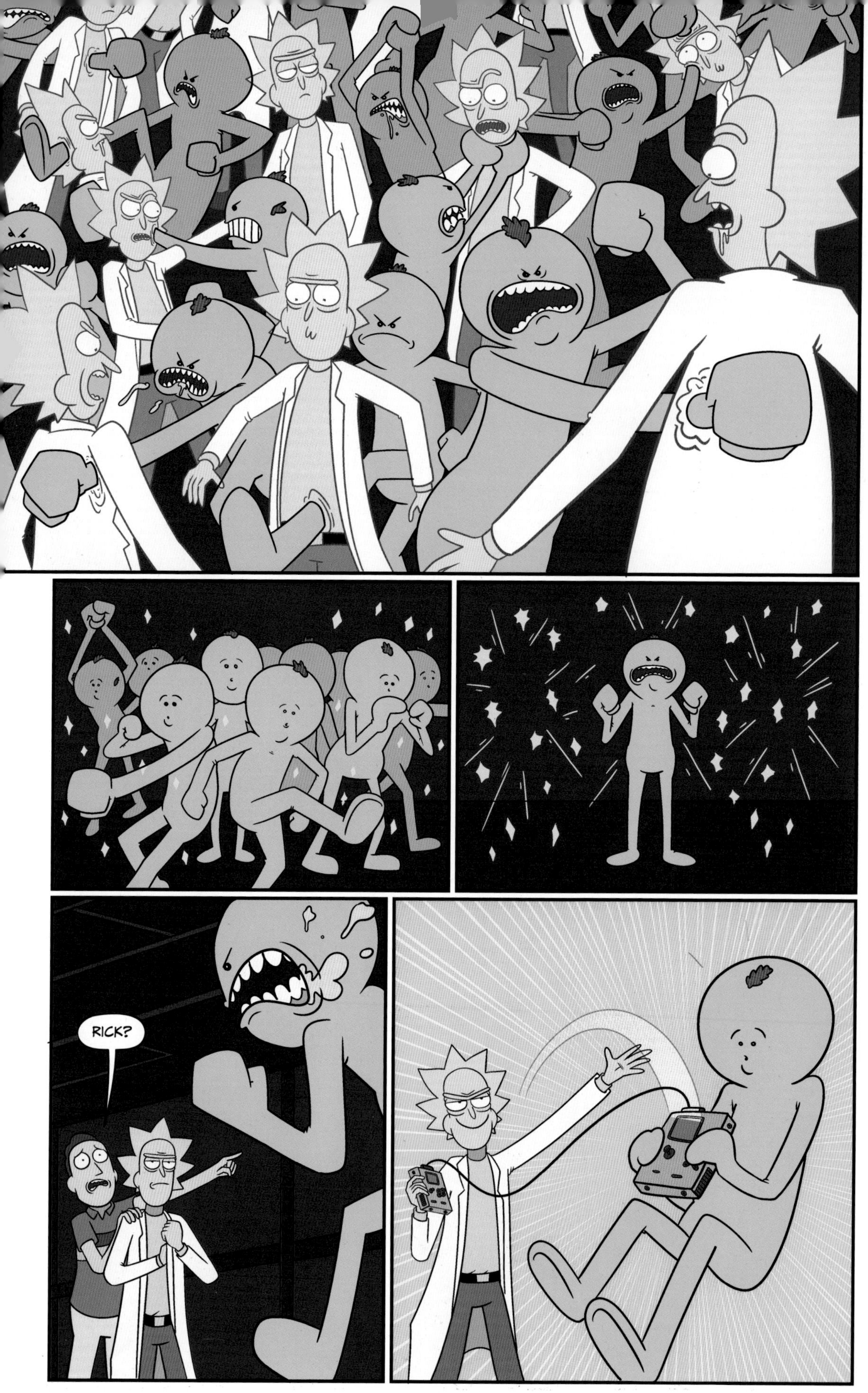
RICK?

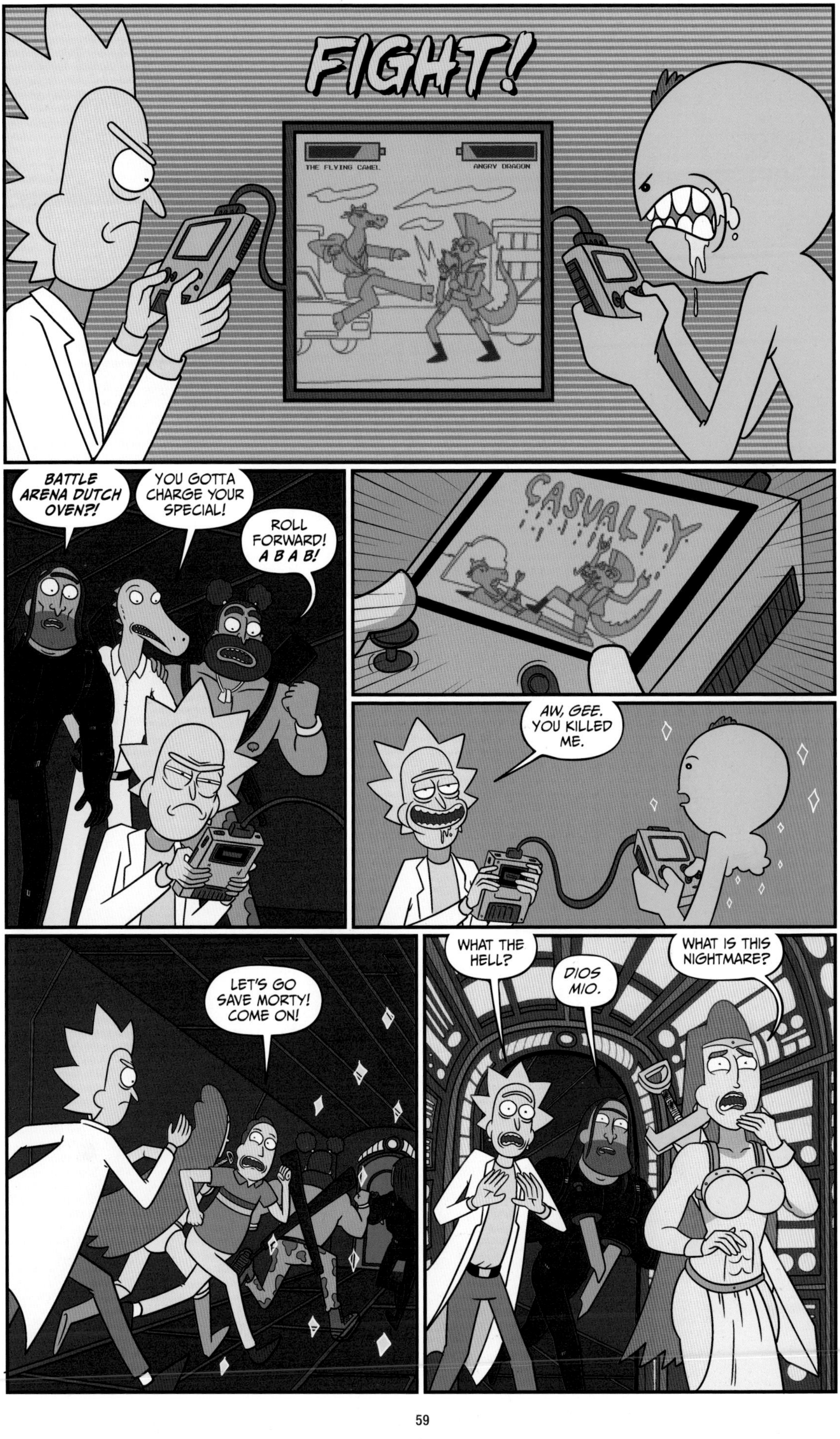

FIGHT!
THE FLYING CAMEL
ANGRY DRAGON
BATTLE ARENA DUTCH OVEN?!
YOU GOTTA CHARGE YOUR SPECIAL!
ROLL FORWARD! A B A B!
CASUALTY
AW, GEE. YOU KILLED ME.
LET'S GO SAVE MORTY! COME ON!
WHAT THE HELL?
DIOS MIO.
WHAT IS THIS NIGHTMARE?

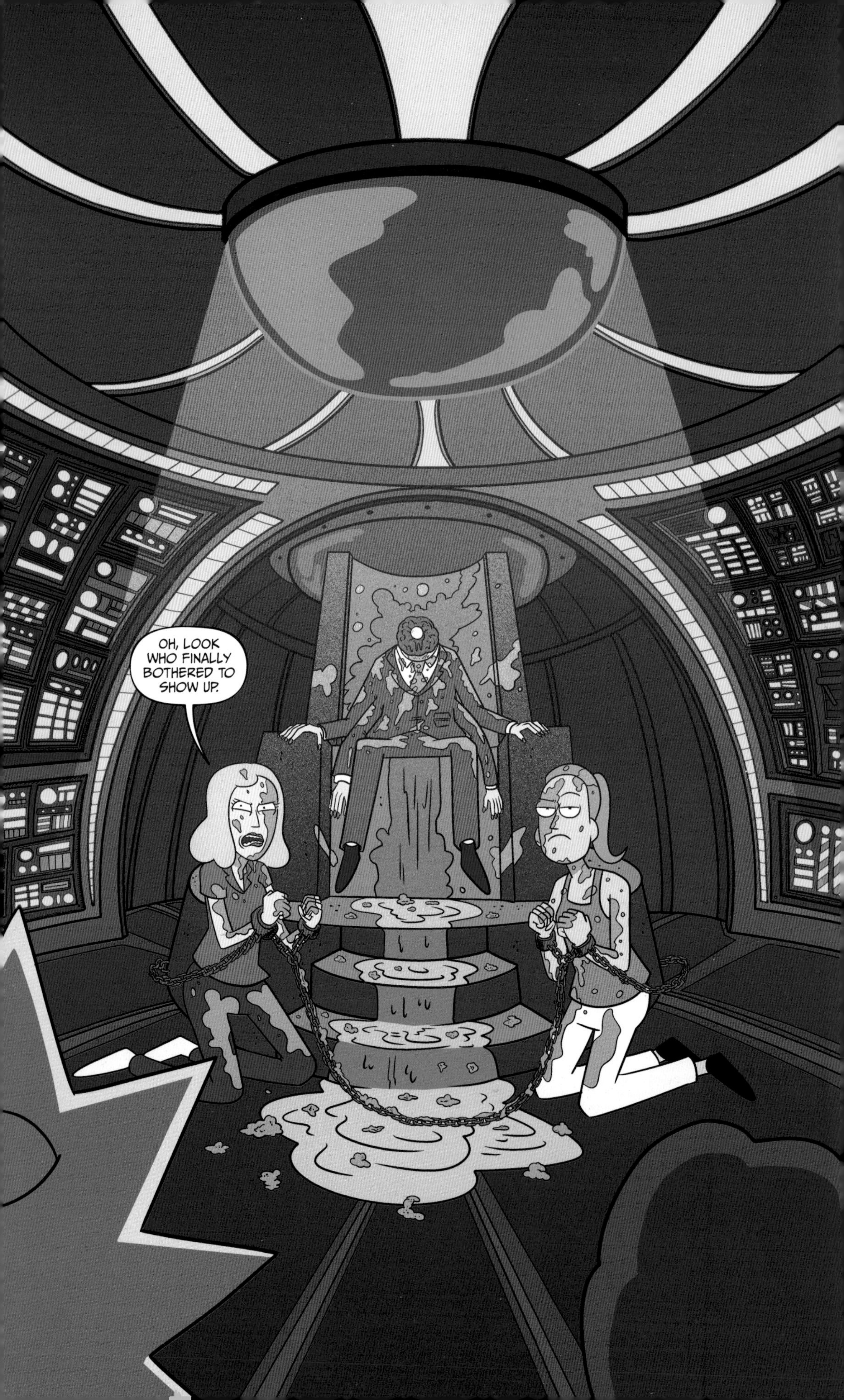
OH, LOOK WHO FINALLY BOTHERED TO SHOW UP.

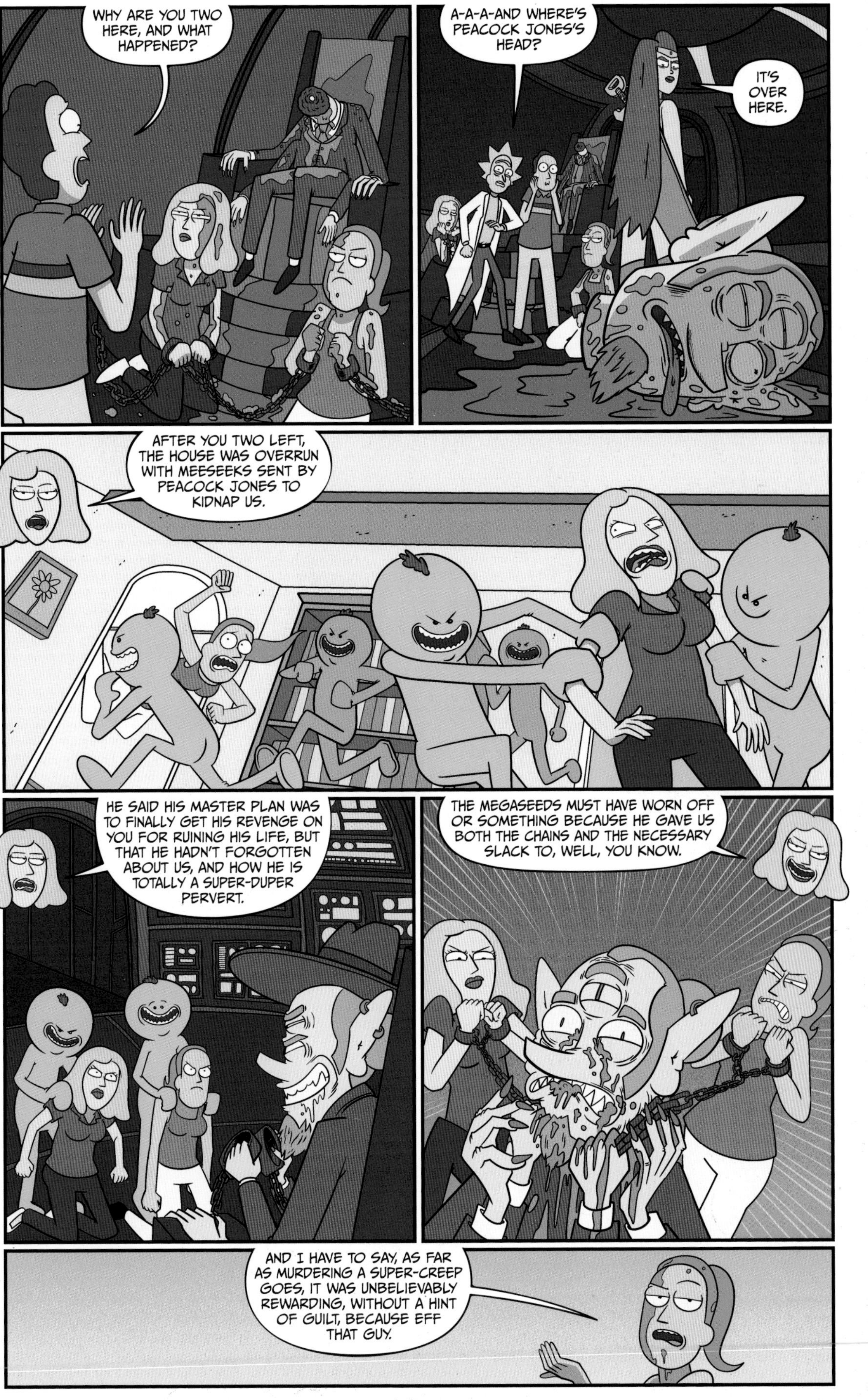
WHY ARE YOU TWO HERE, AND WHAT HAPPENED?
A-A-A-AND WHERE'S PEACOCK JONES'S HEAD?
IT'S OVER HERE.
AFTER YOU TWO LEFT, THE HOUSE WAS OVERRUN WITH MEESEEKS SENT BY PEACOCK JONES TO KIDNAP US.
HE SAID HIS MASTER PLAN WAS TO FINALLY GET HIS REVENGE ON YOU FOR RUINING HIS LIFE, BUT THAT HE HADN'T FORGOTTEN ABOUT US, AND HOW HE IS TOTALLY A SUPER-DUPER PERVERT.
THE MEGASEEDS MUST HAVE WORN OFF OR SOMETHING BECAUSE HE GAVE US BOTH THE CHAINS AND THE NECESSARY SLACK TO, WELL, YOU KNOW.
AND I HAVE TO SAY, AS FAR AS MURDERING A SUPER-CREEP GOES, IT WAS UNBELIEVABLY REWARDING, WITHOUT A HINT OF GUILT, BECAUSE EFF THAT GUY.

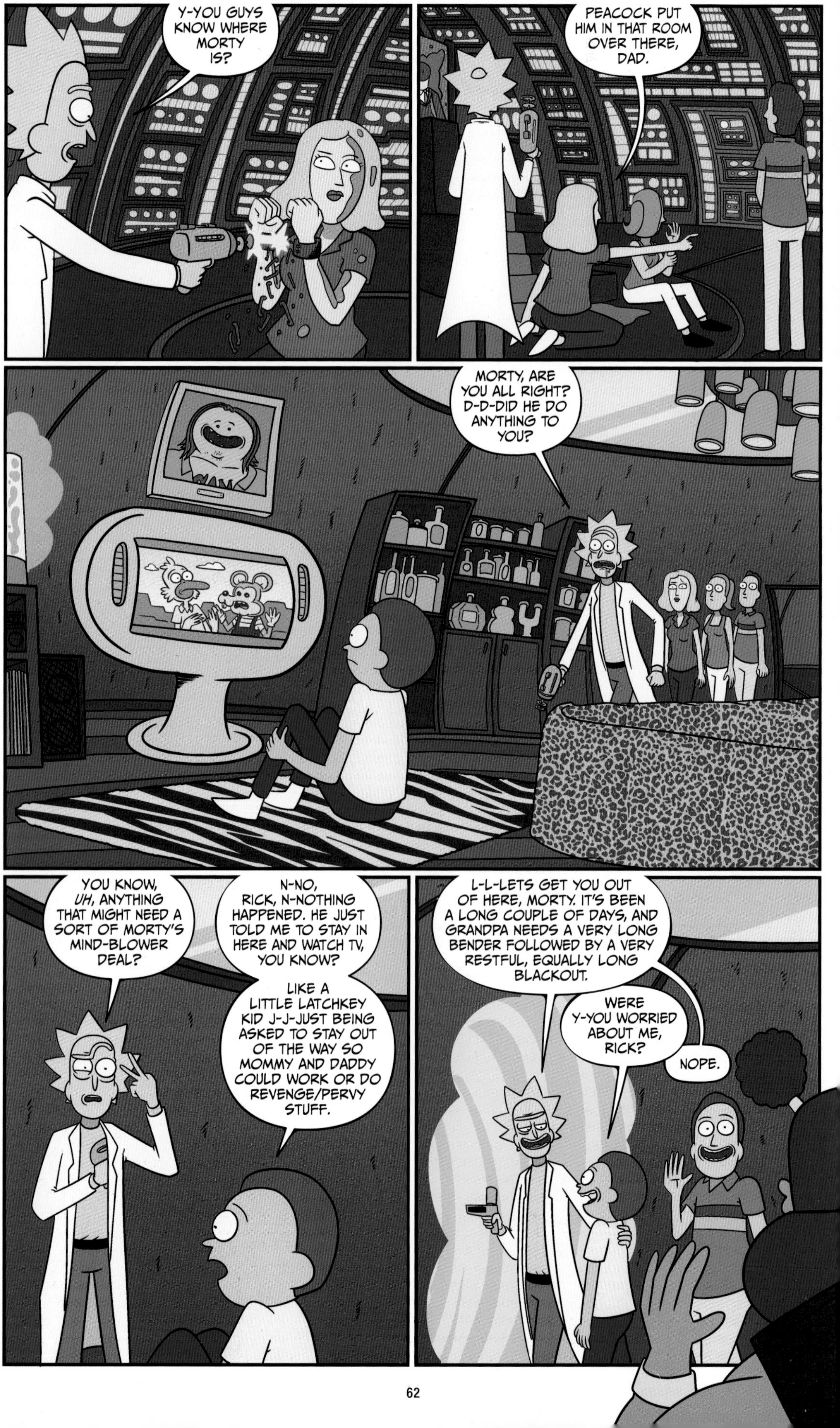
Y-YOU GUYS KNOW WHERE MORTY IS?
PEACOCK PUT HIM IN THAT ROOM OVER THERE, DAD.
MORTY, ARE YOU ALL RIGHT? D-D-DID HE DO ANYTHING TO YOU?
YOU KNOW, *UH*, ANYTHING THAT MIGHT NEED A SORT OF MORTY'S MIND-BLOWER DEAL?
N-NO, RICK, N-NOTHING HAPPENED. HE JUST TOLD ME TO STAY IN HERE AND WATCH TV, YOU KNOW?
LIKE A LITTLE LATCHKEY KID J-J-JUST BEING ASKED TO STAY OUT OF THE WAY SO MOMMY AND DADDY COULD WORK OR DO REVENGE/PERVY STUFF.
L-L-LETS GET YOU OUT OF HERE, MORTY. IT'S BEEN A LONG COUPLE OF DAYS, AND GRANDPA NEEDS A VERY LONG BENDER FOLLOWED BY A VERY RESTFUL, EQUALLY LONG BLACKOUT.
WERE Y-YOU WORRIED ABOUT ME, RICK?
NOPE.

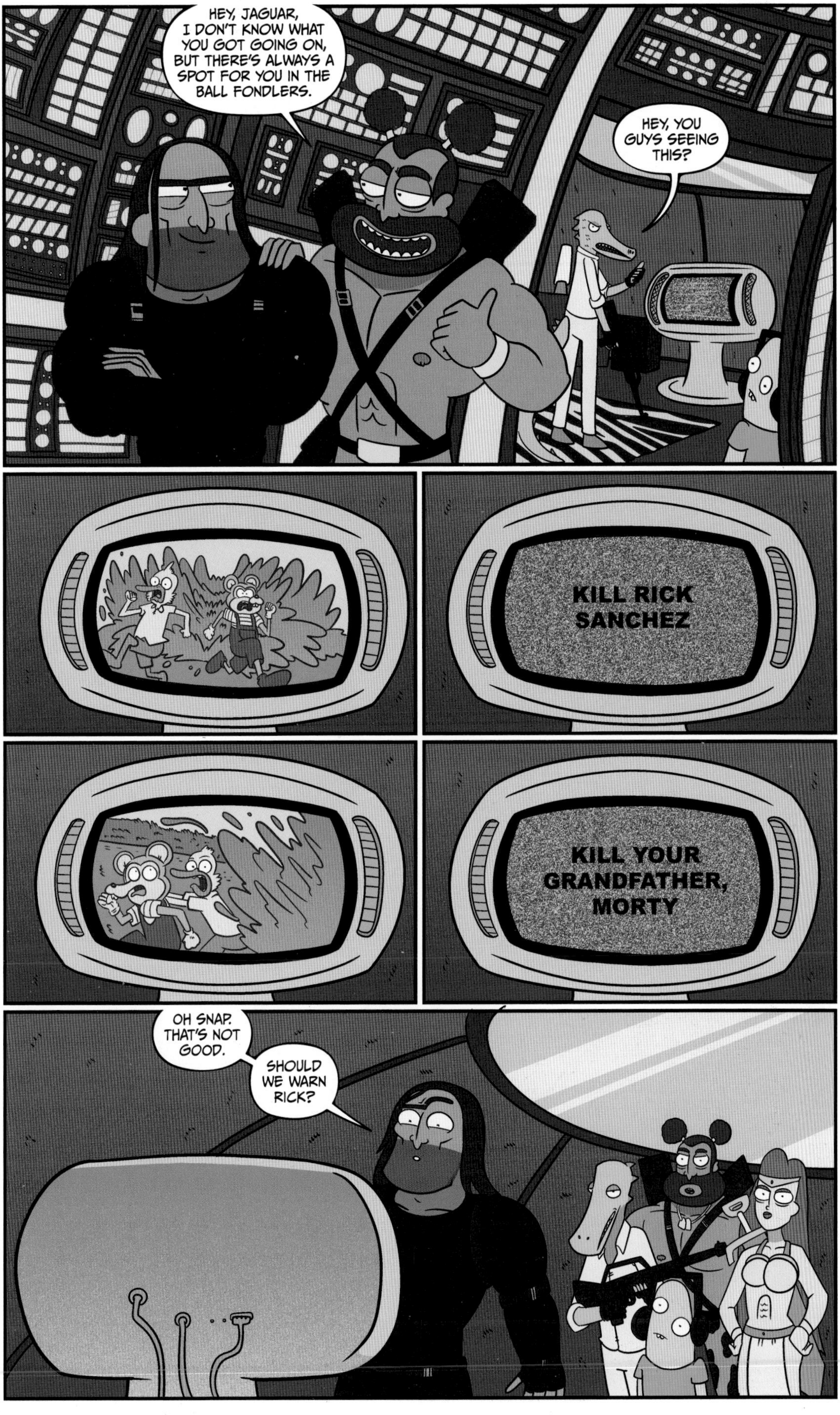
HEY, JAGUAR, I DON'T KNOW WHAT YOU GOT GOING ON, BUT THERE'S ALWAYS A SPOT FOR YOU IN THE BALL FONDLERS.
HEY, YOU GUYS SEEING THIS?
KILL RICK SANCHEZ
KILL YOUR GRANDFATHER, MORTY
OH SNAP. THAT'S NOT GOOD.
SHOULD WE WARN RICK?

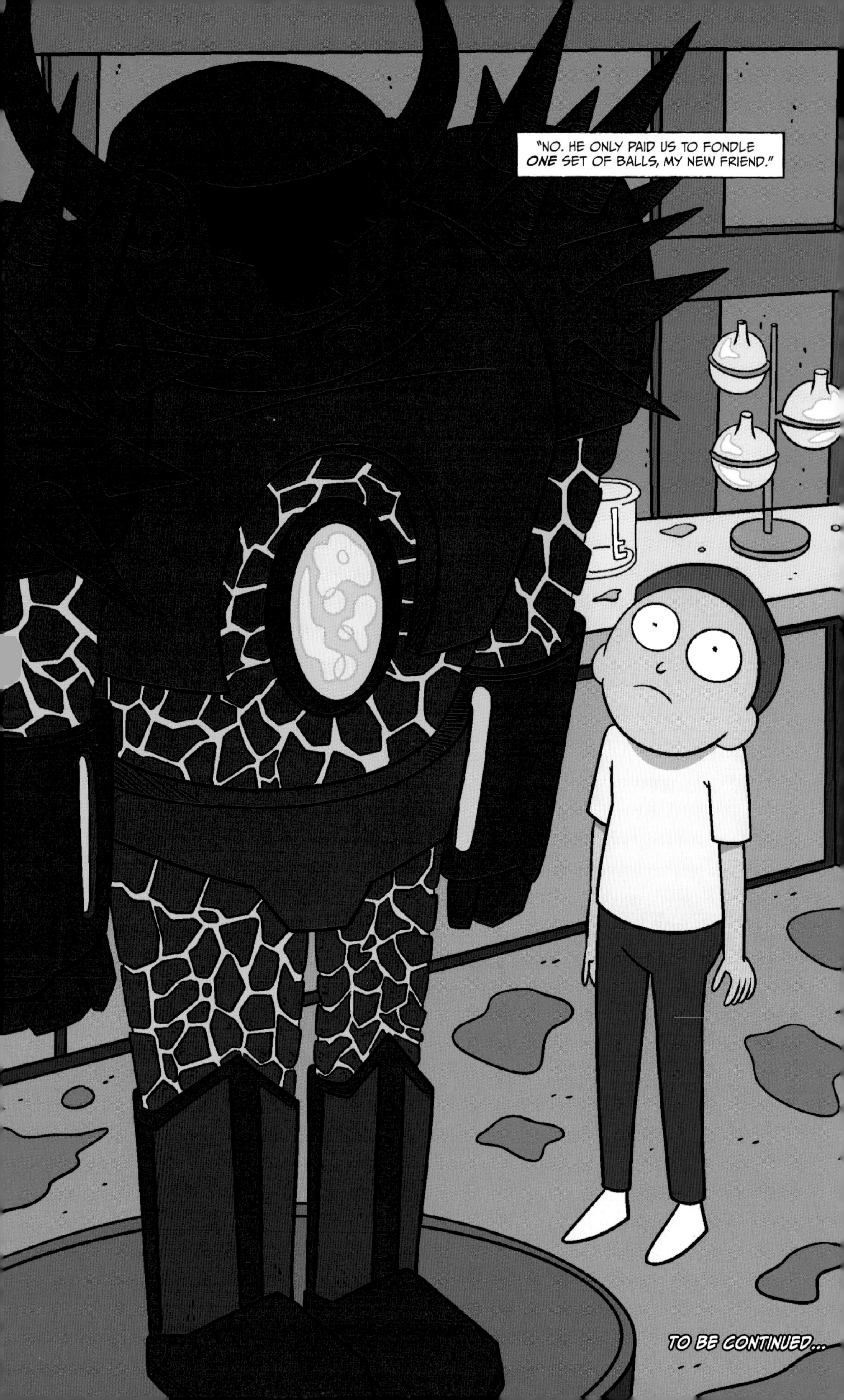
"NO. HE ONLY PAID US TO FONDLE *ONE* SET OF BALLS, MY NEW FRIEND."
TO BE CONTINUED...

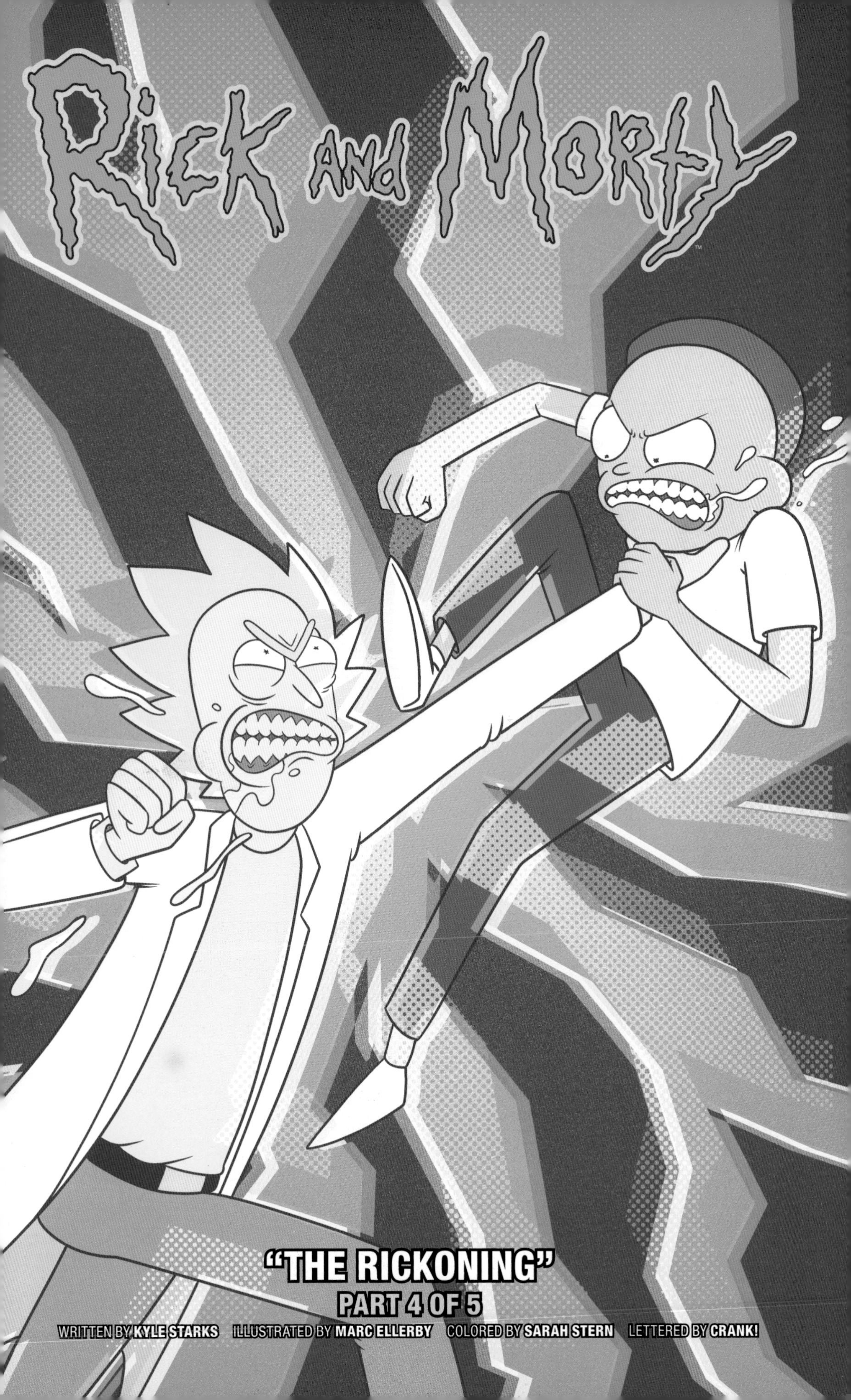
Rick and Morty™
"THE RICKONING"
PART 4 OF 5
WRITTEN BY KYLE STARKS ILLUSTRATED BY MARC ELLERBY COLORED BY SARAH STERN LETTERED BY CRANK!

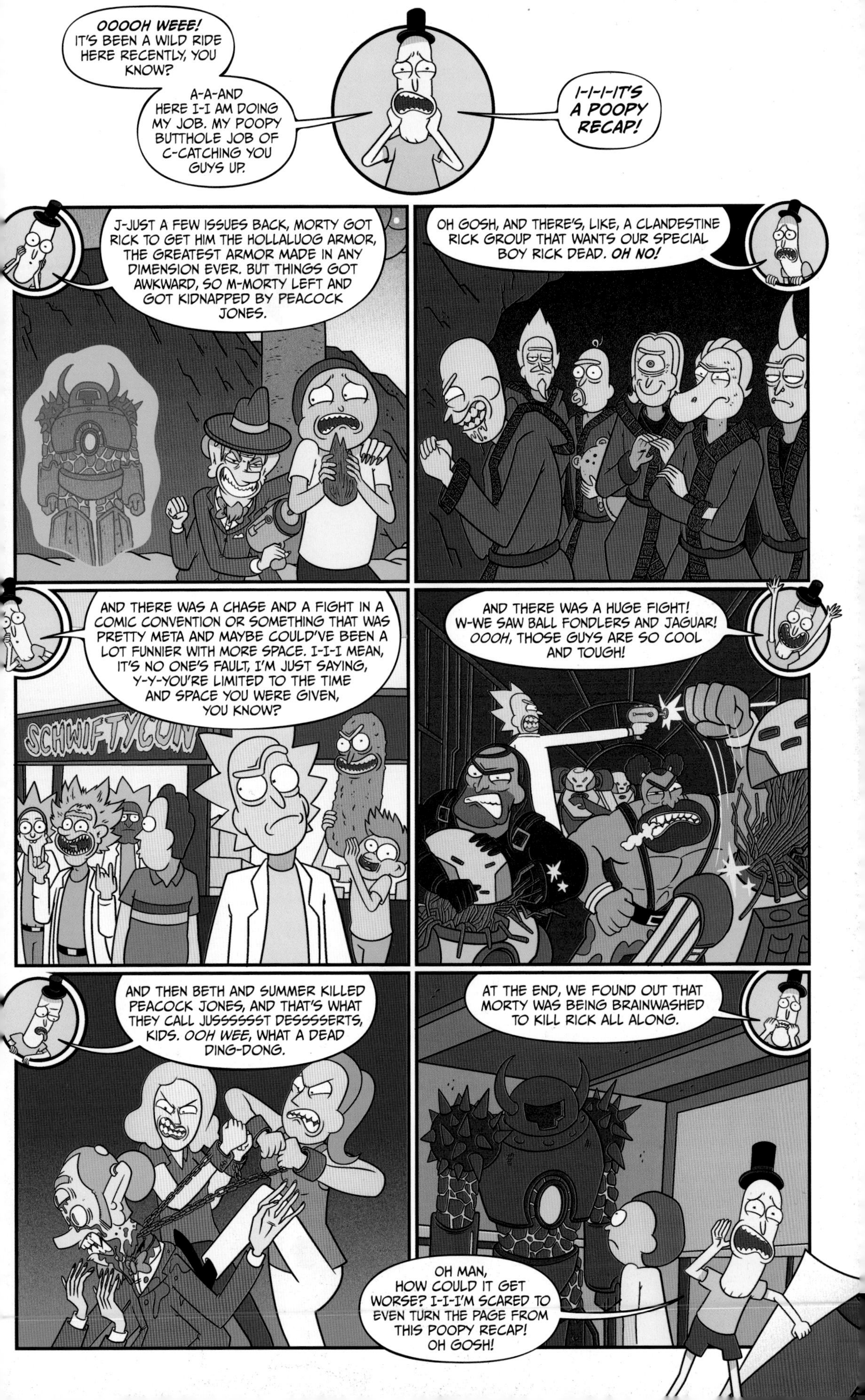

OOOOH WEEE! IT'S BEEN A WILD RIDE HERE RECENTLY, YOU KNOW?
A-A-AND HERE I-I AM DOING MY JOB. MY POOPY BUTTHOLE JOB OF C-CATCHING YOU GUYS UP.
I-I-I-IT'S A POOPY RECAP!
J-JUST A FEW ISSUES BACK, MORTY GOT RICK TO GET HIM THE HOLLALUOG ARMOR, THE GREATEST ARMOR MADE IN ANY DIMENSION EVER. BUT THINGS GOT AWKWARD, SO M-MORTY LEFT AND GOT KIDNAPPED BY PEACOCK JONES.
OH GOSH, AND THERE'S, LIKE, A CLANDESTINE RICK GROUP THAT WANTS OUR SPECIAL BOY RICK DEAD. OH NO!
AND THERE WAS A CHASE AND A FIGHT IN A COMIC CONVENTION OR SOMETHING THAT WAS PRETTY META AND MAYBE COULD'VE BEEN A LOT FUNNIER WITH MORE SPACE. I-I-I MEAN, IT'S NO ONE'S FAULT, I'M JUST SAYING, Y-Y-YOU'RE LIMITED TO THE TIME AND SPACE YOU WERE GIVEN, YOU KNOW?
SCHWIFTYCON
AND THERE WAS A HUGE FIGHT! W-WE SAW BALL FONDLERS AND JAGUAR! OOOH, THOSE GUYS ARE SO COOL AND TOUGH!
AND THEN BETH AND SUMMER KILLED PEACOCK JONES, AND THAT'S WHAT THEY CALL JUSSSSSST DESSSSERTS, KIDS. OOH WEE, WHAT A DEAD DING-DONG.
AT THE END, WE FOUND OUT THAT MORTY WAS BEING BRAINWASHED TO KILL RICK ALL ALONG.
OH MAN, HOW COULD IT GET WORSE? I-I-I'M SCARED TO EVEN TURN THE PAGE FROM THIS POOPY RECAP! OH GOSH!

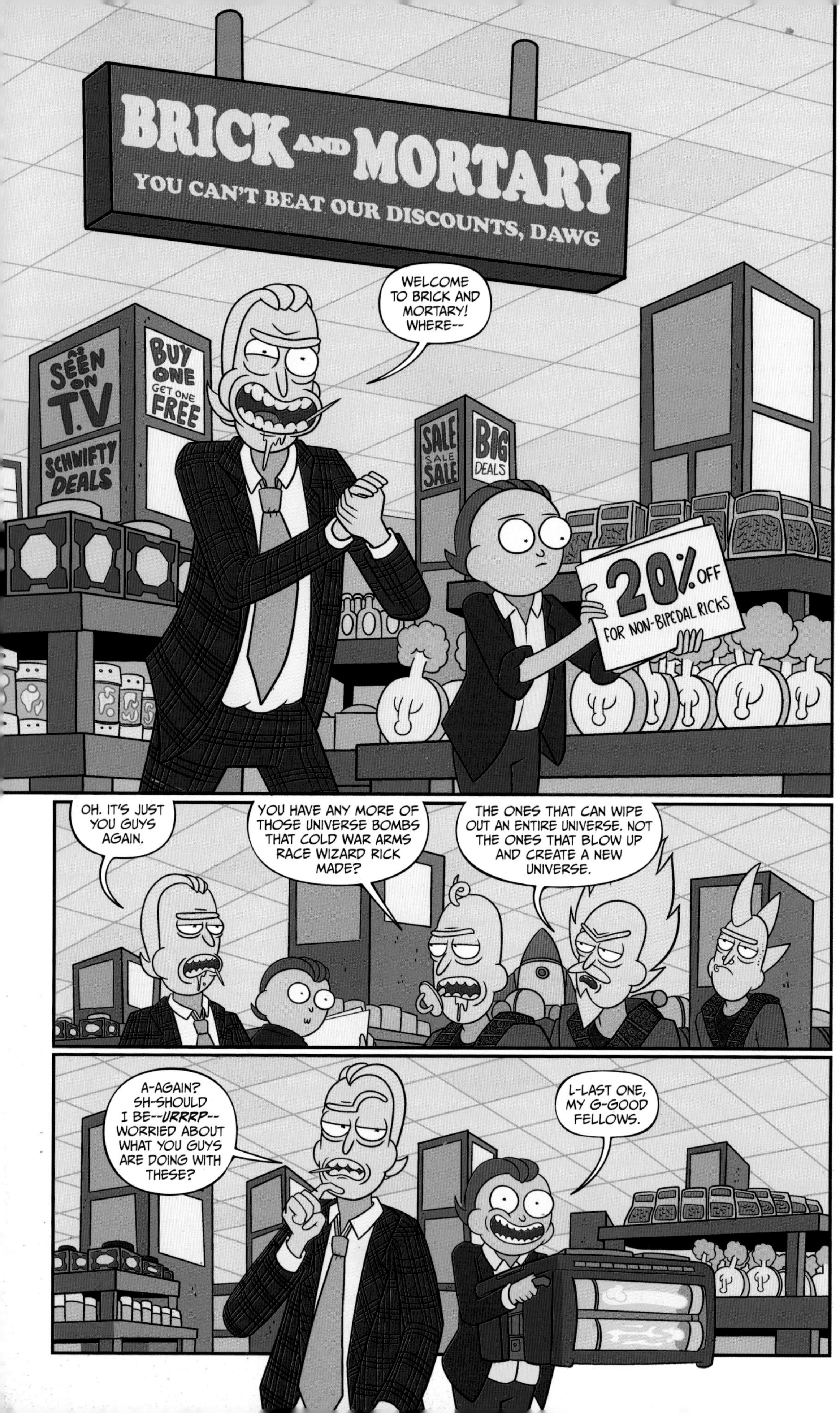
BRICK AND MORTARY
YOU CAN'T BEAT OUR DISCOUNTS, DAWG
WELCOME TO BRICK AND MORTARY! WHERE--
AS SEEN ON T.V
BUY ONE GET ONE FREE
SCHWIFTY DEALS
SALE SALE SALE
BIG DEALS
20% OFF FOR NON-BIPEDAL RICKS
OH. IT'S JUST YOU GUYS AGAIN.
YOU HAVE ANY MORE OF THOSE UNIVERSE BOMBS THAT COLD WAR ARMS RACE WIZARD RICK MADE?
THE ONES THAT CAN WIPE OUT AN ENTIRE UNIVERSE. NOT THE ONES THAT BLOW UP AND CREATE A NEW UNIVERSE.
A-AGAIN? SH-SHOULD I BE--URRRP--WORRIED ABOUT WHAT YOU GUYS ARE DOING WITH THESE?
L-LAST ONE, MY G-GOOD FELLOWS.

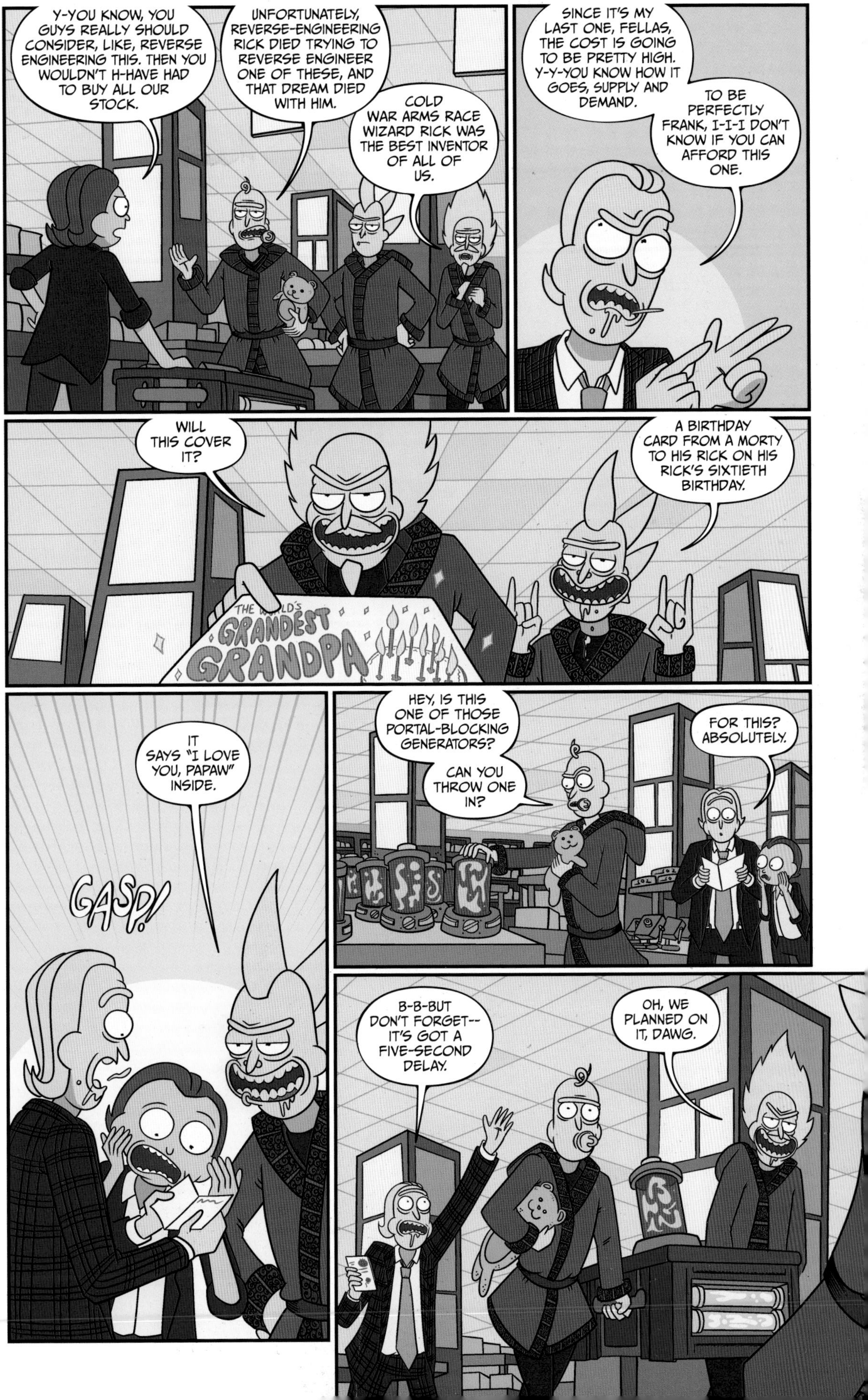
Y-YOU KNOW, YOU GUYS REALLY SHOULD CONSIDER, LIKE, REVERSE ENGINEERING THIS. THEN YOU WOULDN'T H-HAVE HAD TO BUY ALL OUR STOCK.
UNFORTUNATELY, REVERSE-ENGINEERING RICK DIED TRYING TO REVERSE ENGINEER ONE OF THESE, AND THAT DREAM DIED WITH HIM.
COLD WAR ARMS RACE WIZARD RICK WAS THE BEST INVENTOR OF ALL OF US.
SINCE IT'S MY LAST ONE, FELLAS, THE COST IS GOING TO BE PRETTY HIGH. Y-Y-YOU KNOW HOW IT GOES, SUPPLY AND DEMAND.
TO BE PERFECTLY FRANK, I-I-I DON'T KNOW IF YOU CAN AFFORD THIS ONE.
WILL THIS COVER IT?
A BIRTHDAY CARD FROM A MORTY TO HIS RICK ON HIS RICK'S SIXTIETH BIRTHDAY.
GRANDEST GRANDPA
IT SAYS "I LOVE YOU, PAPAW" INSIDE.
GASP!
HEY, IS THIS ONE OF THOSE PORTAL-BLOCKING GENERATORS?
CAN YOU THROW ONE IN?
FOR THIS? ABSOLUTELY.
B-B-BUT DON'T FORGET-- IT'S GOT A FIVE-SECOND DELAY.
OH, WE PLANNED ON IT, DAWG.

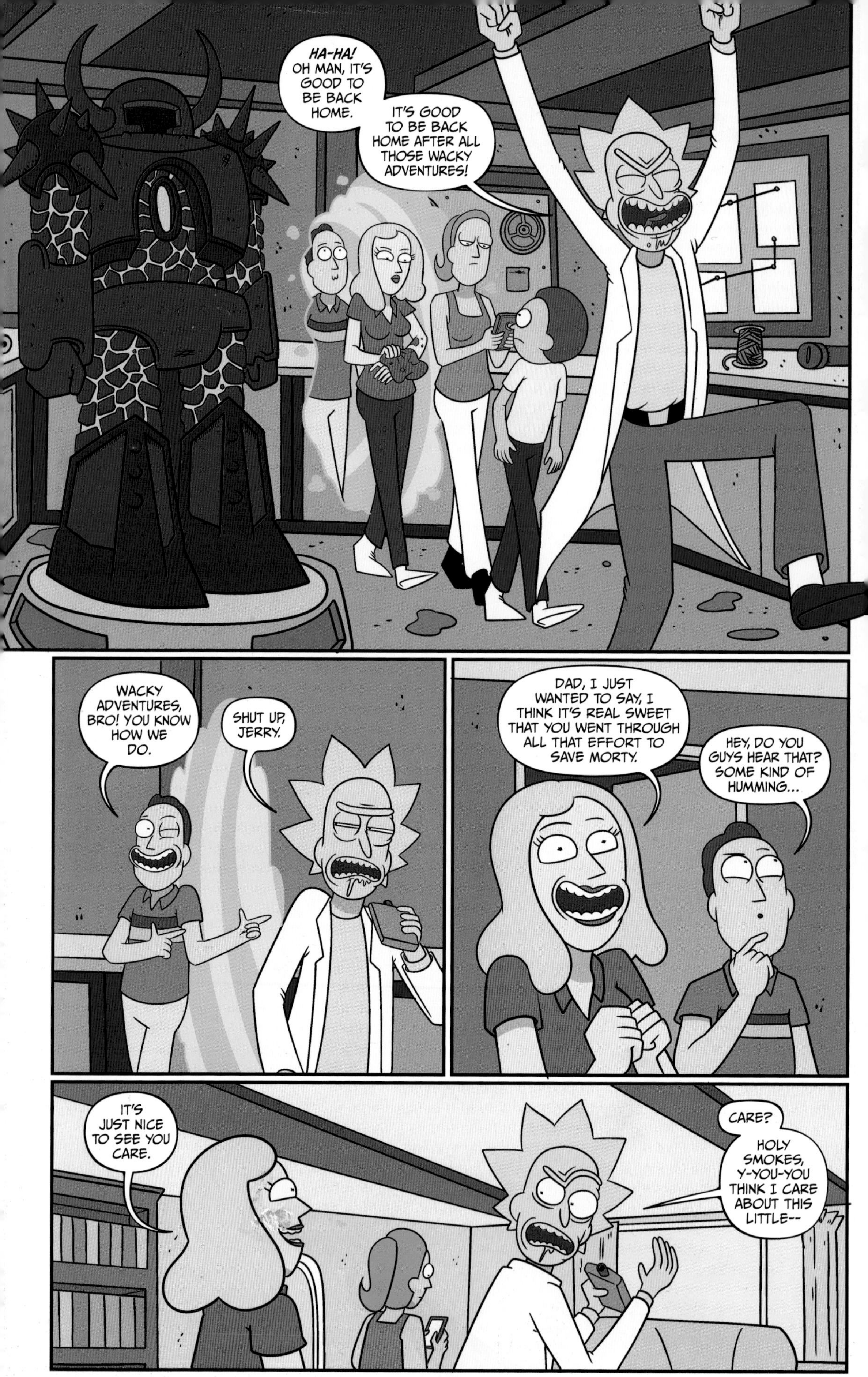
HA-HA! OH MAN, IT'S GOOD TO BE BACK HOME.
IT'S GOOD TO BE BACK HOME AFTER ALL THOSE WACKY ADVENTURES!
WACKY ADVENTURES, BRO! YOU KNOW HOW WE DO.
SHUT UP, JERRY.
DAD, I JUST WANTED TO SAY, I THINK IT'S REAL SWEET THAT YOU WENT THROUGH ALL THAT EFFORT TO SAVE MORTY.
HEY, DO YOU GUYS HEAR THAT? SOME KIND OF HUMMING...
IT'S JUST NICE TO SEE YOU CARE.
CARE?
HOLY SMOKES, Y-YOU-YOU THINK I CARE ABOUT THIS LITTLE--

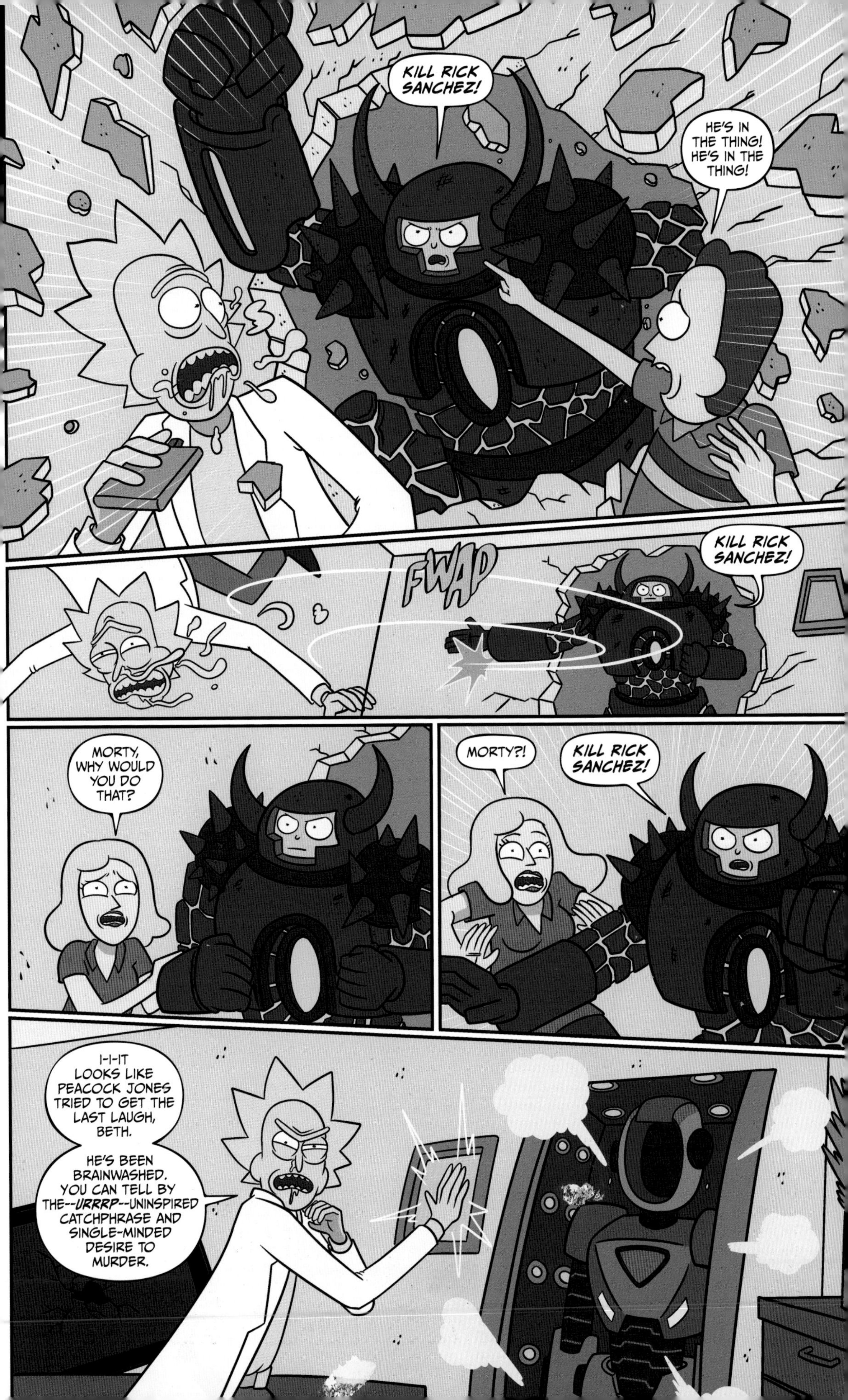
KILL RICK SANCHEZ!
HE'S IN THE THING! HE'S IN THE THING!
FWAP
KILL RICK SANCHEZ!
MORTY, WHY WOULD YOU DO THAT?
MORTY?!
KILL RICK SANCHEZ!
I-I-IT LOOKS LIKE PEACOCK JONES TRIED TO GET THE LAST LAUGH, BETH.
HE'S BEEN BRAINWASHED. YOU CAN TELL BY THE--URRRP--UNINSPIRED CATCHPHRASE AND SINGLE-MINDED DESIRE TO MURDER.

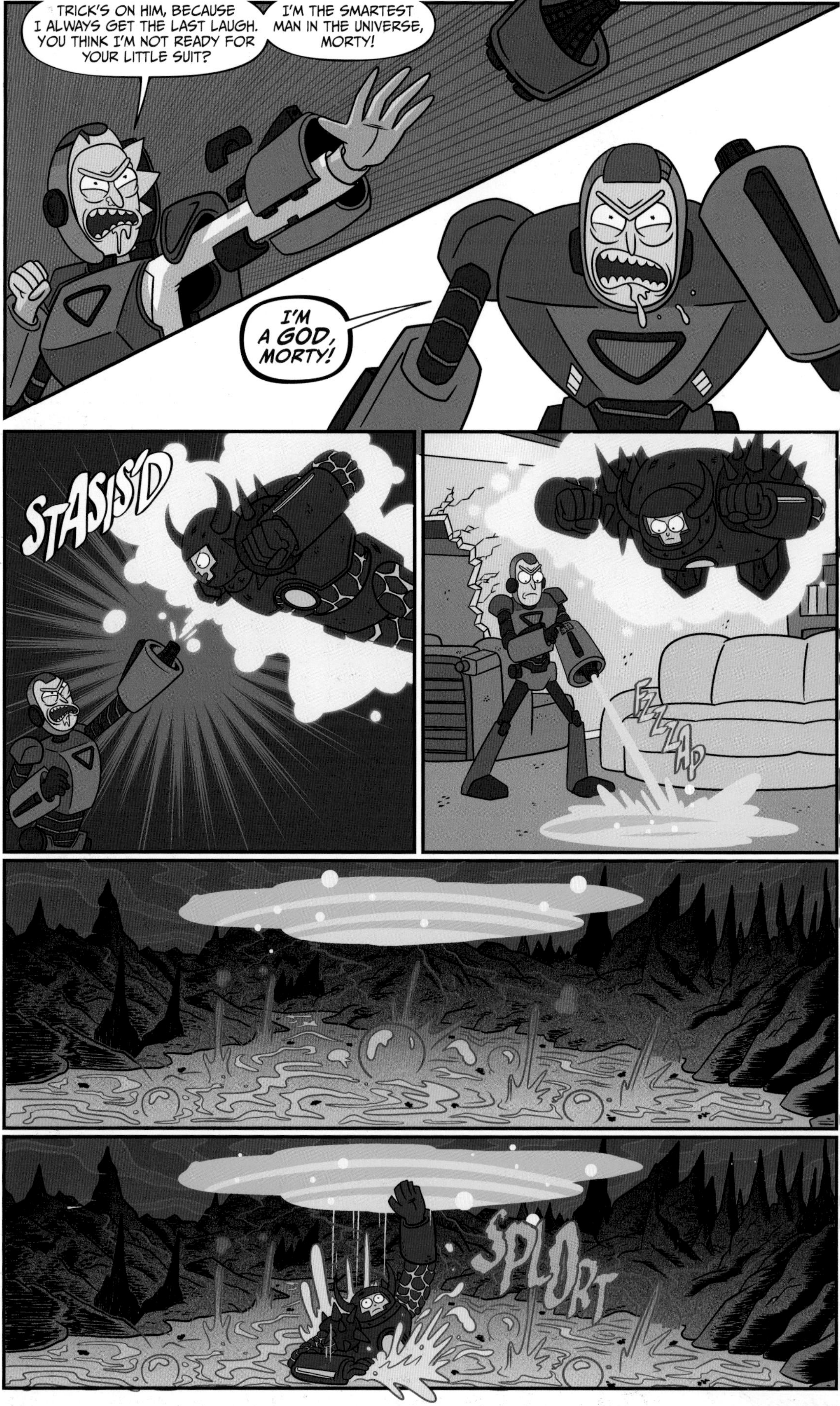
TRICK'S ON HIM, BECAUSE I ALWAYS GET THE LAST LAUGH. YOU THINK I'M NOT READY FOR YOUR LITTLE SUIT?
I'M THE SMARTEST MAN IN THE UNIVERSE, MORTY!
I'M A GOD, MORTY!
STASIS'D
FZZZAP
SPLORT

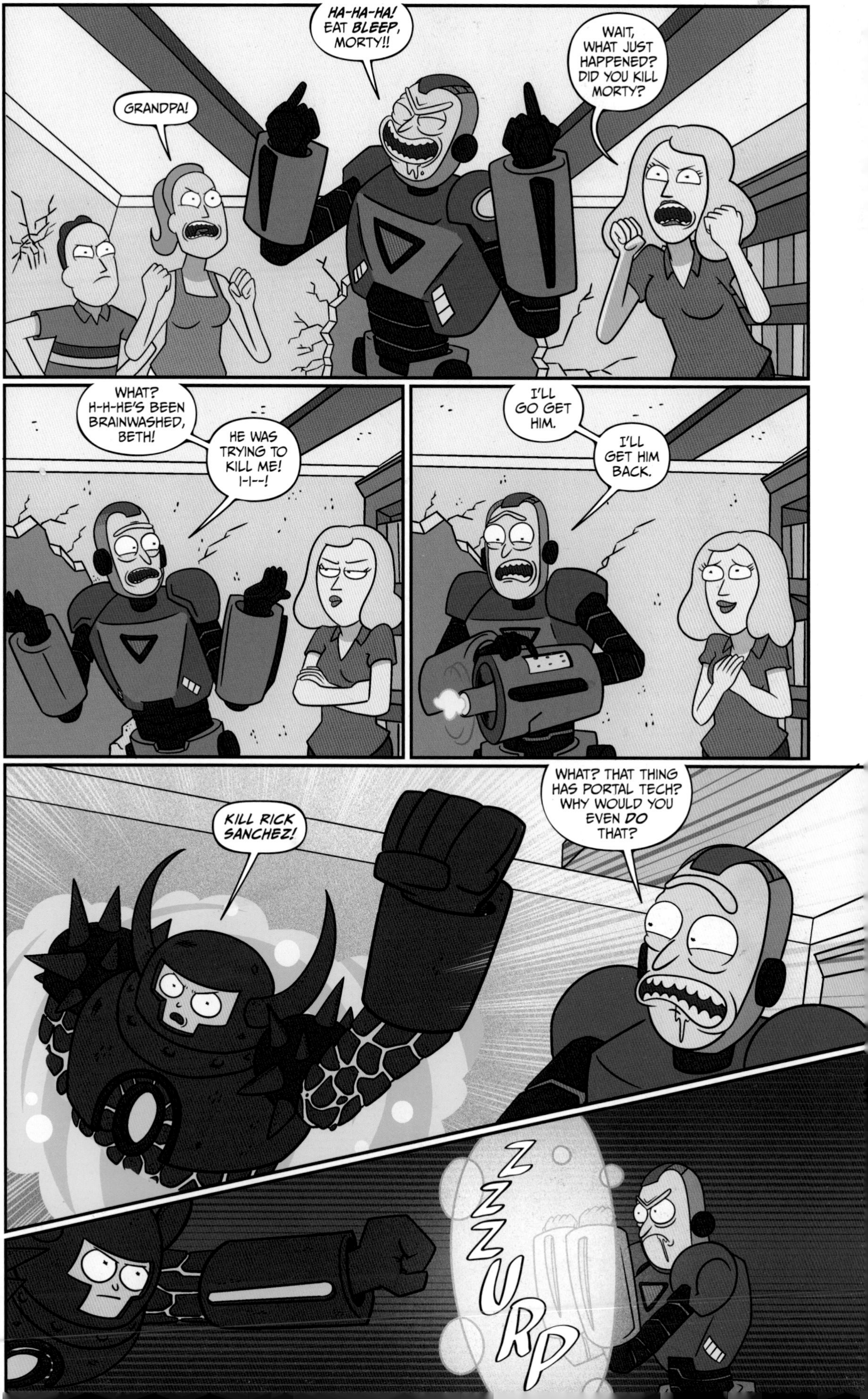
HA-HA-HA! EAT BLEEP, MORTY!!
GRANDPA!
WAIT, WHAT JUST HAPPENED? DID YOU KILL MORTY?
WHAT? H-H-HE'S BEEN BRAINWASHED, BETH!
HE WAS TRYING TO KILL ME! I-I--!
I'LL GO GET HIM.
I'LL GET HIM BACK.
KILL RICK SANCHEZ!
WHAT? THAT THING HAS PORTAL TECH? WHY WOULD YOU EVEN DO THAT?
ZZZURP

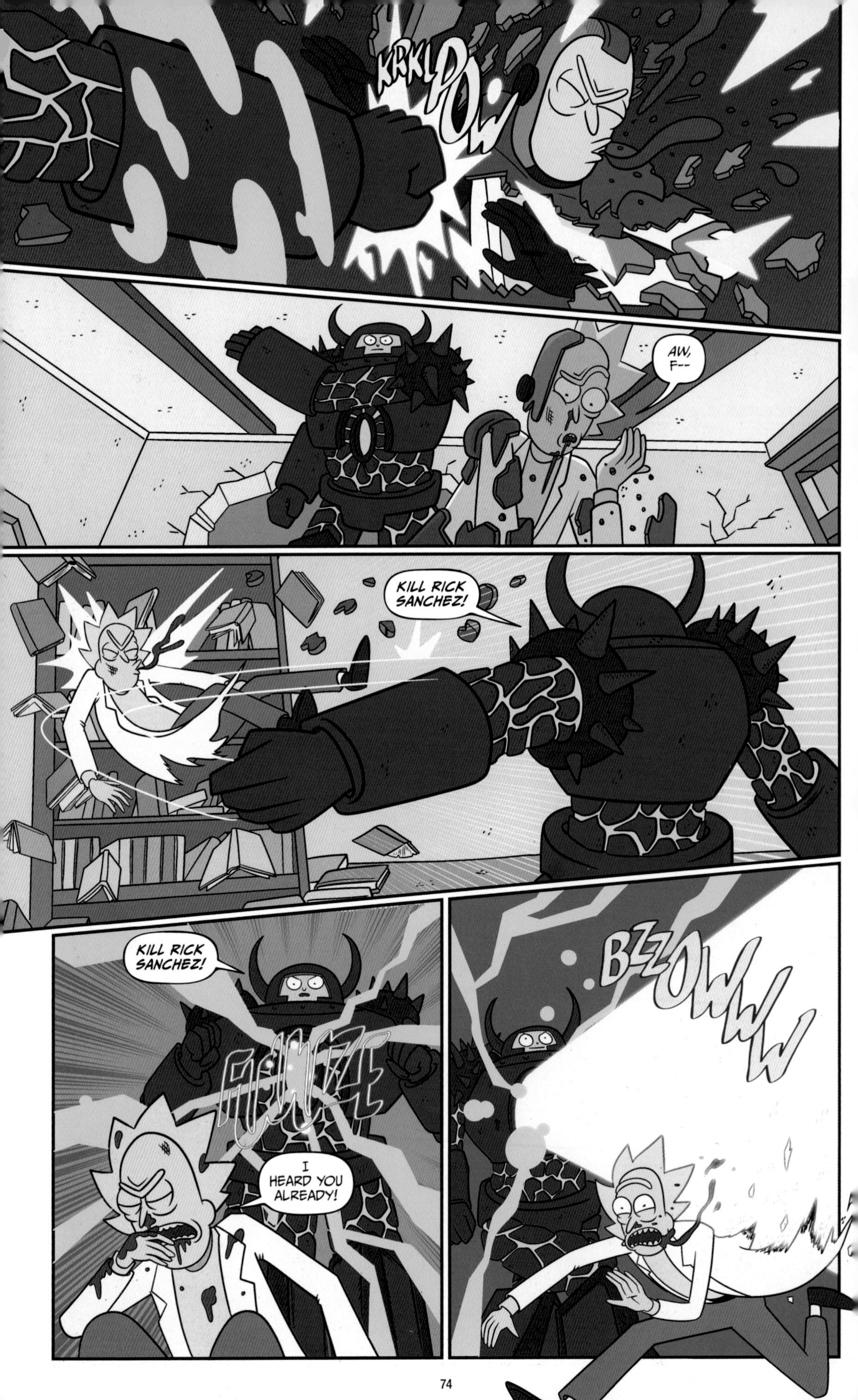
KRKLPOW
AW, F--
KILL RICK SANCHEZ!
KILL RICK SANCHEZ!
I HEARD YOU ALREADY!
BZZOWWW

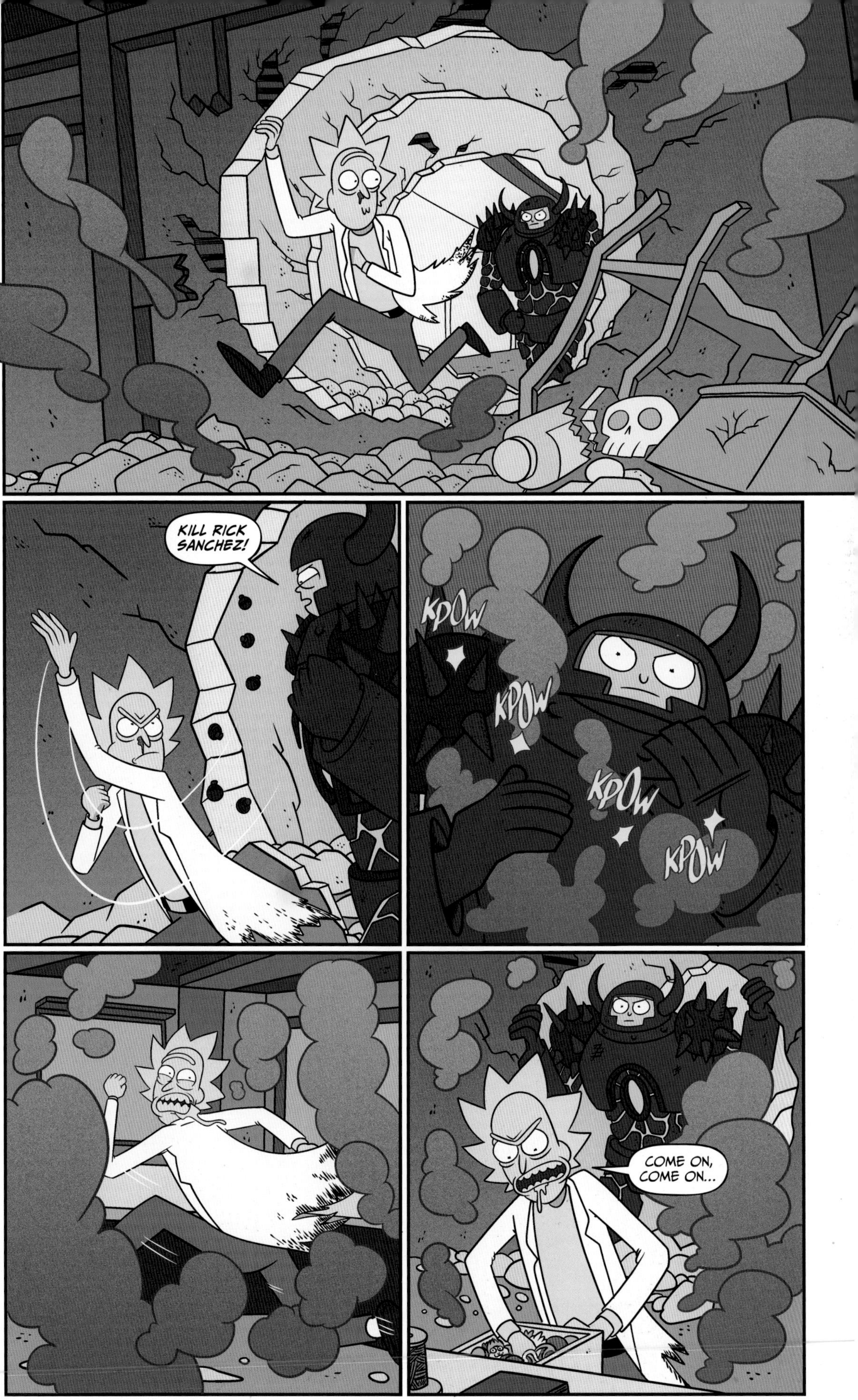
KILL RICK SANCHEZ!
KPOW
KPOW
KPOW
KPOW
COME ON, COME ON...

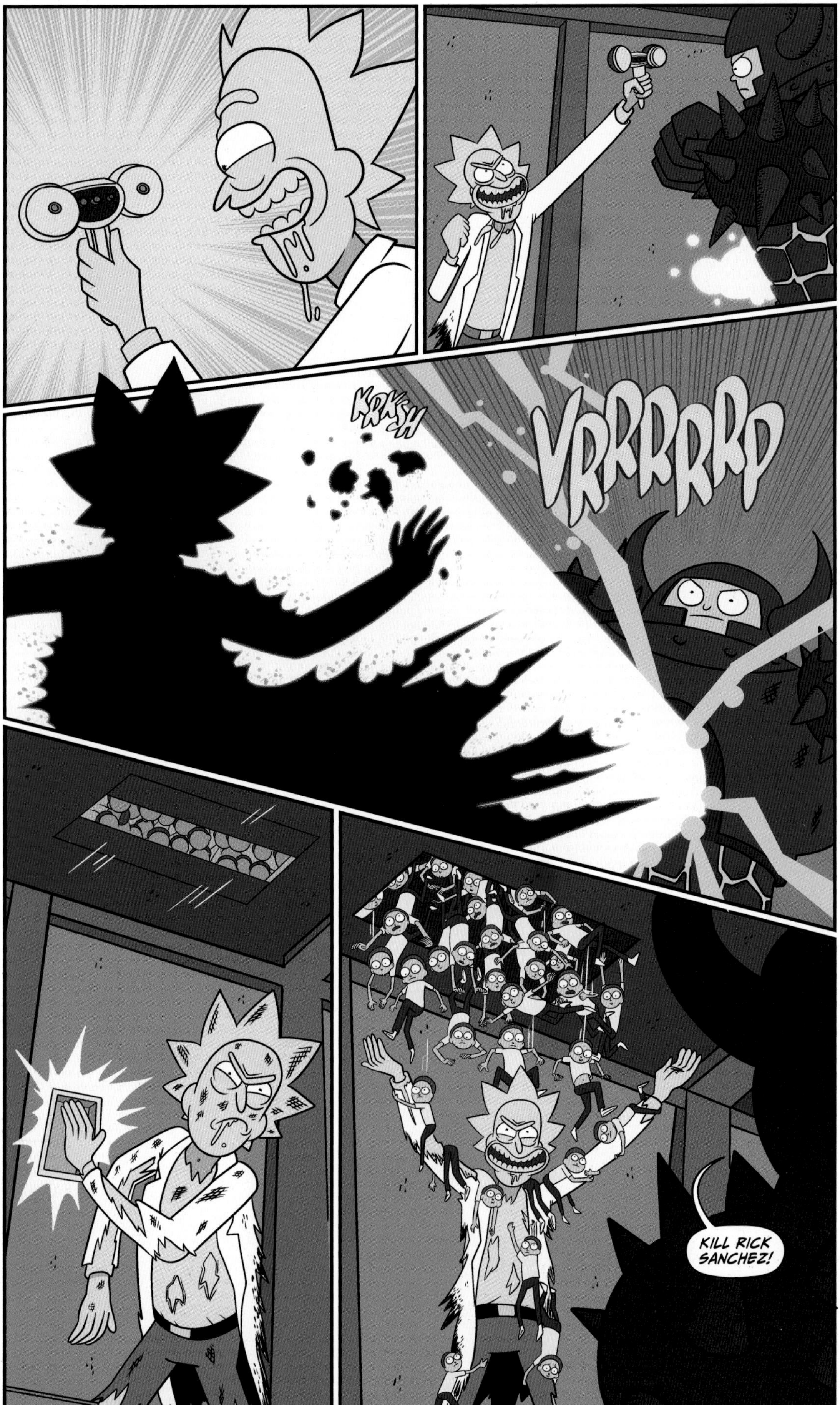
KRKSH
VRRRRRP
KILL RICK SANCHEZ!

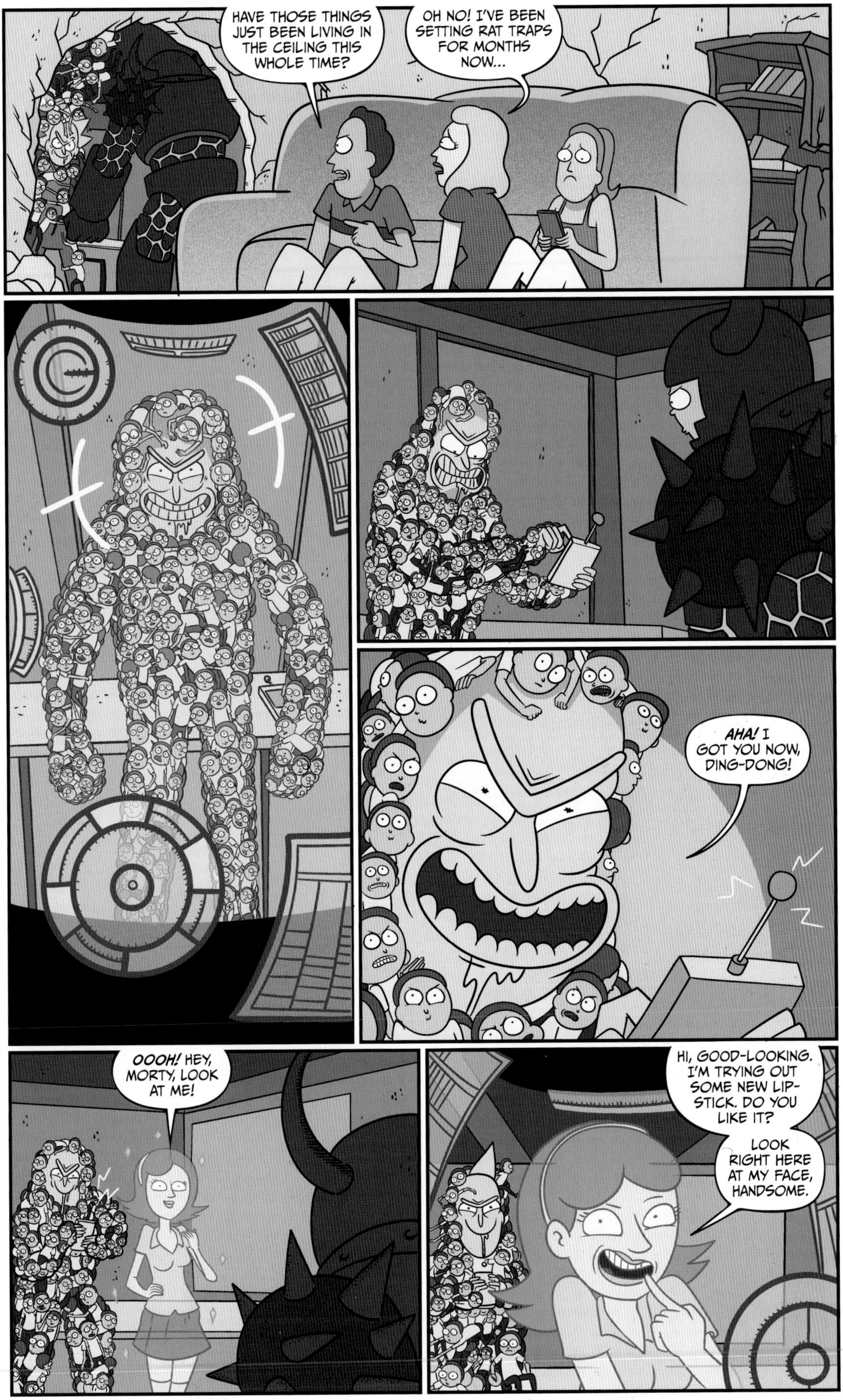
HAVE THOSE THINGS JUST BEEN LIVING IN THE CEILING THIS WHOLE TIME?
OH NO! I'VE BEEN SETTING RAT TRAPS FOR MONTHS NOW...
AHA! I GOT YOU NOW, DING-DONG!
OOOH! HEY, MORTY, LOOK AT ME!
HI, GOOD-LOOKING. I'M TRYING OUT SOME NEW LIP-STICK. DO YOU LIKE IT?
LOOK RIGHT HERE AT MY FACE, HANDSOME.

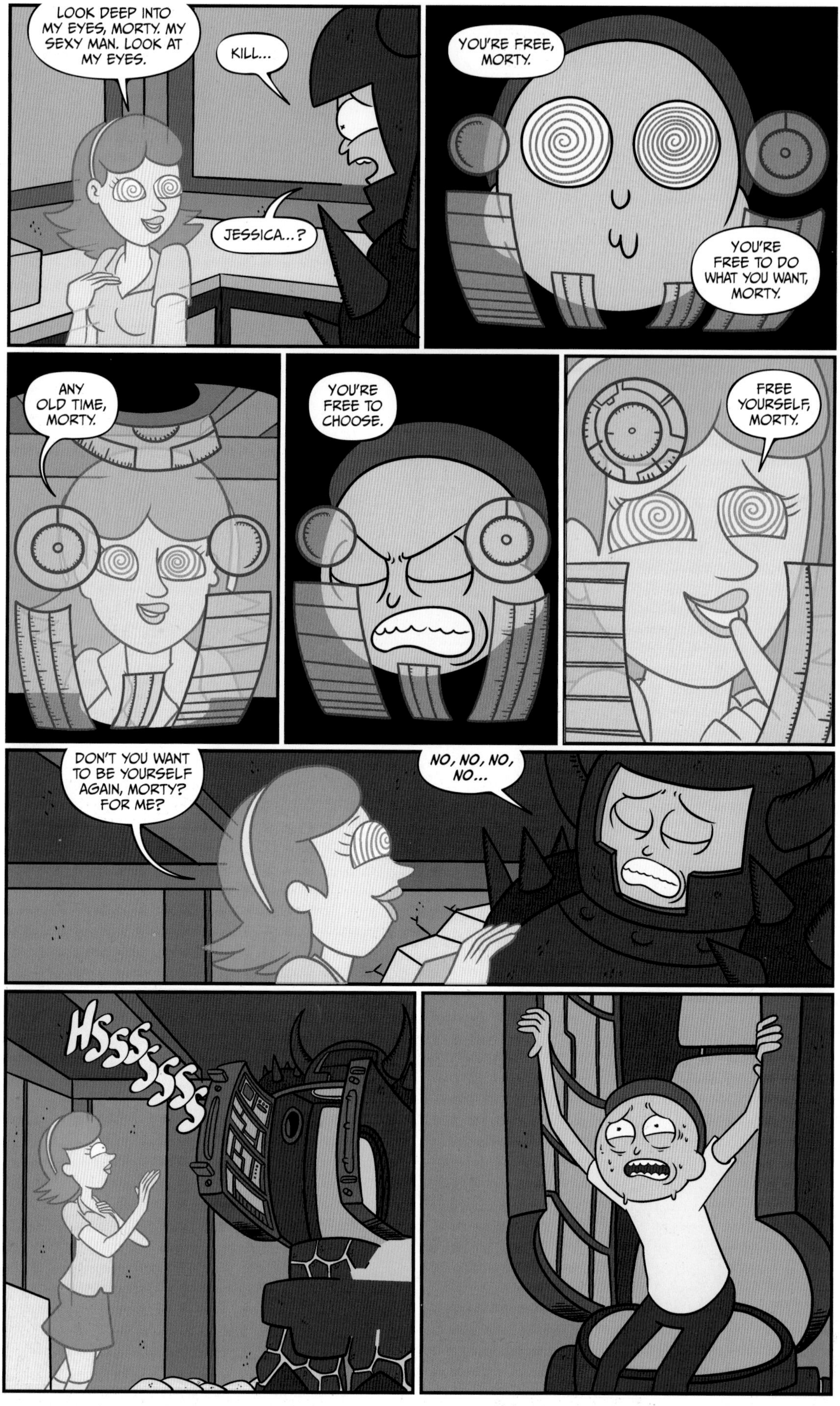
LOOK DEEP INTO MY EYES, MORTY. MY SEXY MAN. LOOK AT MY EYES.
KILL...
JESSICA...?
YOU'RE FREE, MORTY.
YOU'RE FREE TO DO WHAT YOU WANT, MORTY.
ANY OLD TIME, MORTY.
YOU'RE FREE TO CHOOSE.
FREE YOURSELF, MORTY.
DON'T YOU WANT TO BE YOURSELF AGAIN, MORTY? FOR ME?
NO, NO, NO, NO...
HSSSSSSSS

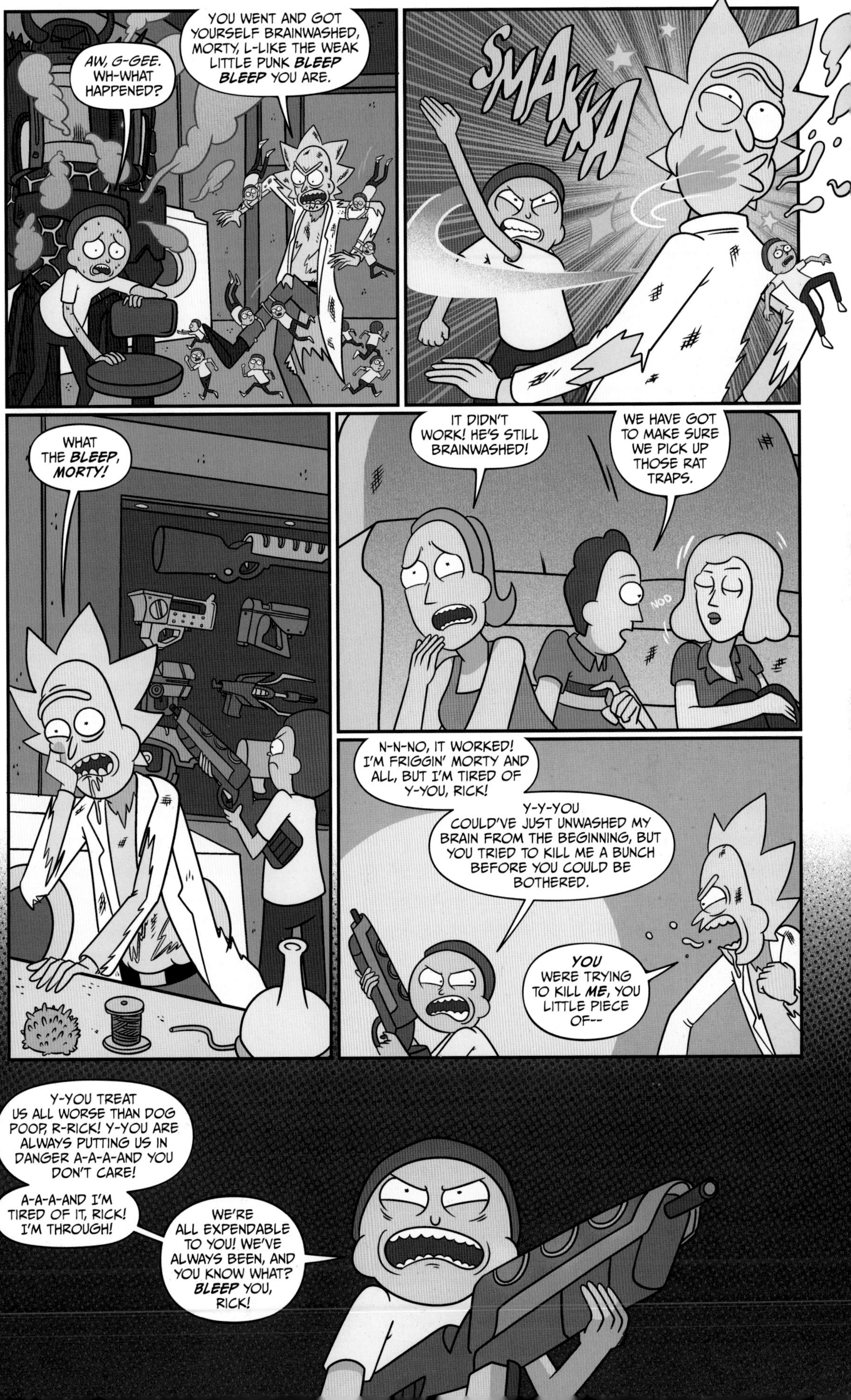
AW, G-GEE. WH-WHAT HAPPENED?
YOU WENT AND GOT YOURSELF BRAINWASHED, MORTY, L-LIKE THE WEAK LITTLE PUNK BLEEP BLEEP YOU ARE.
SMAKKA
WHAT THE BLEEP, MORTY!
IT DIDN'T WORK! HE'S STILL BRAINWASHED!
WE HAVE GOT TO MAKE SURE WE PICK UP THOSE RAT TRAPS.
NOD
N-N-NO, IT WORKED! I'M FRIGGIN' MORTY AND ALL, BUT I'M TIRED OF Y-YOU, RICK!
Y-Y-YOU COULD'VE JUST UNWASHED MY BRAIN FROM THE BEGINNING, BUT YOU TRIED TO KILL ME A BUNCH BEFORE YOU COULD BE BOTHERED.
YOU WERE TRYING TO KILL ME, YOU LITTLE PIECE OF--
Y-YOU TREAT US ALL WORSE THAN DOG POOP, R-RICK! Y-YOU ARE ALWAYS PUTTING US IN DANGER A-A-A-AND YOU DON'T CARE!
A-A-A-AND I'M TIRED OF IT, RICK! I'M THROUGH!
WE'RE ALL EXPENDABLE TO YOU! WE'VE ALWAYS BEEN, AND YOU KNOW WHAT? BLEEP YOU, RICK!

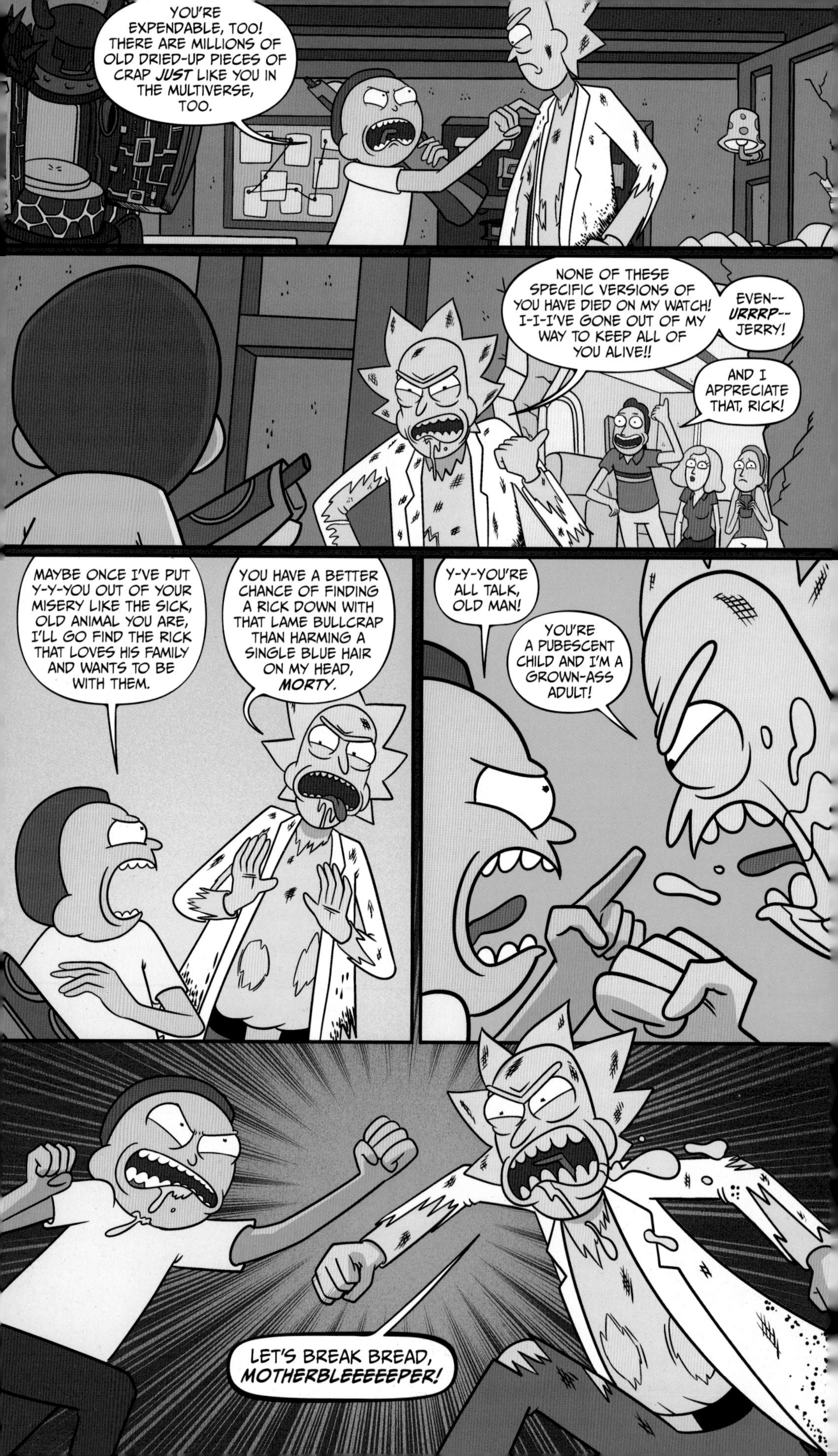
YOU'RE EXPENDABLE, TOO! THERE ARE MILLIONS OF OLD DRIED-UP PIECES OF CRAP JUST LIKE YOU IN THE MULTIVERSE, TOO.
NONE OF THESE SPECIFIC VERSIONS OF YOU HAVE DIED ON MY WATCH! I-I-I'VE GONE OUT OF MY WAY TO KEEP ALL OF YOU ALIVE!!
EVEN-- URRRP-- JERRY!
AND I APPRECIATE THAT, RICK!
MAYBE ONCE I'VE PUT Y-Y-YOU OUT OF YOUR MISERY LIKE THE SICK, OLD ANIMAL YOU ARE, I'LL GO FIND THE RICK THAT LOVES HIS FAMILY AND WANTS TO BE WITH THEM.
YOU HAVE A BETTER CHANCE OF FINDING A RICK DOWN WITH THAT LAME BULLCRAP THAN HARMING A SINGLE BLUE HAIR ON MY HEAD, MORTY.
Y-Y-YOU'RE ALL TALK, OLD MAN!
YOU'RE A PUBESCENT CHILD AND I'M A GROWN-ASS ADULT!
LET'S BREAK BREAD, MOTHERBLEEEEEPER!

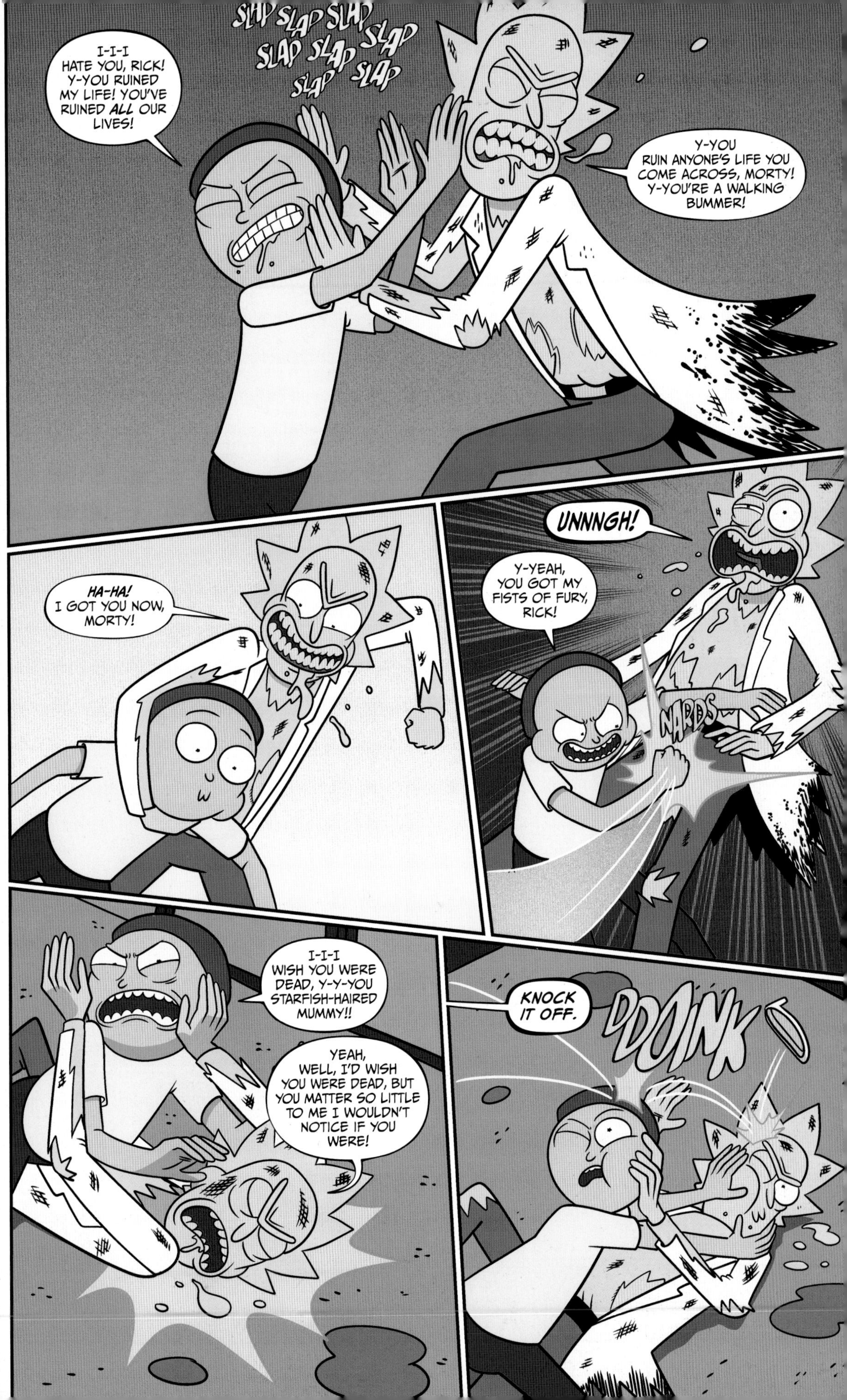

SLAP SLAP SLAP SLAP SLAP SLAP SLAP SLAP
I-I-I HATE YOU, RICK! Y-YOU RUINED MY LIFE! YOU'VE RUINED ALL OUR LIVES!
Y-YOU RUIN ANYONE'S LIFE YOU COME ACROSS, MORTY! Y-YOU'RE A WALKING BUMMER!
HA-HA! I GOT YOU NOW, MORTY!
UNNNGH!
Y-YEAH, YOU GOT MY FISTS OF FURY, RICK!
NARDS
I-I-I WISH YOU WERE DEAD, Y-Y-YOU STARFISH-HAIRED MUMMY!!
YEAH, WELL, I'D WISH YOU WERE DEAD, BUT YOU MATTER SO LITTLE TO ME I WOULDN'T NOTICE IF YOU WERE!
KNOCK IT OFF.
DDOINK

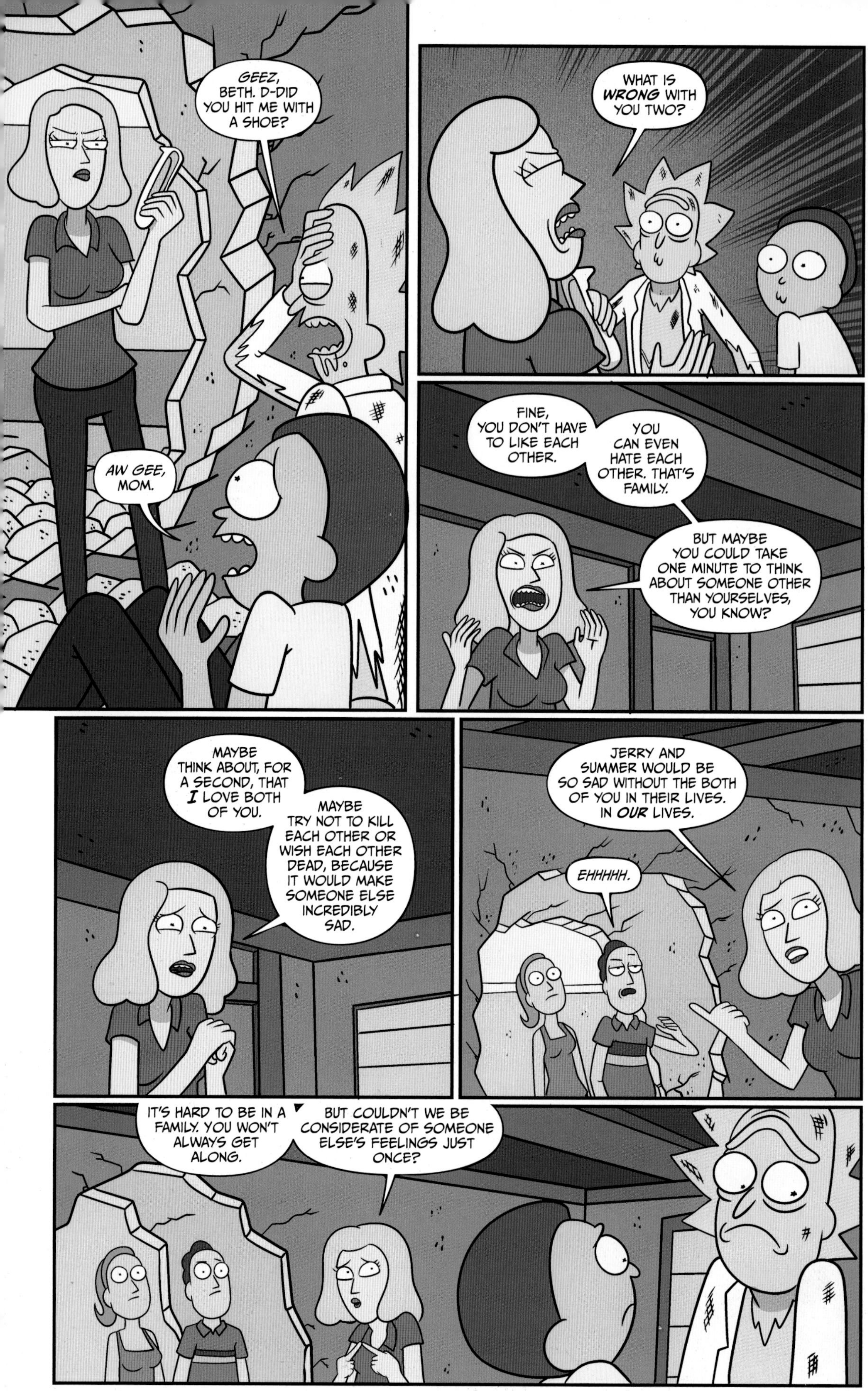
GEEZ, BETH. D-DID YOU HIT ME WITH A SHOE?
AW GEE, MOM.
WHAT IS WRONG WITH YOU TWO?
FINE, YOU DON'T HAVE TO LIKE EACH OTHER.
YOU CAN EVEN HATE EACH OTHER. THAT'S FAMILY.
BUT MAYBE YOU COULD TAKE ONE MINUTE TO THINK ABOUT SOMEONE OTHER THAN YOURSELVES, YOU KNOW?
MAYBE THINK ABOUT, FOR A SECOND, THAT I LOVE BOTH OF YOU.
MAYBE TRY NOT TO KILL EACH OTHER OR WISH EACH OTHER DEAD, BECAUSE IT WOULD MAKE SOMEONE ELSE INCREDIBLY SAD.
JERRY AND SUMMER WOULD BE SO SAD WITHOUT THE BOTH OF YOU IN THEIR LIVES. IN OUR LIVES.
EHHHHH.
IT'S HARD TO BE IN A FAMILY. YOU WON'T ALWAYS GET ALONG.
BUT COULDN'T WE BE CONSIDERATE OF SOMEONE ELSE'S FEELINGS JUST ONCE?

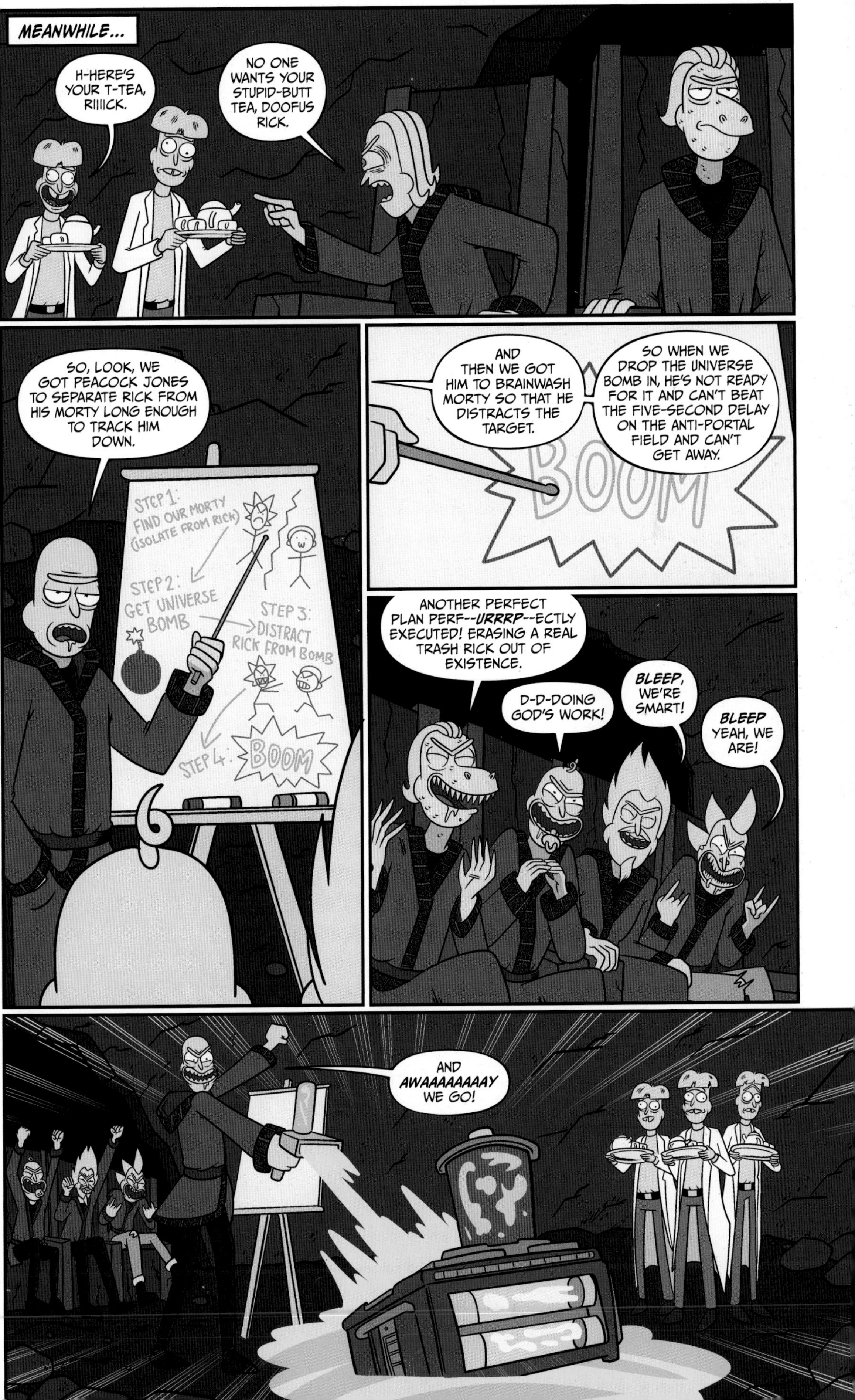
MEANWHILE...
H-HERE'S YOUR T-TEA, RIIIICK.
NO ONE WANTS YOUR STUPID-BUTT TEA, DOOFUS RICK.
SO, LOOK, WE GOT PEACOCK JONES TO SEPARATE RICK FROM HIS MORTY LONG ENOUGH TO TRACK HIM DOWN.
STEP 1: FIND OUR MORTY (ISOLATE FROM RICK)
STEP 2: GET UNIVERSE BOMB
STEP 3: DISTRACT RICK FROM BOMB
STEP 4: BOOM
AND THEN WE GOT HIM TO BRAINWASH MORTY SO THAT HE DISTRACTS THE TARGET.
SO WHEN WE DROP THE UNIVERSE BOMB IN, HE'S NOT READY FOR IT AND CAN'T BEAT THE FIVE-SECOND DELAY ON THE ANTI-PORTAL FIELD AND CAN'T GET AWAY.
BOOM
ANOTHER PERFECT PLAN PERF--URRRP--ECTLY EXECUTED! ERASING A REAL TRASH RICK OUT OF EXISTENCE.
D-D-DOING GOD'S WORK!
BLEEP, WE'RE SMART!
BLEEP YEAH, WE ARE!
AND AWAAAAAAAAY WE GO!

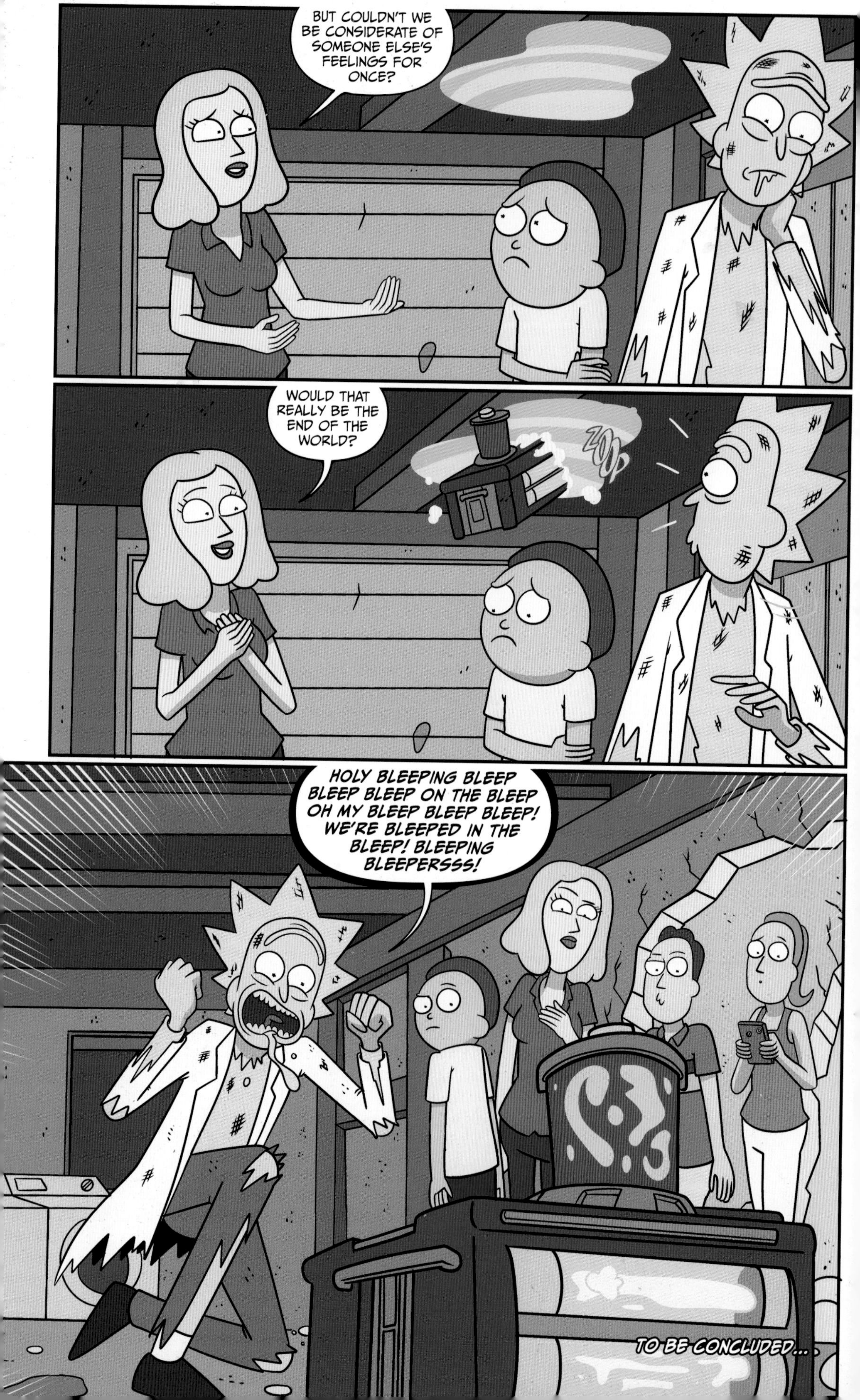
BUT COULDN'T WE BE CONSIDERATE OF SOMEONE ELSE'S FEELINGS FOR ONCE?
WOULD THAT REALLY BE THE END OF THE WORLD?
ZOOP
HOLY BLEEPING BLEEP BLEEP BLEEP ON THE BLEEP OH MY BLEEP BLEEP BLEEP! WE'RE BLEEPED IN THE BLEEP! BLEEPING BLEEPERSSS!
TO BE CONCLUDED...

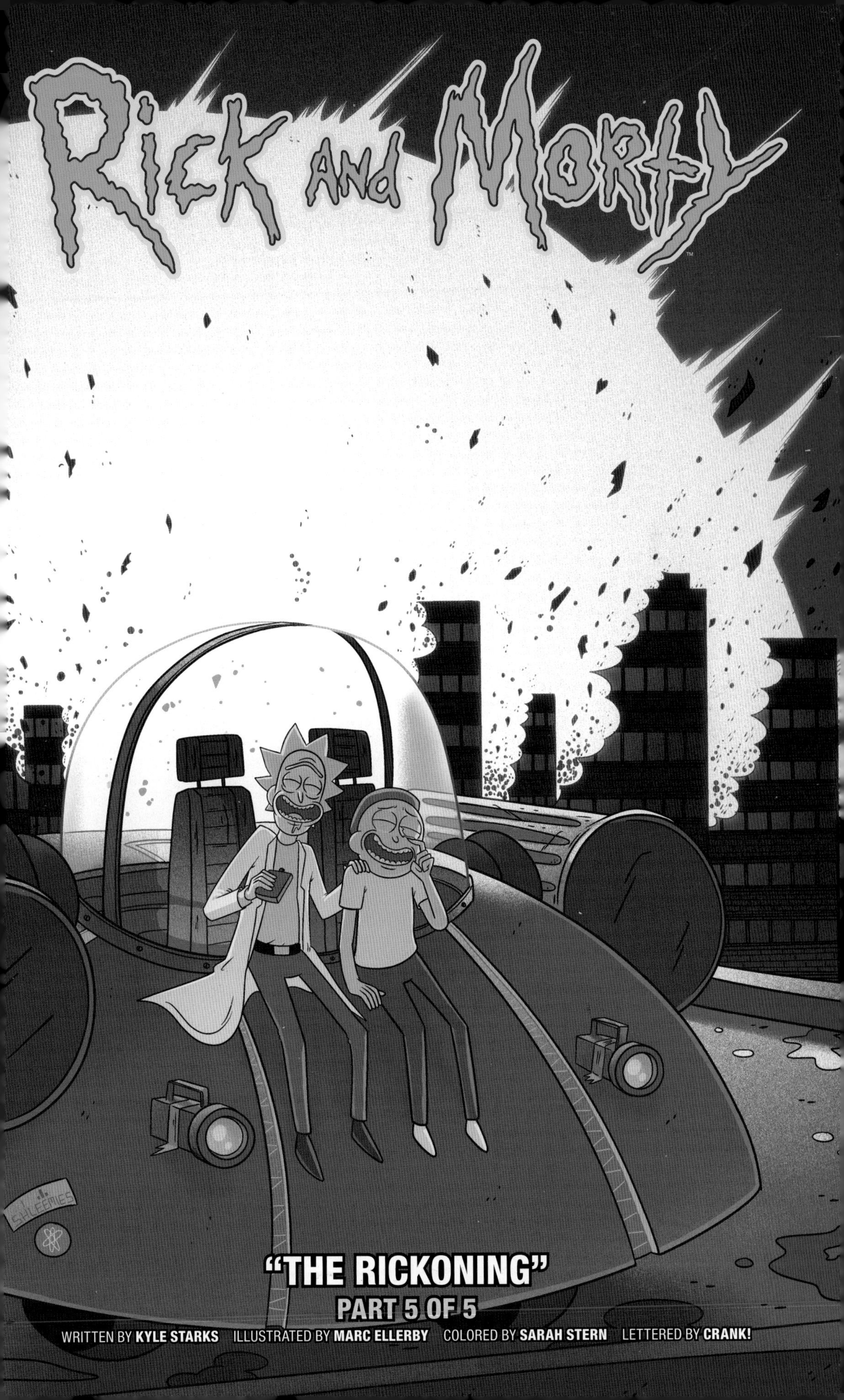
Rick and Morty

# "THE RICKONING"

## PART 5 OF 5

WRITTEN BY **KYLE STARKS** ILLUSTRATED BY **MARC ELLERBY** COLORED BY **SARAH STERN** LETTERED BY **CRANK!**

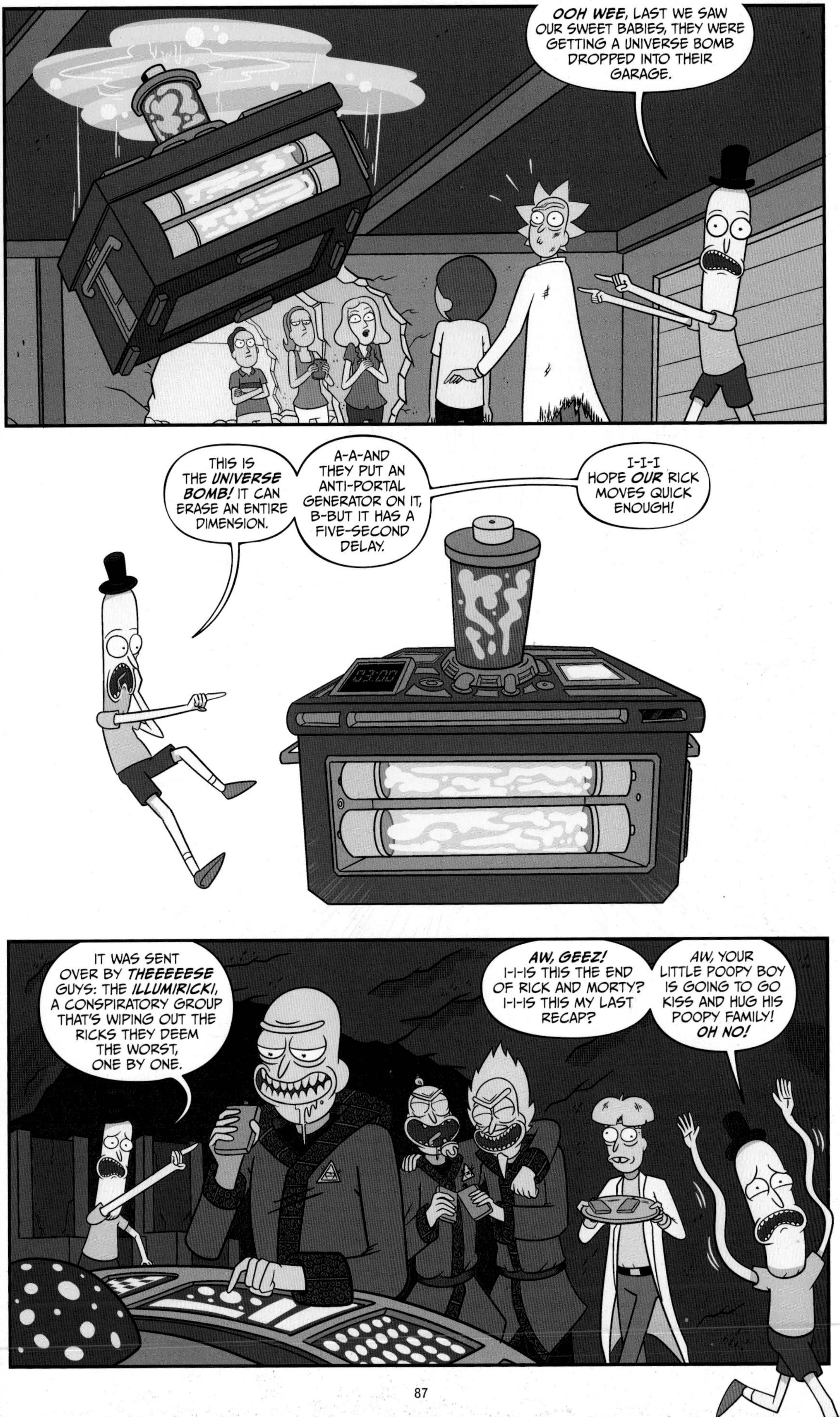
OOH WEE, LAST WE SAW OUR SWEET BABIES, THEY WERE GETTING A UNIVERSE BOMB DROPPED INTO THEIR GARAGE.
THIS IS THE UNIVERSE BOMB! IT CAN ERASE AN ENTIRE DIMENSION.
A-A-AND THEY PUT AN ANTI-PORTAL GENERATOR ON IT, B-BUT IT HAS A FIVE-SECOND DELAY.
I-I-I HOPE OUR RICK MOVES QUICK ENOUGH!
IT WAS SENT OVER BY THEEEEESE GUYS: THE ILLUMIRICKI, A CONSPIRATORY GROUP THAT'S WIPING OUT THE RICKS THEY DEEM THE WORST, ONE BY ONE.
AW, GEEZ! I-I-IS THIS THE END OF RICK AND MORTY? I-I-IS THIS MY LAST RECAP?
AW, YOUR LITTLE POOPY BOY IS GOING TO GO KISS AND HUG HIS POOPY FAMILY! OH NO!

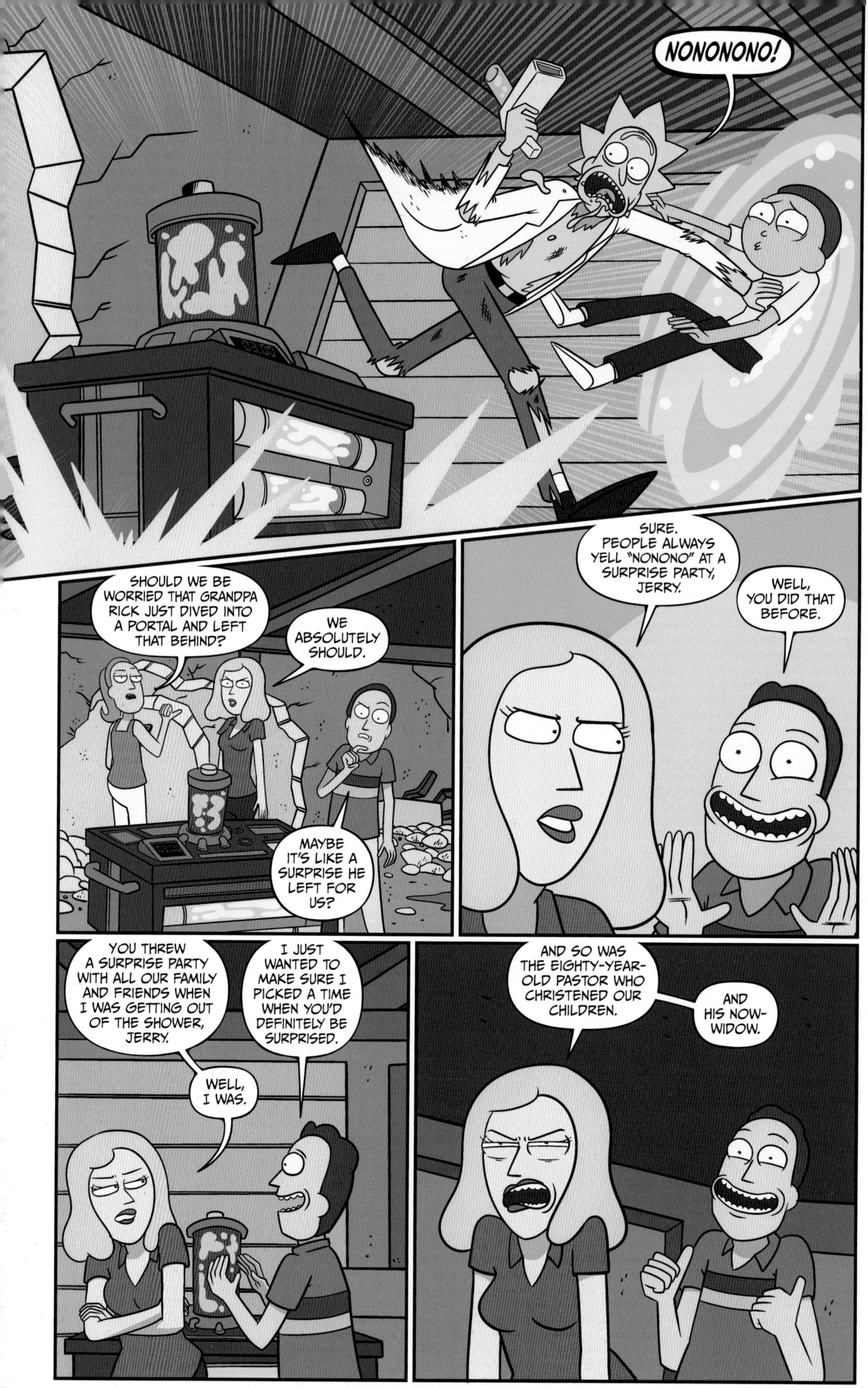
NONONONO!
SHOULD WE BE WORRIED THAT GRANDPA RICK JUST DIVED INTO A PORTAL AND LEFT THAT BEHIND?
WE ABSOLUTELY SHOULD.
MAYBE IT'S LIKE A SURPRISE HE LEFT FOR US?
SURE. PEOPLE ALWAYS YELL "NONONO" AT A SURPRISE PARTY, JERRY.
WELL, YOU DID THAT BEFORE.
YOU THREW A SURPRISE PARTY WITH ALL OUR FAMILY AND FRIENDS WHEN I WAS GETTING OUT OF THE SHOWER, JERRY.
WELL, I WAS.
I JUST WANTED TO MAKE SURE I PICKED A TIME WHEN YOU'D DEFINITELY BE SURPRISED.
AND SO WAS THE EIGHTY-YEAR-OLD PASTOR WHO CHRISTENED OUR CHILDREN.
AND HIS NOW-WIDOW.

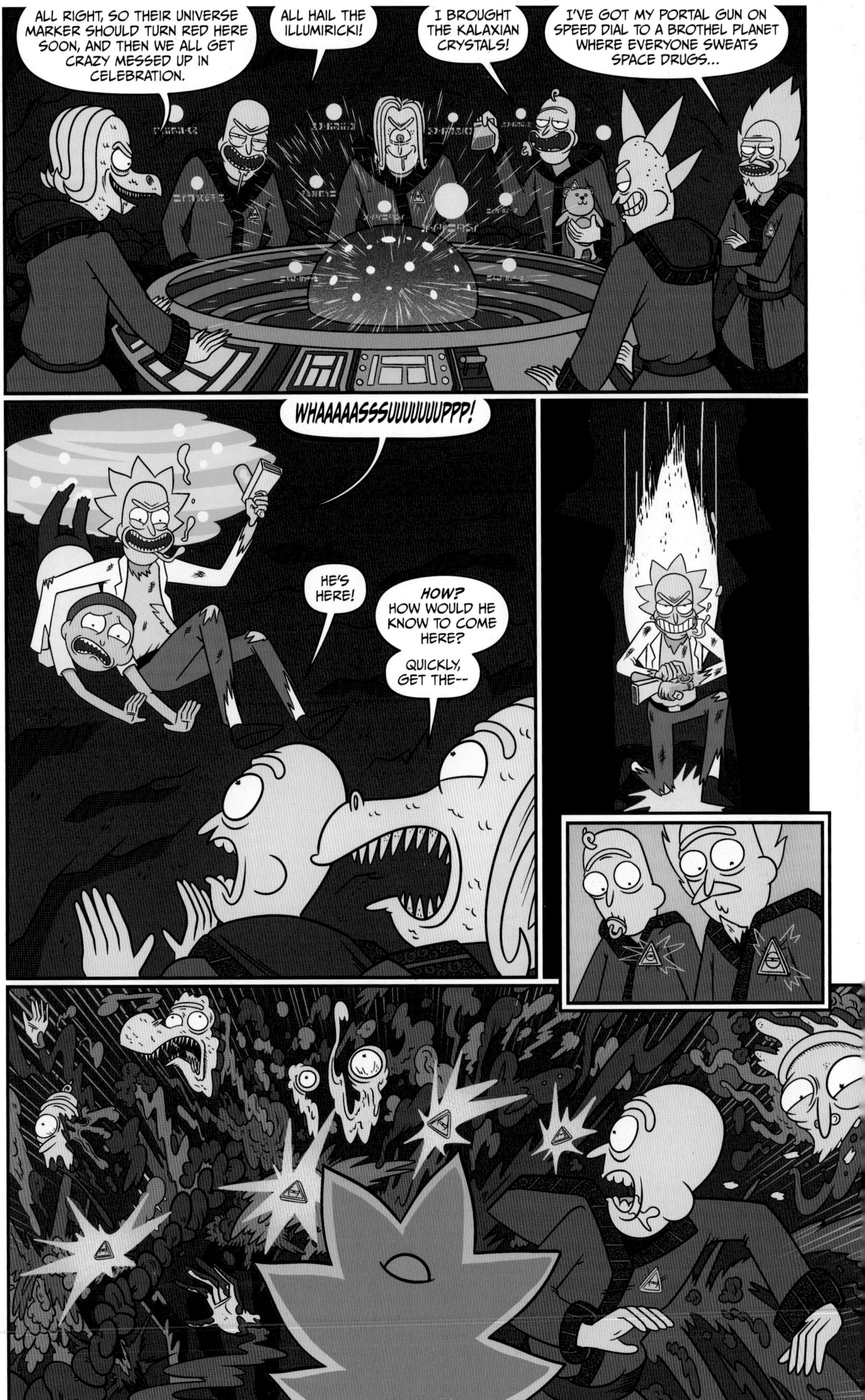
ALL RIGHT, SO THEIR UNIVERSE MARKER SHOULD TURN RED HERE SOON, AND THEN WE ALL GET CRAZY MESSED UP IN CELEBRATION.
ALL HAIL THE ILLUMIRICK!
I BROUGHT THE KALAXIAN CRYSTALS!
I'VE GOT MY PORTAL GUN ON SPEED DIAL TO A BROTHEL PLANET WHERE EVERYONE SWEATS SPACE DRUGS...
WHAAAAASSSUUUUUUUPPP!
HE'S HERE!
HOW? HOW WOULD HE KNOW TO COME HERE?
QUICKLY, GET THE--

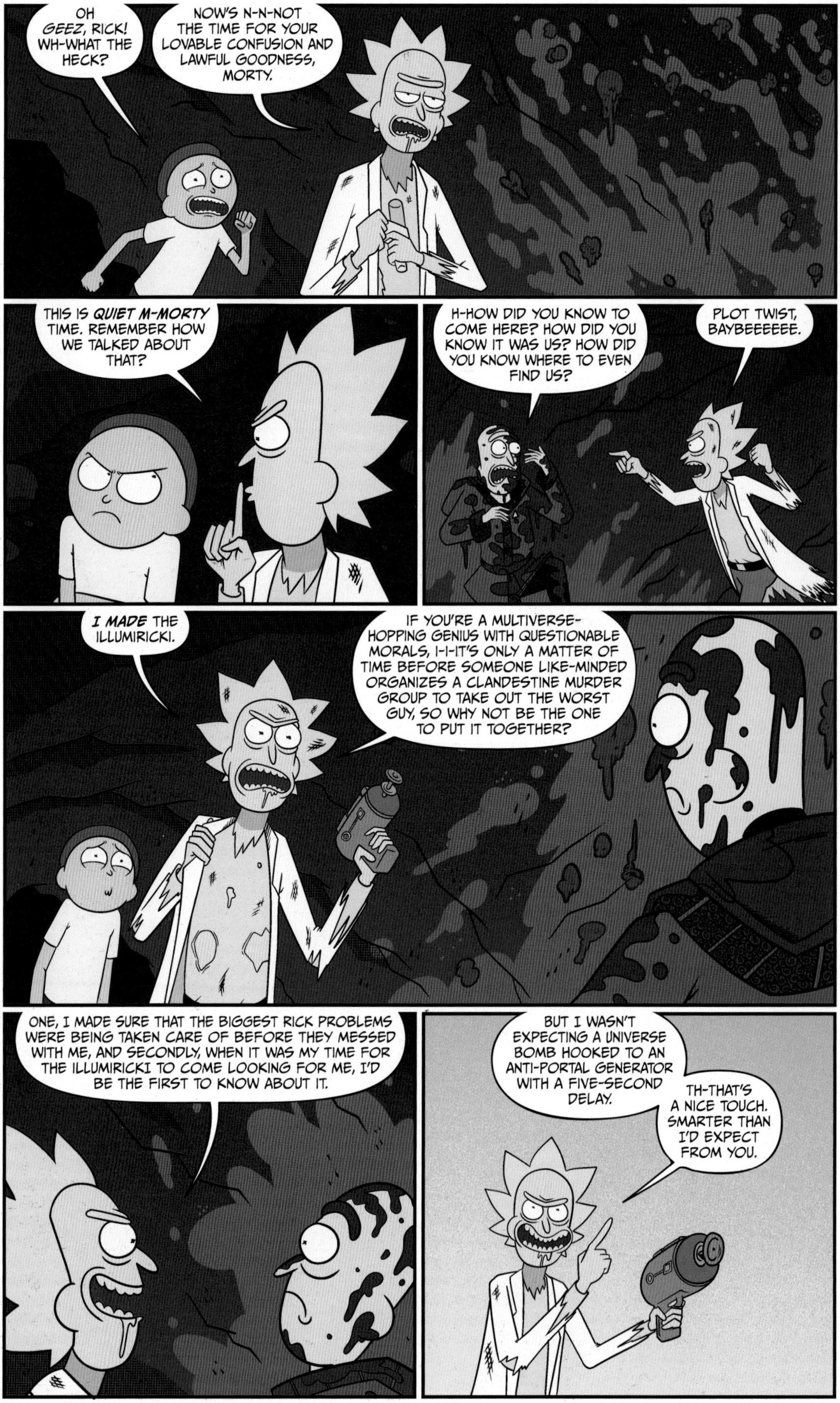
OH GEEZ, RICK! WH-WHAT THE HECK?
NOW'S N-N-NOT THE TIME FOR YOUR LOVABLE CONFUSION AND LAWFUL GOODNESS, MORTY.
THIS IS *QUIET M-MORTY* TIME. REMEMBER HOW WE TALKED ABOUT THAT?
H-HOW DID YOU KNOW TO COME HERE? HOW DID YOU KNOW IT WAS US? HOW DID YOU KNOW WHERE TO EVEN FIND US?
PLOT TWIST, BAYBEEEEEE.
*I MADE* THE ILLUMIRICKI.
IF YOU'RE A MULTIVERSE-HOPPING GENIUS WITH QUESTIONABLE MORALS, I-I-IT'S ONLY A MATTER OF TIME BEFORE SOMEONE LIKE-MINDED ORGANIZES A CLANDESTINE MURDER GROUP TO TAKE OUT THE WORST GUY, SO WHY NOT BE THE ONE TO PUT IT TOGETHER?
ONE, I MADE SURE THAT THE BIGGEST RICK PROBLEMS WERE BEING TAKEN CARE OF BEFORE THEY MESSED WITH ME, AND SECONDLY, WHEN IT WAS MY TIME FOR THE ILLUMIRICKI TO COME LOOKING FOR ME, I'D BE THE FIRST TO KNOW ABOUT IT.
BUT I WASN'T EXPECTING A UNIVERSE BOMB HOOKED TO AN ANTI-PORTAL GENERATOR WITH A FIVE-SECOND DELAY.
TH-THAT'S A NICE TOUCH. SMARTER THAN I'D EXPECT FROM YOU.

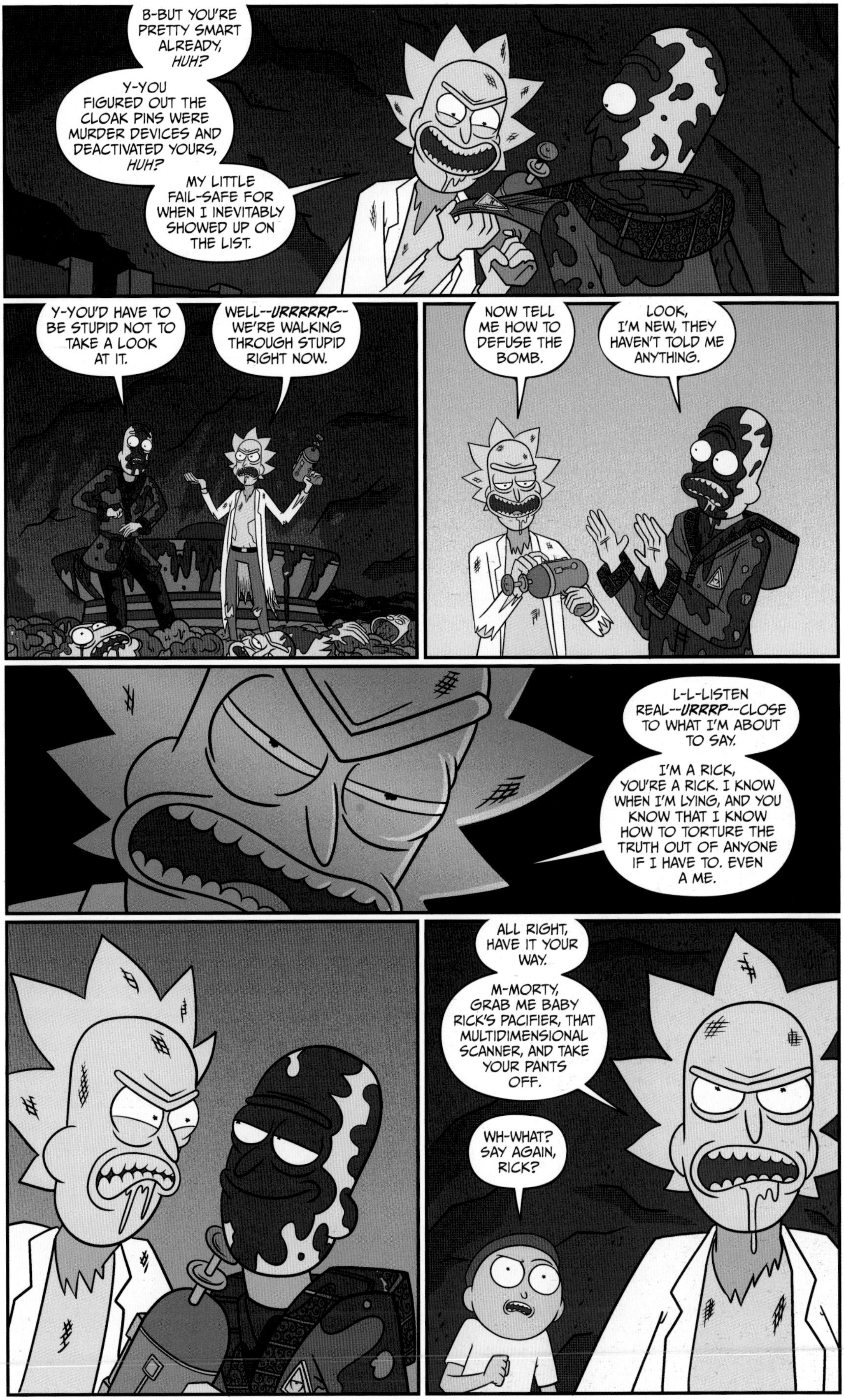
B-BUT YOU'RE PRETTY SMART ALREADY, *HUH?*
Y-YOU FIGURED OUT THE CLOAK PINS WERE MURDER DEVICES AND DEACTIVATED YOURS, *HUH?*
MY LITTLE FAIL-SAFE FOR WHEN I INEVITABLY SHOWED UP ON THE LIST.
Y-YOU'D HAVE TO BE STUPID NOT TO TAKE A LOOK AT IT.
WELL--*URRRRRP*--WE'RE WALKING THROUGH STUPID RIGHT NOW.
NOW TELL ME HOW TO DEFUSE THE BOMB.
LOOK, I'M NEW, THEY HAVEN'T TOLD ME ANYTHING.
L-L-LISTEN REAL--*URRRP*--CLOSE TO WHAT I'M ABOUT TO SAY.
I'M A RICK, YOU'RE A RICK. I KNOW WHEN I'M LYING, AND YOU KNOW THAT I KNOW HOW TO TORTURE THE TRUTH OUT OF ANYONE IF I HAVE TO. EVEN A ME.
ALL RIGHT, HAVE IT YOUR WAY.
M-MORTY, GRAB ME BABY RICK'S PACIFIER, THAT MULTIDIMENSIONAL SCANNER, AND TAKE YOUR PANTS OFF.
WH-WHAT? SAY AGAIN, RICK?

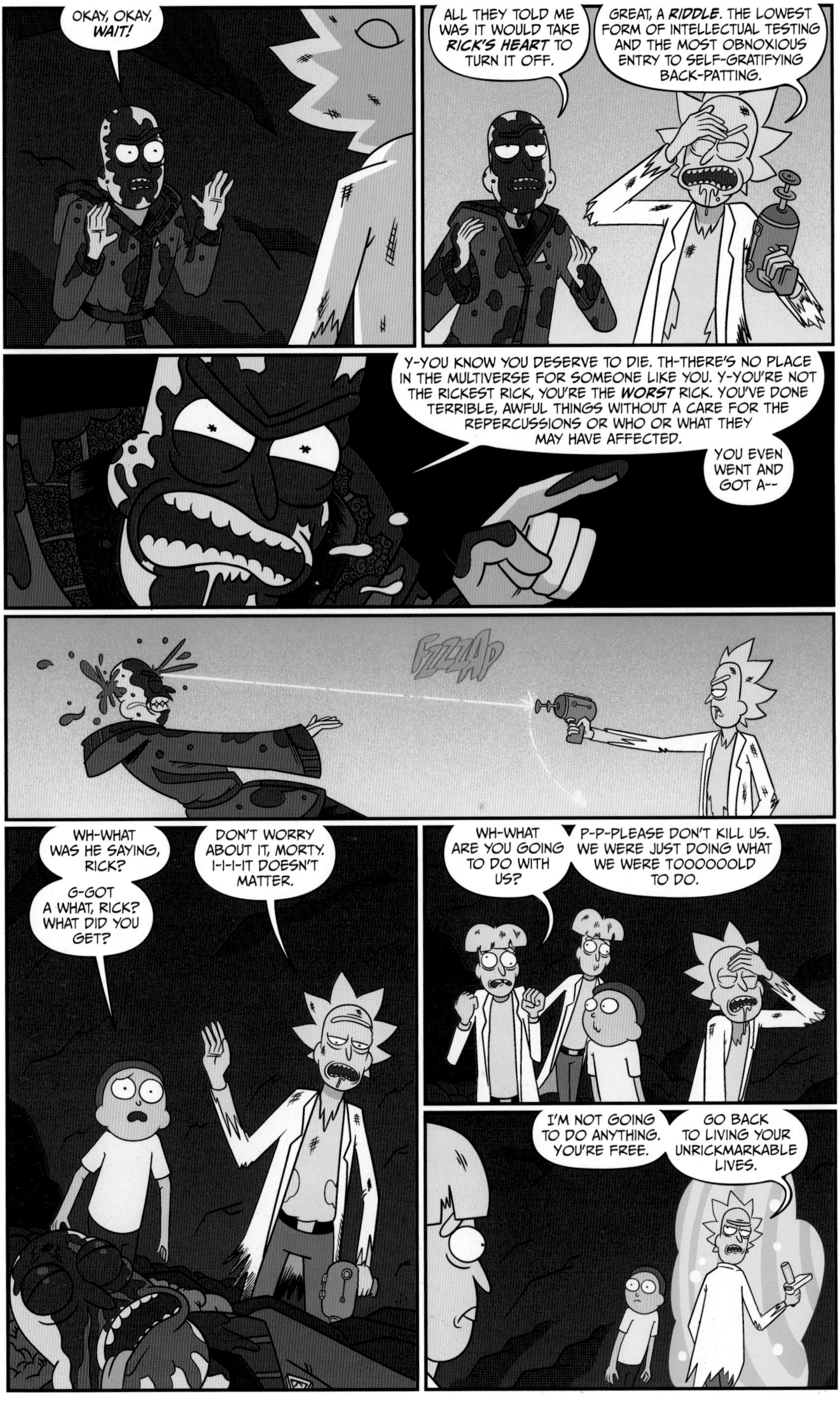
OKAY, OKAY, WAIT!
ALL THEY TOLD ME WAS IT WOULD TAKE RICK'S HEART TO TURN IT OFF.
GREAT, A RIDDLE. THE LOWEST FORM OF INTELLECTUAL TESTING AND THE MOST OBNOXIOUS ENTRY TO SELF-GRATIFYING BACK-PATTING.
Y-YOU KNOW YOU DESERVE TO DIE. TH-THERE'S NO PLACE IN THE MULTIVERSE FOR SOMEONE LIKE YOU. Y-YOU'RE NOT THE RICKEST RICK, YOU'RE THE WORST RICK. YOU'VE DONE TERRIBLE, AWFUL THINGS WITHOUT A CARE FOR THE REPERCUSSIONS OR WHO OR WHAT THEY MAY HAVE AFFECTED.
YOU EVEN WENT AND GOT A--
FZZZAP
WH-WHAT WAS HE SAYING, RICK?
G-GOT A WHAT, RICK? WHAT DID YOU GET?
DON'T WORRY ABOUT IT, MORTY. I-I-I-IT DOESN'T MATTER.
WH-WHAT ARE YOU GOING TO DO WITH US?
P-P-PLEASE DON'T KILL US. WE WERE JUST DOING WHAT WE WERE TOOOOOOLD TO DO.
I'M NOT GOING TO DO ANYTHING. YOU'RE FREE.
GO BACK TO LIVING YOUR UNRICKMARKABLE LIVES.

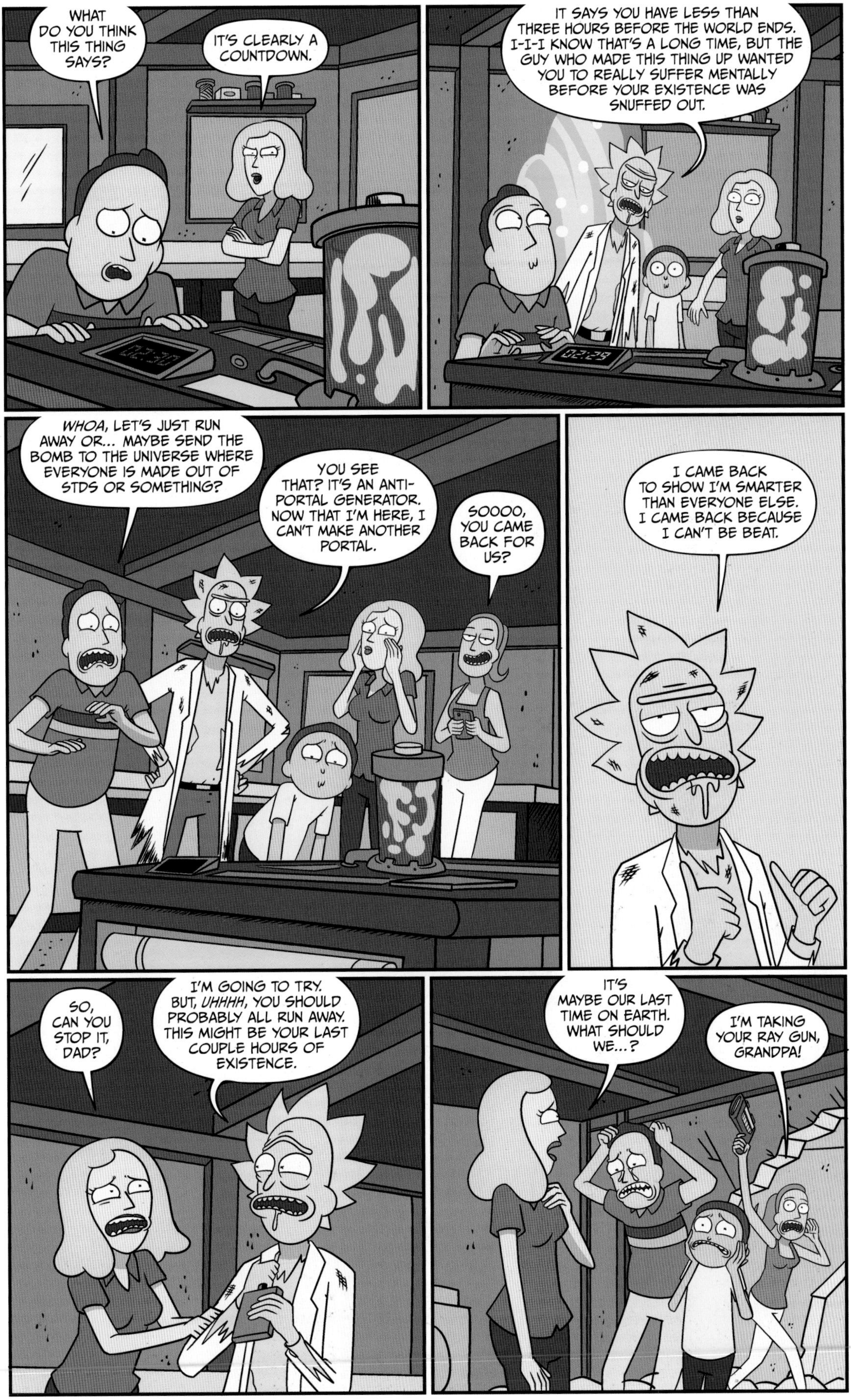
WHAT DO YOU THINK THIS THING SAYS?
IT'S CLEARLY A COUNTDOWN.
IT SAYS YOU HAVE LESS THAN THREE HOURS BEFORE THE WORLD ENDS. I-I-I KNOW THAT'S A LONG TIME, BUT THE GUY WHO MADE THIS THING UP WANTED YOU TO REALLY SUFFER MENTALLY BEFORE YOUR EXISTENCE WAS SNUFFED OUT.
*WHOA*, LET'S JUST RUN AWAY OR... MAYBE SEND THE BOMB TO THE UNIVERSE WHERE EVERYONE IS MADE OUT OF STDS OR SOMETHING?
YOU SEE THAT? IT'S AN ANTI-PORTAL GENERATOR. NOW THAT I'M HERE, I CAN'T MAKE ANOTHER PORTAL.
SOOOO, YOU CAME BACK FOR US?
I CAME BACK TO SHOW I'M SMARTER THAN EVERYONE ELSE. I CAME BACK BECAUSE I CAN'T BE BEAT.
SO, CAN YOU STOP IT, DAD?
I'M GOING TO TRY. BUT, *UHHHH*, YOU SHOULD PROBABLY ALL RUN AWAY. THIS MIGHT BE YOUR LAST COUPLE HOURS OF EXISTENCE.
IT'S MAYBE OUR LAST TIME ON EARTH. WHAT SHOULD WE...?
I'M TAKING YOUR RAY GUN, GRANDPA!

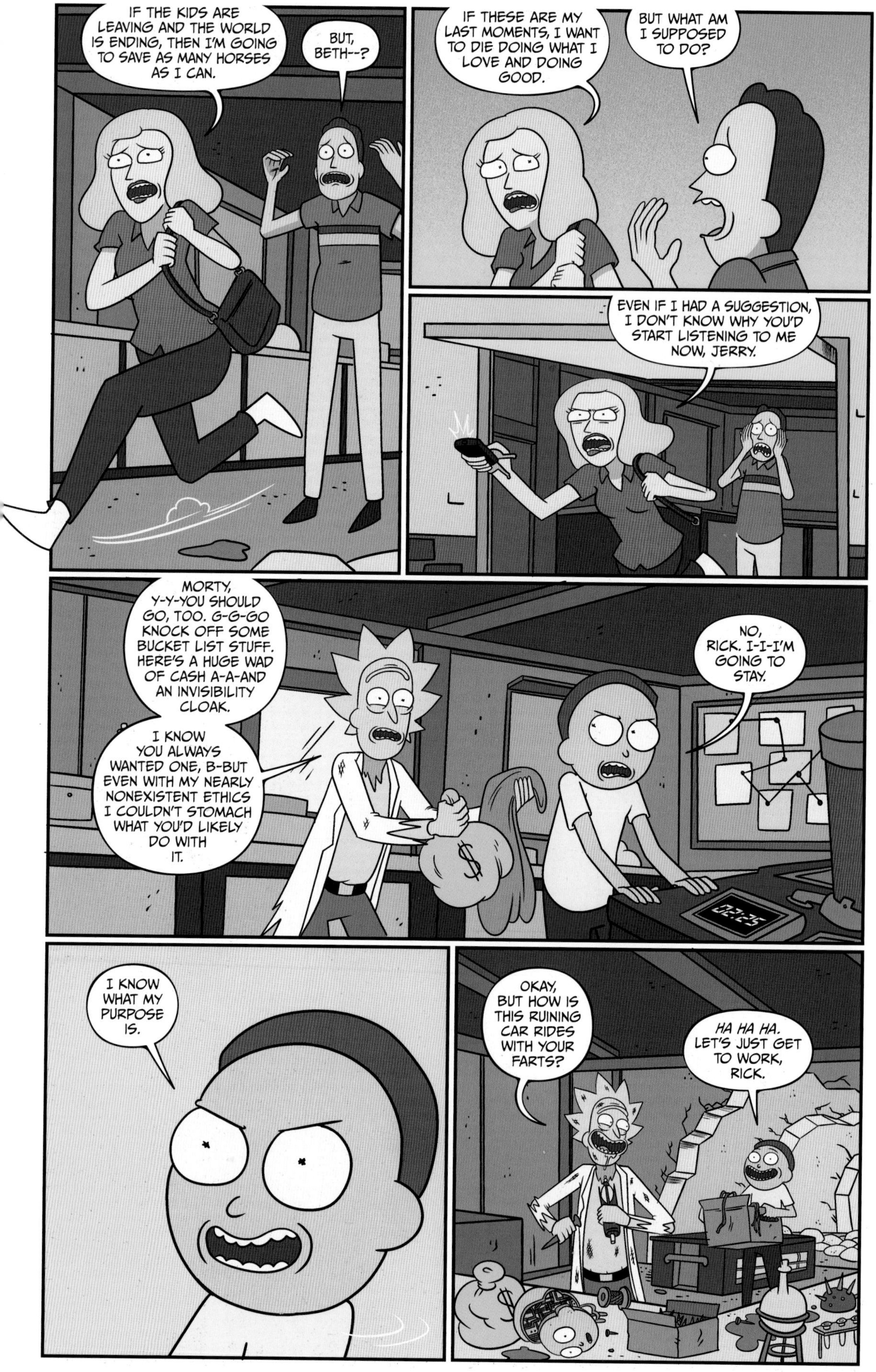
IF THE KIDS ARE LEAVING AND THE WORLD IS ENDING, THEN I'M GOING TO SAVE AS MANY HORSES AS I CAN.
BUT, BETH--?
IF THESE ARE MY LAST MOMENTS, I WANT TO DIE DOING WHAT I LOVE AND DOING GOOD.
BUT WHAT AM I SUPPOSED TO DO?
EVEN IF I HAD A SUGGESTION, I DON'T KNOW WHY YOU'D START LISTENING TO ME NOW, JERRY.
MORTY, Y-Y-YOU SHOULD GO, TOO. G-G-GO KNOCK OFF SOME BUCKET LIST STUFF. HERE'S A HUGE WAD OF CASH A-A-AND AN INVISIBILITY CLOAK.
I KNOW YOU ALWAYS WANTED ONE, B-BUT EVEN WITH MY NEARLY NONEXISTENT ETHICS I COULDN'T STOMACH WHAT YOU'D LIKELY DO WITH IT.
NO, RICK. I-I-I'M GOING TO STAY.
02:25
I KNOW WHAT MY PURPOSE IS.
OKAY, BUT HOW IS THIS RUINING CAR RIDES WITH YOUR FARTS?
*HA HA HA.* LET'S JUST GET TO WORK, RICK.

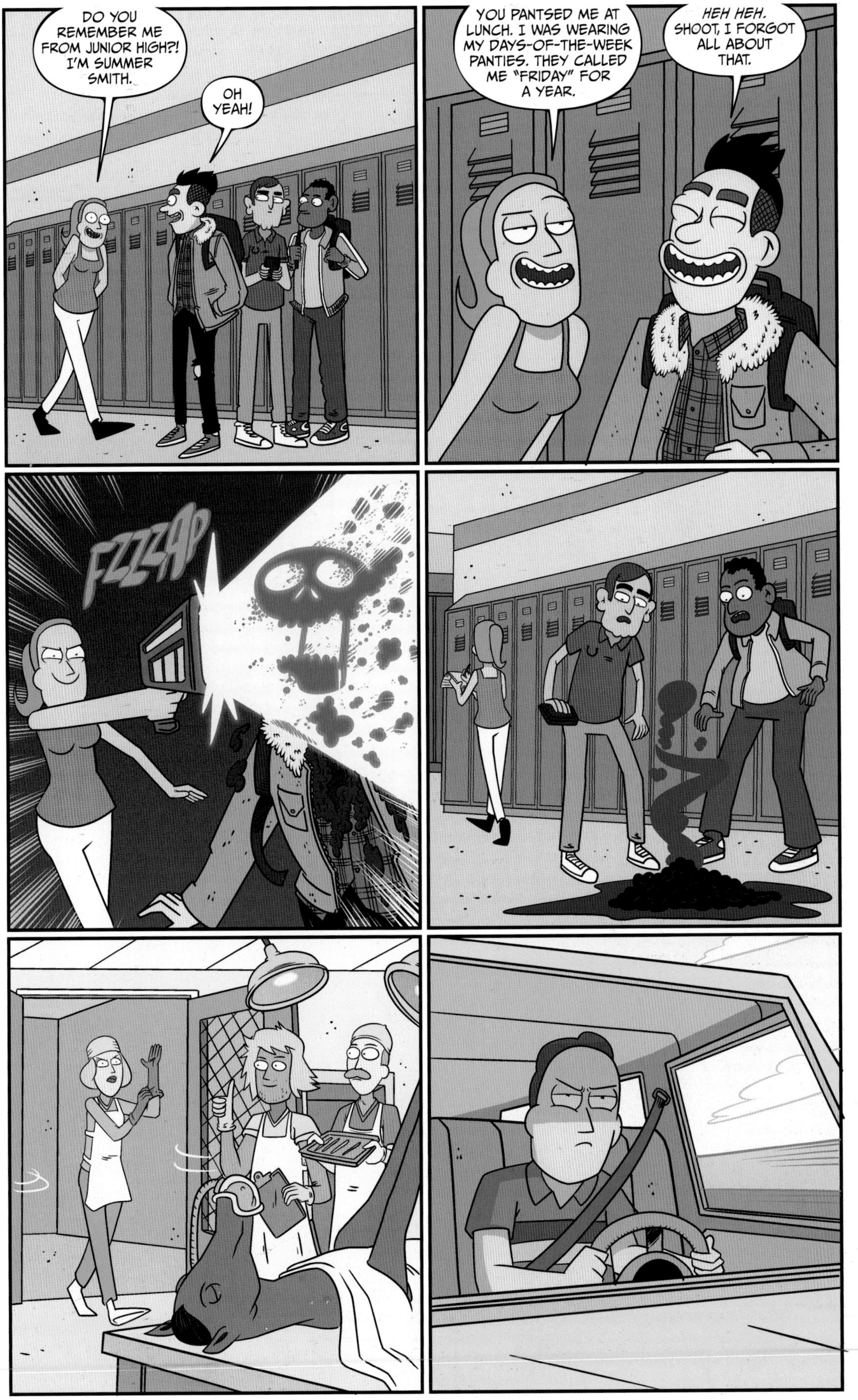
DO YOU REMEMBER ME FROM JUNIOR HIGH?! I'M SUMMER SMITH.
OH YEAH!
YOU PANTSED ME AT LUNCH. I WAS WEARING MY DAYS-OF-THE-WEEK PANTIES. THEY CALLED ME "FRIDAY" FOR A YEAR.
HEH HEH. SHOOT, I FORGOT ALL ABOUT THAT.
FZZZAP

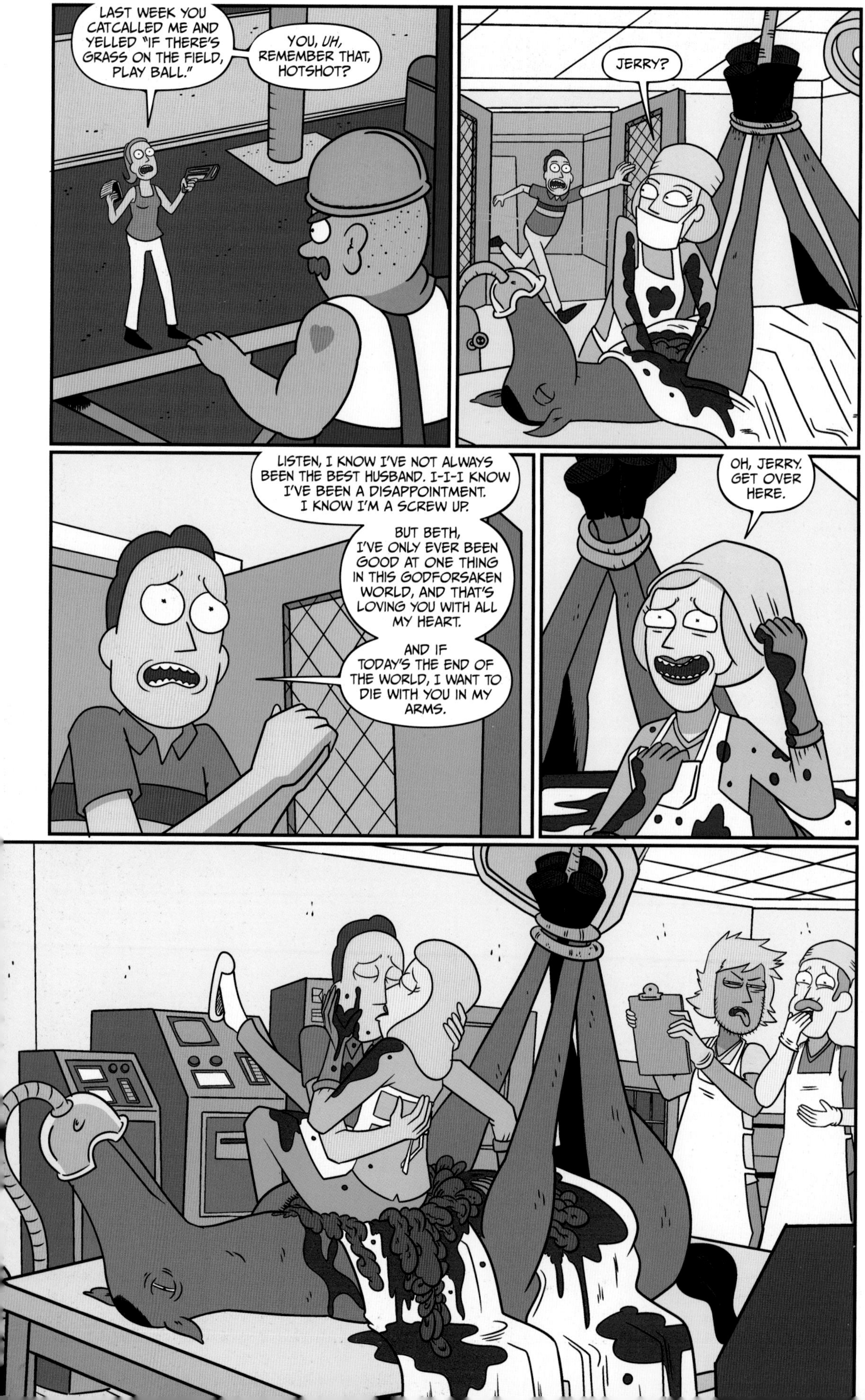
LAST WEEK YOU CATCALLED ME AND YELLED "IF THERE'S GRASS ON THE FIELD, PLAY BALL."
YOU, *UH*, REMEMBER THAT, HOTSHOT?
JERRY?
LISTEN, I KNOW I'VE NOT ALWAYS BEEN THE BEST HUSBAND. I-I-I KNOW I'VE BEEN A DISAPPOINTMENT. I KNOW I'M A SCREW UP.
BUT BETH, I'VE ONLY EVER BEEN GOOD AT ONE THING IN THIS GODFORSAKEN WORLD, AND THAT'S LOVING YOU WITH ALL MY HEART.
AND IF TODAY'S THE END OF THE WORLD, I WANT TO DIE WITH YOU IN MY ARMS.
OH, JERRY. GET OVER HERE.

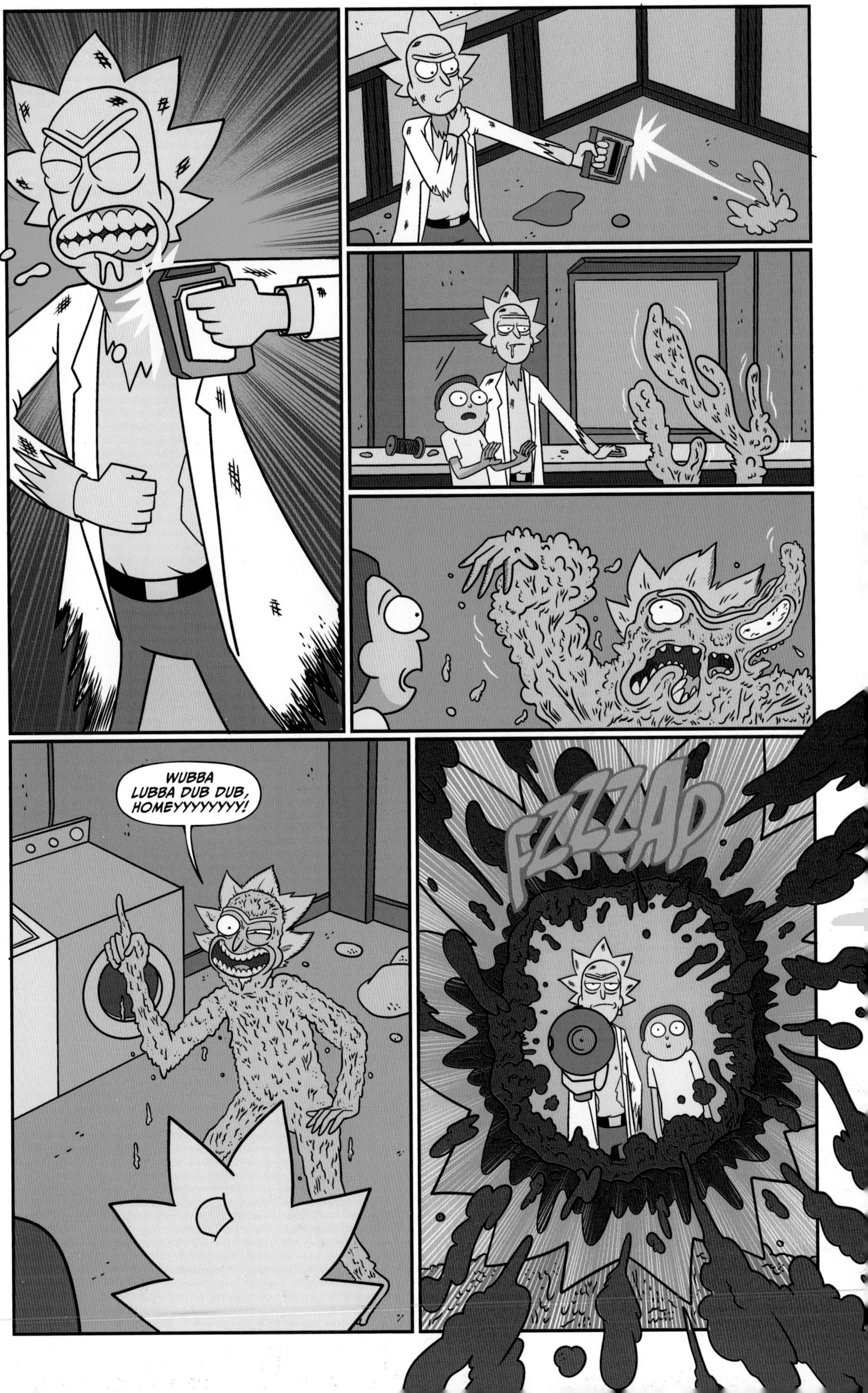
WUBBA LUBBA DUB DUB, HOMEYYYYYYYY!
FZZZAP

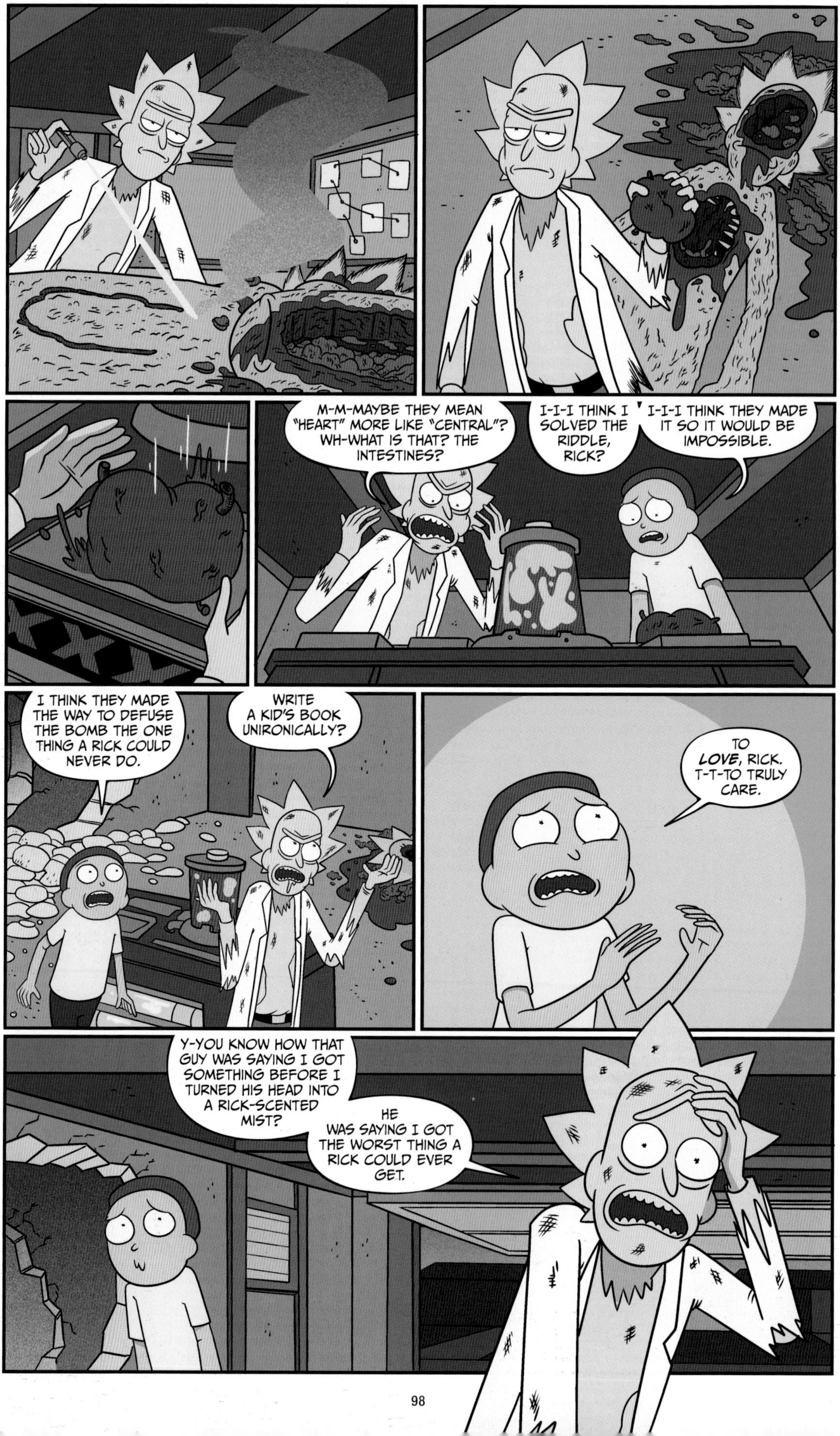
M-M-MAYBE THEY MEAN "HEART" MORE LIKE "CENTRAL"? WH-WHAT IS THAT? THE INTESTINES?
I-I-I THINK I SOLVED THE RIDDLE, RICK?
I-I-I THINK THEY MADE IT SO IT WOULD BE IMPOSSIBLE.
I THINK THEY MADE THE WAY TO DEFUSE THE BOMB THE ONE THING A RICK COULD NEVER DO.
WRITE A KID'S BOOK UNIRONICALLY?
TO *LOVE*, RICK. T-T-TO TRULY CARE.
Y-YOU KNOW HOW THAT GUY WAS SAYING I GOT SOMETHING BEFORE I TURNED HIS HEAD INTO A RICK-SCENTED MIST?
HE WAS SAYING I GOT THE WORST THING A RICK COULD EVER GET.

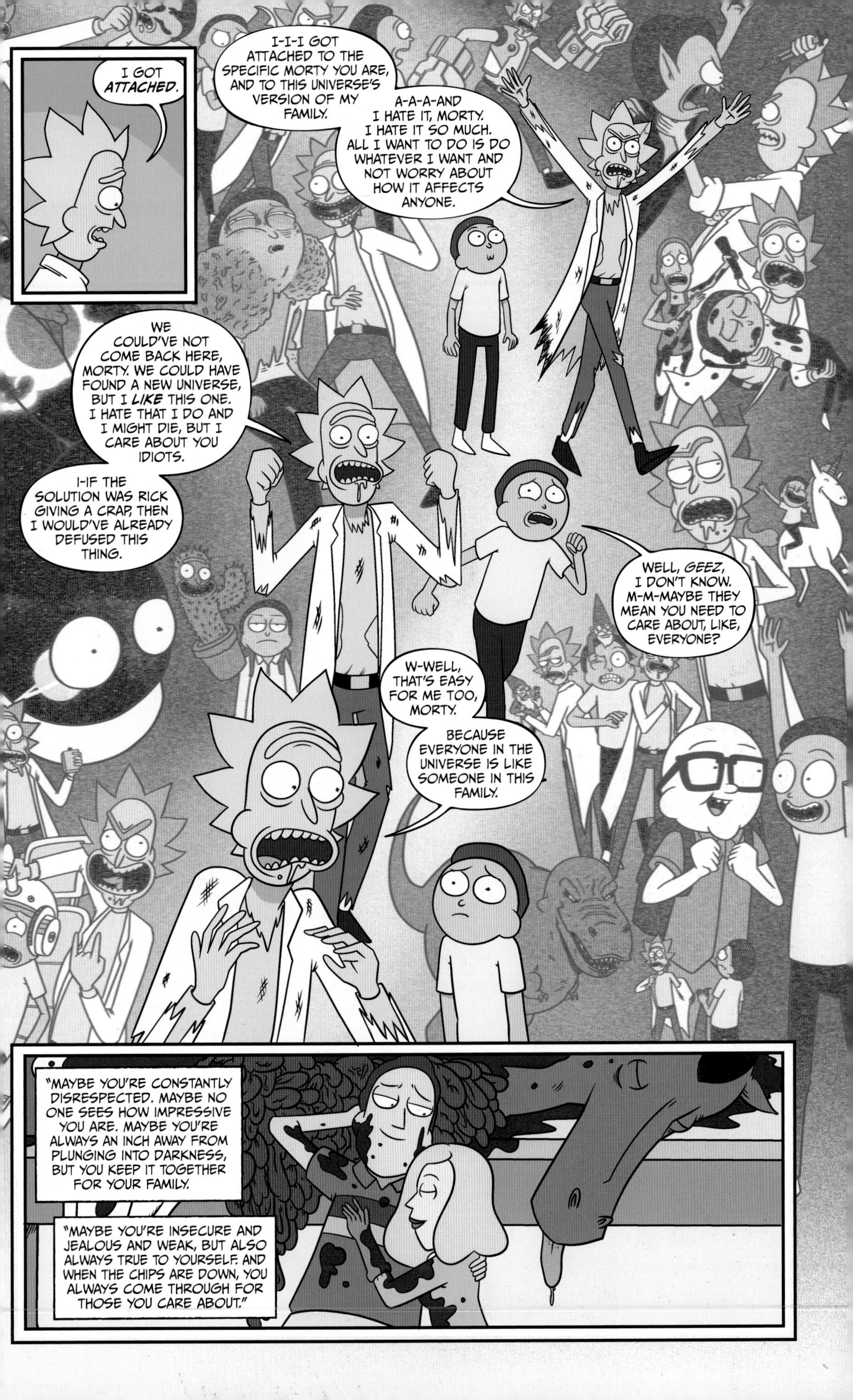
I GOT ATTACHED.
I-I-I GOT ATTACHED TO THE SPECIFIC MORTY YOU ARE, AND TO THIS UNIVERSE'S VERSION OF MY FAMILY.
A-A-A-AND I HATE IT, MORTY. I HATE IT SO MUCH. ALL I WANT TO DO IS DO WHATEVER I WANT AND NOT WORRY ABOUT HOW IT AFFECTS ANYONE.
WE COULD'VE NOT COME BACK HERE, MORTY. WE COULD HAVE FOUND A NEW UNIVERSE, BUT I LIKE THIS ONE. I HATE THAT I DO AND I MIGHT DIE, BUT I CARE ABOUT YOU IDIOTS.
I-IF THE SOLUTION WAS RICK GIVING A CRAP, THEN I WOULD'VE ALREADY DEFUSED THIS THING.
WELL, GEEZ, I DON'T KNOW. M-M-MAYBE THEY MEAN YOU NEED TO CARE ABOUT, LIKE, EVERYONE?
W-WELL, THAT'S EASY FOR ME TOO, MORTY.
BECAUSE EVERYONE IN THE UNIVERSE IS LIKE SOMEONE IN THIS FAMILY.
"MAYBE YOU'RE CONSTANTLY DISRESPECTED. MAYBE NO ONE SEES HOW IMPRESSIVE YOU ARE. MAYBE YOU'RE ALWAYS AN INCH AWAY FROM PLUNGING INTO DARKNESS, BUT YOU KEEP IT TOGETHER FOR YOUR FAMILY.
"MAYBE YOU'RE INSECURE AND JEALOUS AND WEAK, BUT ALSO ALWAYS TRUE TO YOURSELF. AND WHEN THE CHIPS ARE DOWN, YOU ALWAYS COME THROUGH FOR THOSE YOU CARE ABOUT."

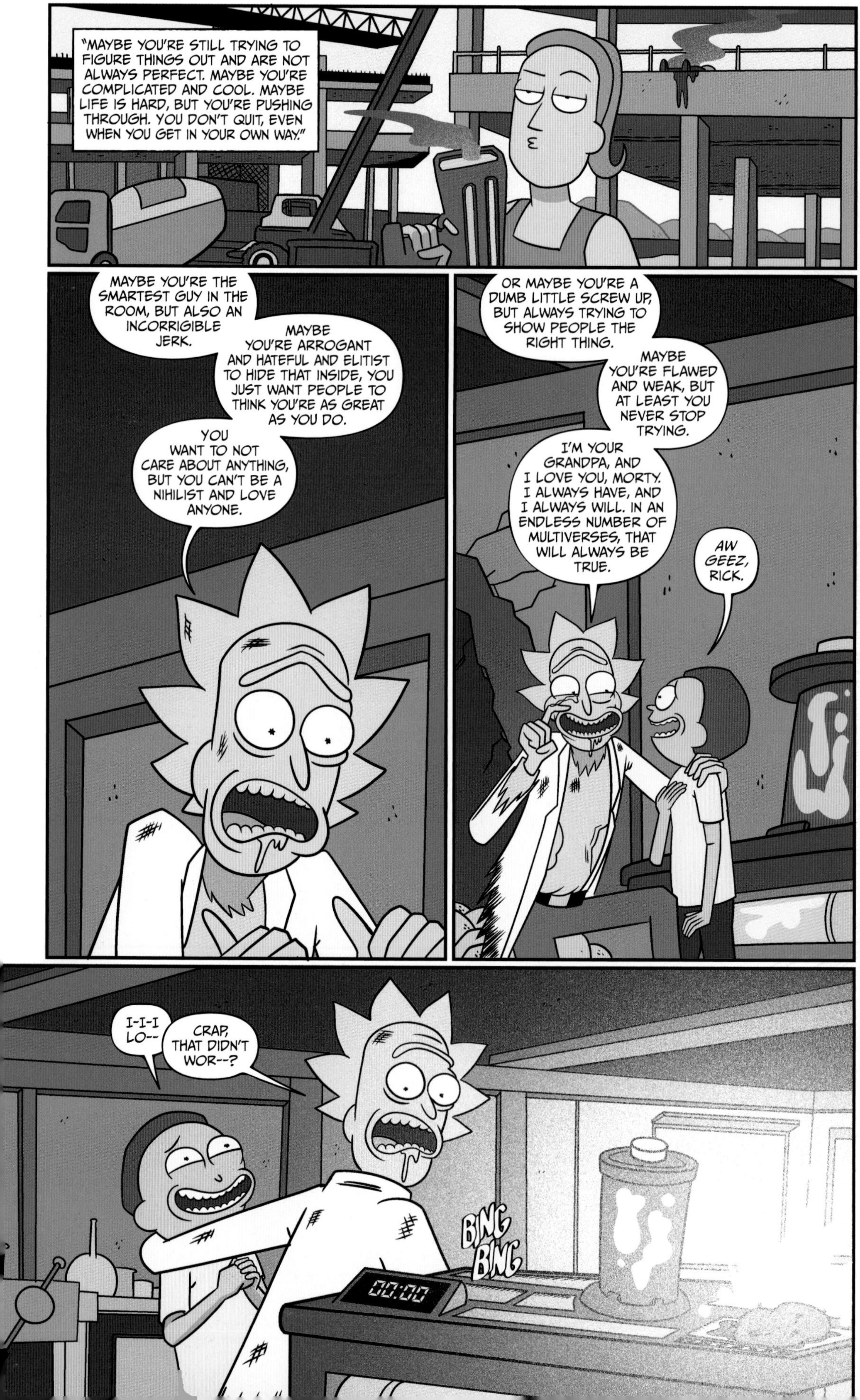
"MAYBE YOU'RE STILL TRYING TO FIGURE THINGS OUT AND ARE NOT ALWAYS PERFECT. MAYBE YOU'RE COMPLICATED AND COOL. MAYBE LIFE IS HARD, BUT YOU'RE PUSHING THROUGH. YOU DON'T QUIT, EVEN WHEN YOU GET IN YOUR OWN WAY."
MAYBE YOU'RE THE SMARTEST GUY IN THE ROOM, BUT ALSO AN INCORRIGIBLE JERK.
MAYBE YOU'RE ARROGANT AND HATEFUL AND ELITIST TO HIDE THAT INSIDE, YOU JUST WANT PEOPLE TO THINK YOU'RE AS GREAT AS YOU DO.
YOU WANT TO NOT CARE ABOUT ANYTHING, BUT YOU CAN'T BE A NIHILIST AND LOVE ANYONE.
OR MAYBE YOU'RE A DUMB LITTLE SCREW UP, BUT ALWAYS TRYING TO SHOW PEOPLE THE RIGHT THING.
MAYBE YOU'RE FLAWED AND WEAK, BUT AT LEAST YOU NEVER STOP TRYING.
I'M YOUR GRANDPA, AND I LOVE YOU, MORTY. I ALWAYS HAVE, AND I ALWAYS WILL. IN AN ENDLESS NUMBER OF MULTIVERSES, THAT WILL ALWAYS BE TRUE.
AW GEEZ, RICK.
I-I-I LO--
CRAP, THAT DIDN'T WOR--?
BING BING
00:00

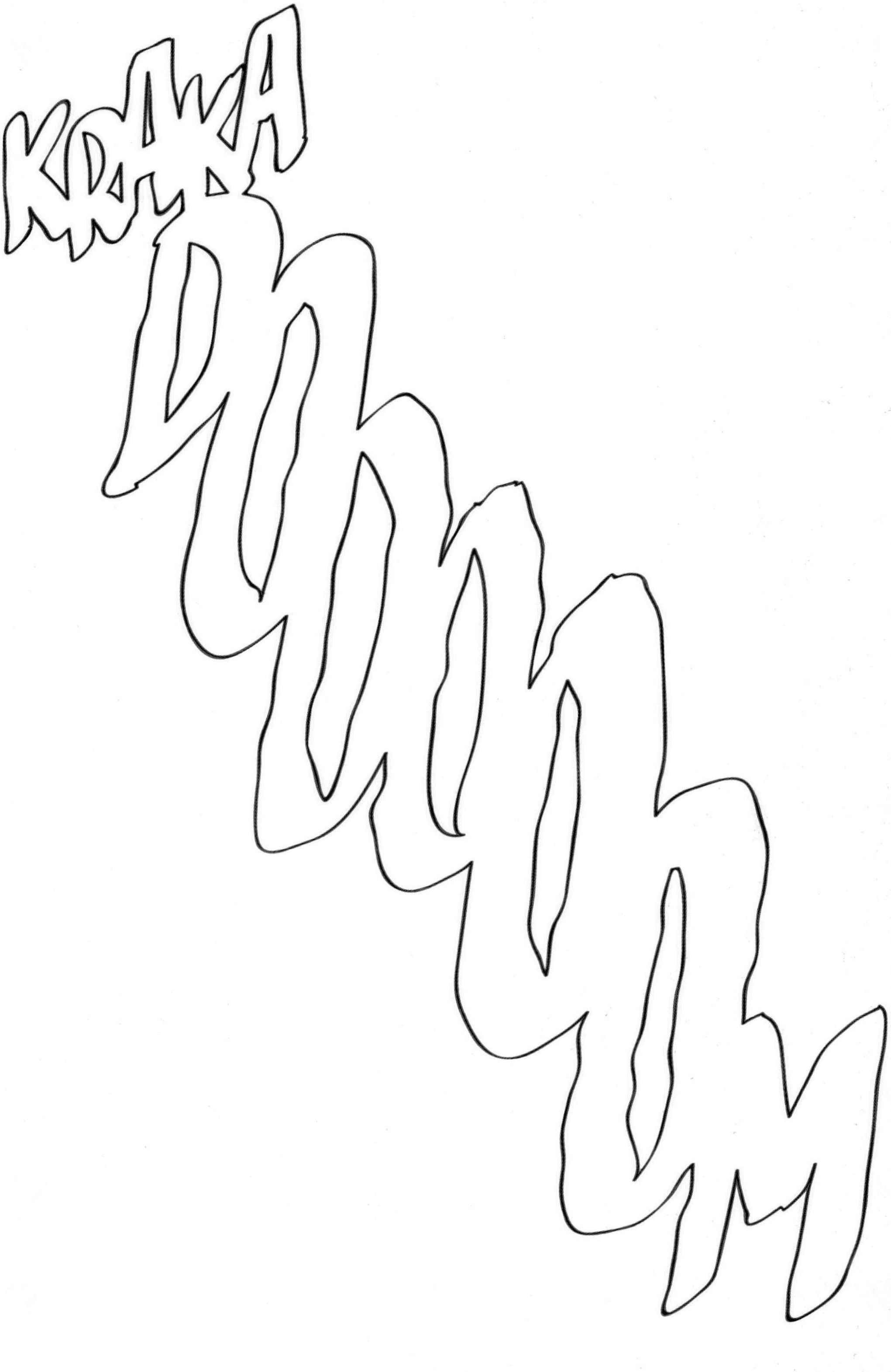
KRAKA

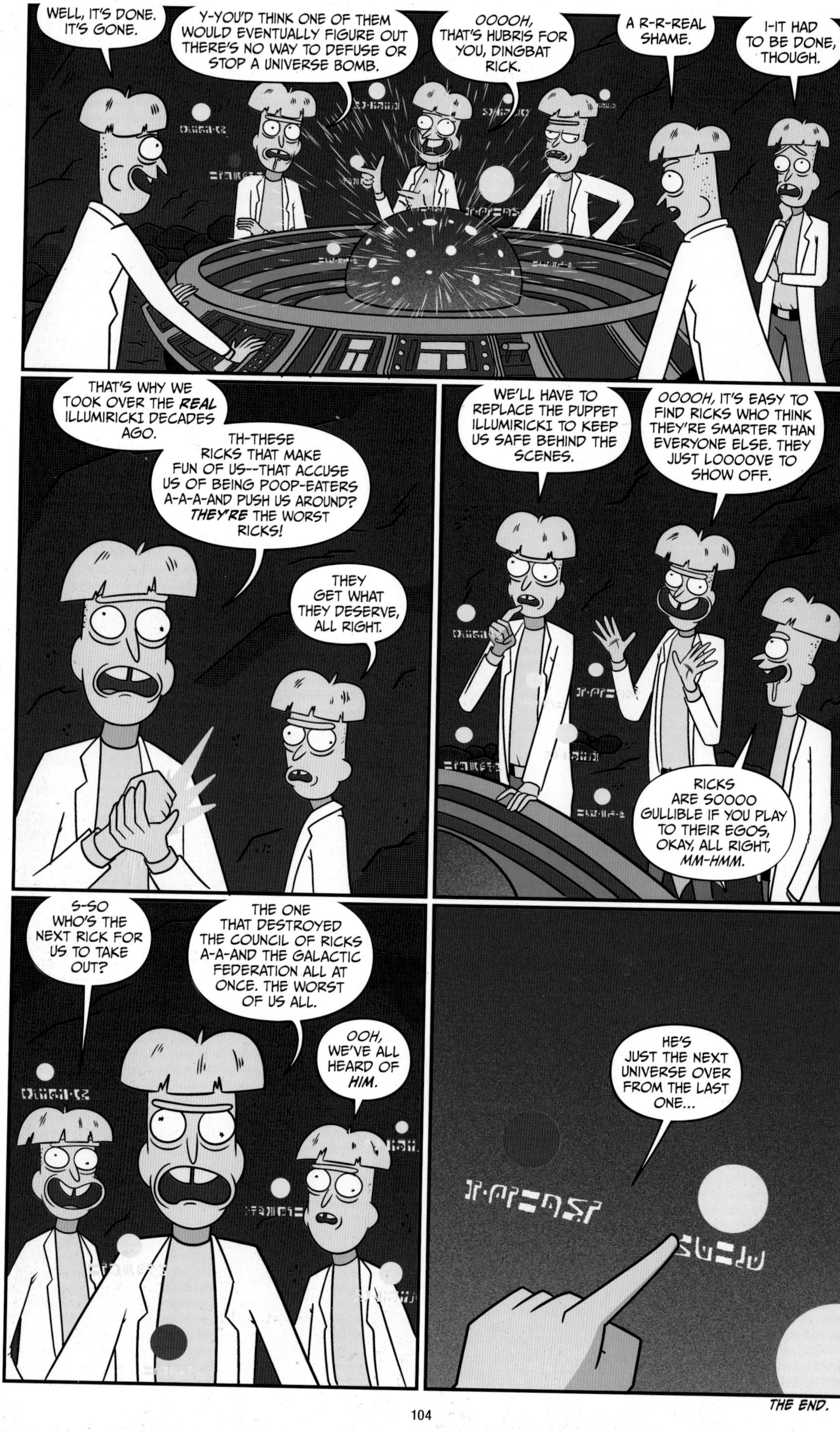
WELL, IT'S DONE. IT'S GONE.
Y-YOU'D THINK ONE OF THEM WOULD EVENTUALLY FIGURE OUT THERE'S NO WAY TO DEFUSE OR STOP A UNIVERSE BOMB.
OOOOH, THAT'S HUBRIS FOR YOU, DINGBAT RICK.
A R-R-REAL SHAME.
I-IT HAD TO BE DONE, THOUGH.
THAT'S WHY WE TOOK OVER THE REAL ILLUMIRICKI DECADES AGO.
TH-THESE RICKS THAT MAKE FUN OF US--THAT ACCUSE US OF BEING POOP-EATERS A-A-A-AND PUSH US AROUND? THEY'RE THE WORST RICKS!
THEY GET WHAT THEY DESERVE, ALL RIGHT.
WE'LL HAVE TO REPLACE THE PUPPET ILLUMIRICKI TO KEEP US SAFE BEHIND THE SCENES.
OOOOH, IT'S EASY TO FIND RICKS WHO THINK THEY'RE SMARTER THAN EVERYONE ELSE. THEY JUST LOOOOVE TO SHOW OFF.
RICKS ARE SOOOO GULLIBLE IF YOU PLAY TO THEIR EGOS, OKAY, ALL RIGHT, MM-HMM.
S-SO WHO'S THE NEXT RICK FOR US TO TAKE OUT?
THE ONE THAT DESTROYED THE COUNCIL OF RICKS A-A-AND THE GALACTIC FEDERATION ALL AT ONCE. THE WORST OF US ALL.
OOH, WE'VE ALL HEARD OF HIM.
HE'S JUST THE NEXT UNIVERSE OVER FROM THE LAST ONE...
THE END.

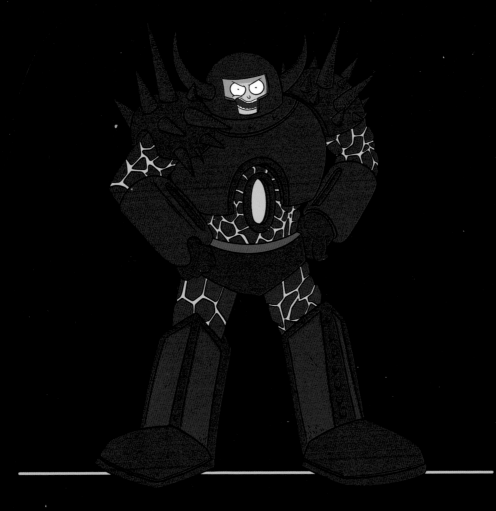

# BONUS STORIES

## BITTY CRITTYS

## BLUBBER

## BABY DON'T HURT ME

## LIKES AND FOLLOWS

## ATTACK THE VIRUS

ALL STORIES WRITTEN BY **TERRY BLAS**
ALL STORIES ILLUSTRATED & COLORED BY **BENJAMIN DEWEY**
ALL STORIES LETTERED BY **CRANK!**

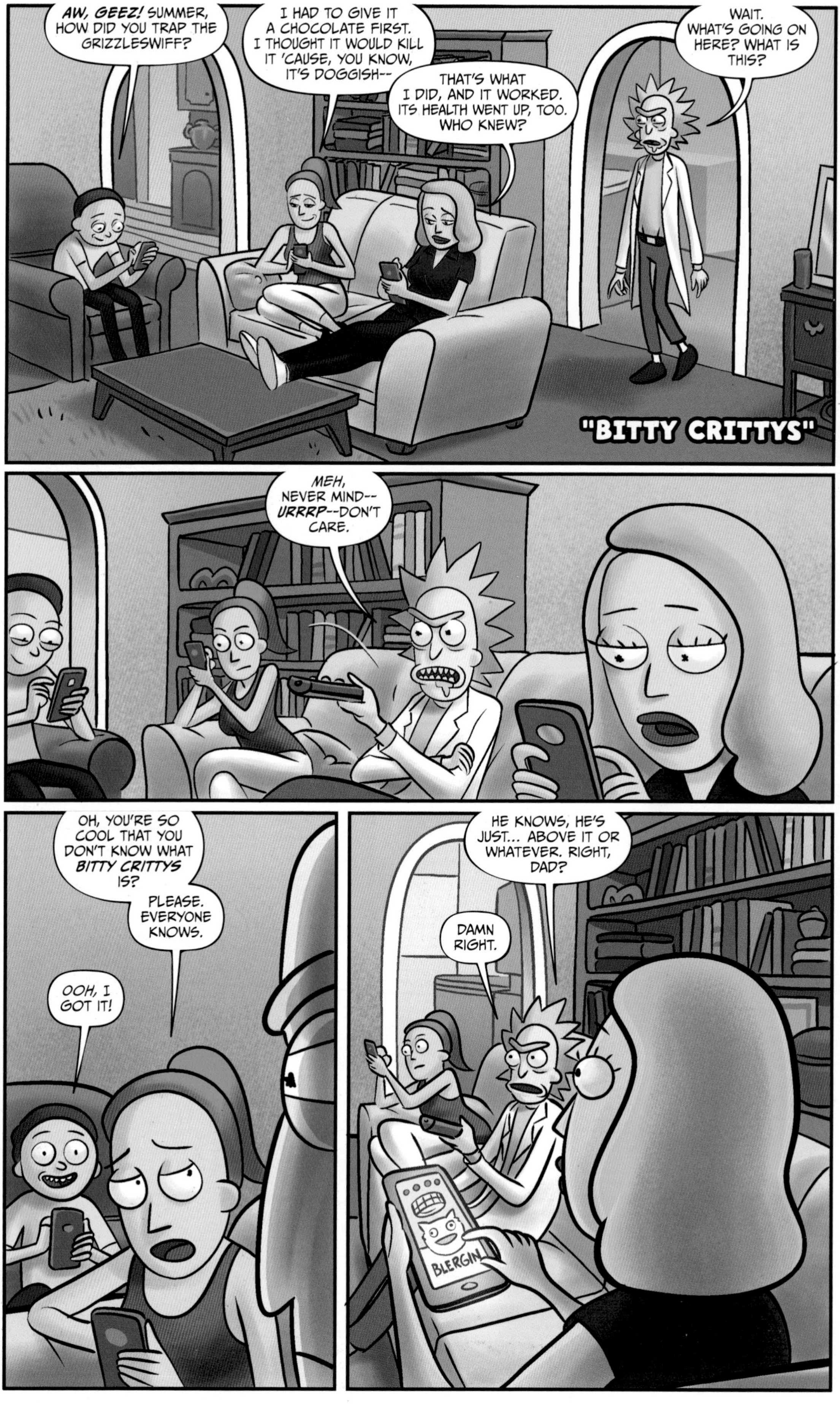
AW, GEEZ! SUMMER, HOW DID YOU TRAP THE GRIZZLESWIFF?
I HAD TO GIVE IT A CHOCOLATE FIRST. I THOUGHT IT WOULD KILL IT 'CAUSE, YOU KNOW, IT'S DOGGISH--
THAT'S WHAT I DID, AND IT WORKED. ITS HEALTH WENT UP, TOO. WHO KNEW?
WAIT. WHAT'S GOING ON HERE? WHAT IS THIS?
"BITTY CRITTYS"
MEH, NEVER MIND-- URRRP--DON'T CARE.
OH, YOU'RE SO COOL THAT YOU DON'T KNOW WHAT BITTY CRITTYS IS?
PLEASE. EVERYONE KNOWS.
OOH, I GOT IT!
HE KNOWS, HE'S JUST... ABOVE IT OR WHATEVER. RIGHT, DAD?
DAMN RIGHT.
BLERGIN

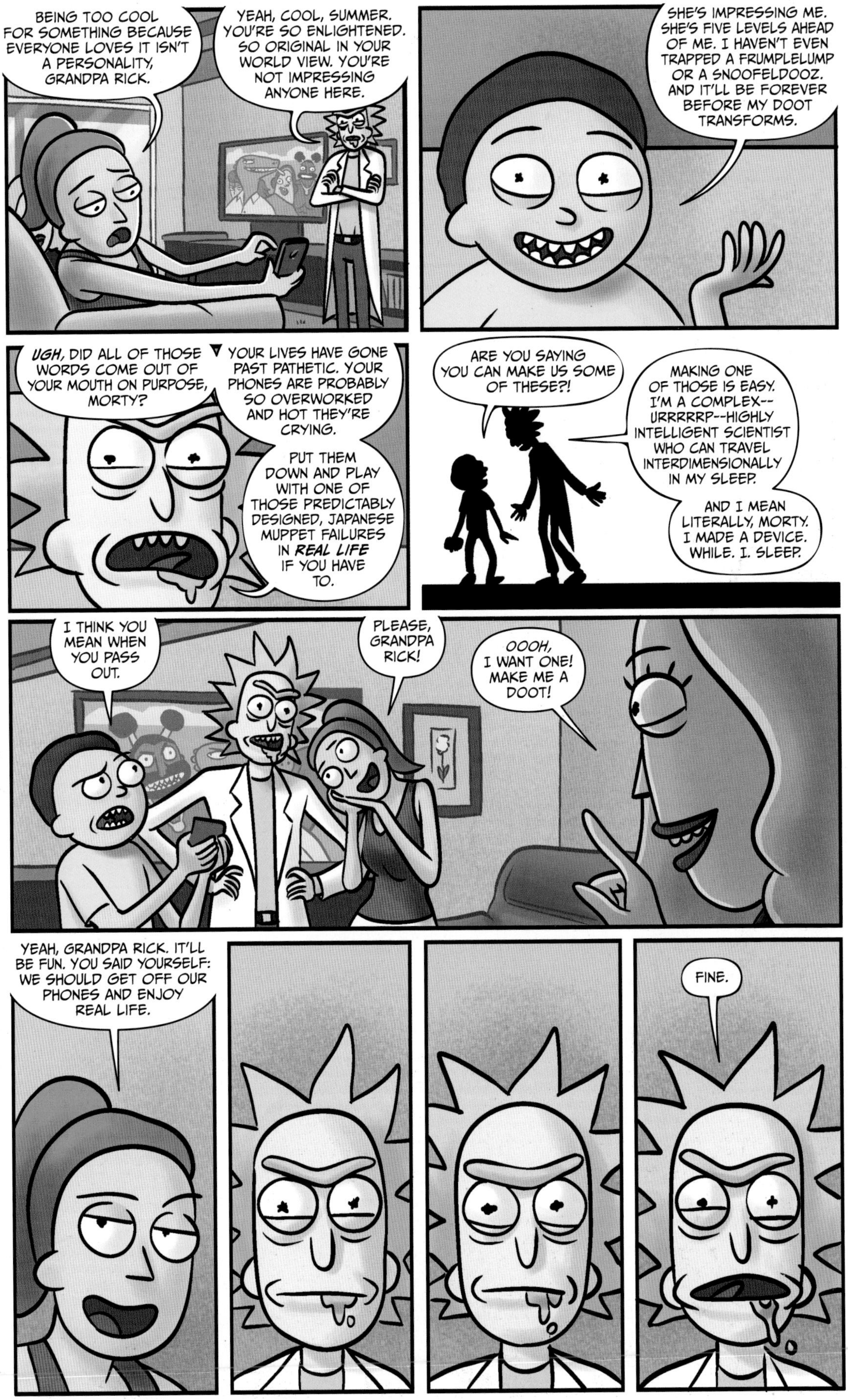
BEING TOO COOL FOR SOMETHING BECAUSE EVERYONE LOVES IT ISN'T A PERSONALITY, GRANDPA RICK.
YEAH, COOL, SUMMER. YOU'RE SO ENLIGHTENED. SO ORIGINAL IN YOUR WORLD VIEW. YOU'RE NOT IMPRESSING ANYONE HERE.
SHE'S IMPRESSING ME. SHE'S FIVE LEVELS AHEAD OF ME. I HAVEN'T EVEN TRAPPED A FRUMPLELUMP OR A SNOOFELDOOZ. AND IT'LL BE FOREVER BEFORE MY DOOT TRANSFORMS.
UGH, DID ALL OF THOSE WORDS COME OUT OF YOUR MOUTH ON PURPOSE, MORTY?
YOUR LIVES HAVE GONE PAST PATHETIC. YOUR PHONES ARE PROBABLY SO OVERWORKED AND HOT THEY'RE CRYING.
PUT THEM DOWN AND PLAY WITH ONE OF THOSE PREDICTABLY DESIGNED, JAPANESE MUPPET FAILURES IN REAL LIFE IF YOU HAVE TO.
ARE YOU SAYING YOU CAN MAKE US SOME OF THESE?!
MAKING ONE OF THOSE IS EASY. I'M A COMPLEX-- URRRRRP--HIGHLY INTELLIGENT SCIENTIST WHO CAN TRAVEL INTERDIMENSIONALLY IN MY SLEEP.
AND I MEAN LITERALLY, MORTY. I MADE A DEVICE. WHILE. I. SLEEP.
I THINK YOU MEAN WHEN YOU PASS OUT.
PLEASE, GRANDPA RICK!
OOOH, I WANT ONE! MAKE ME A DOOT!
YEAH, GRANDPA RICK. IT'LL BE FUN. YOU SAID YOURSELF: WE SHOULD GET OFF OUR PHONES AND ENJOY REAL LIFE.
FINE.

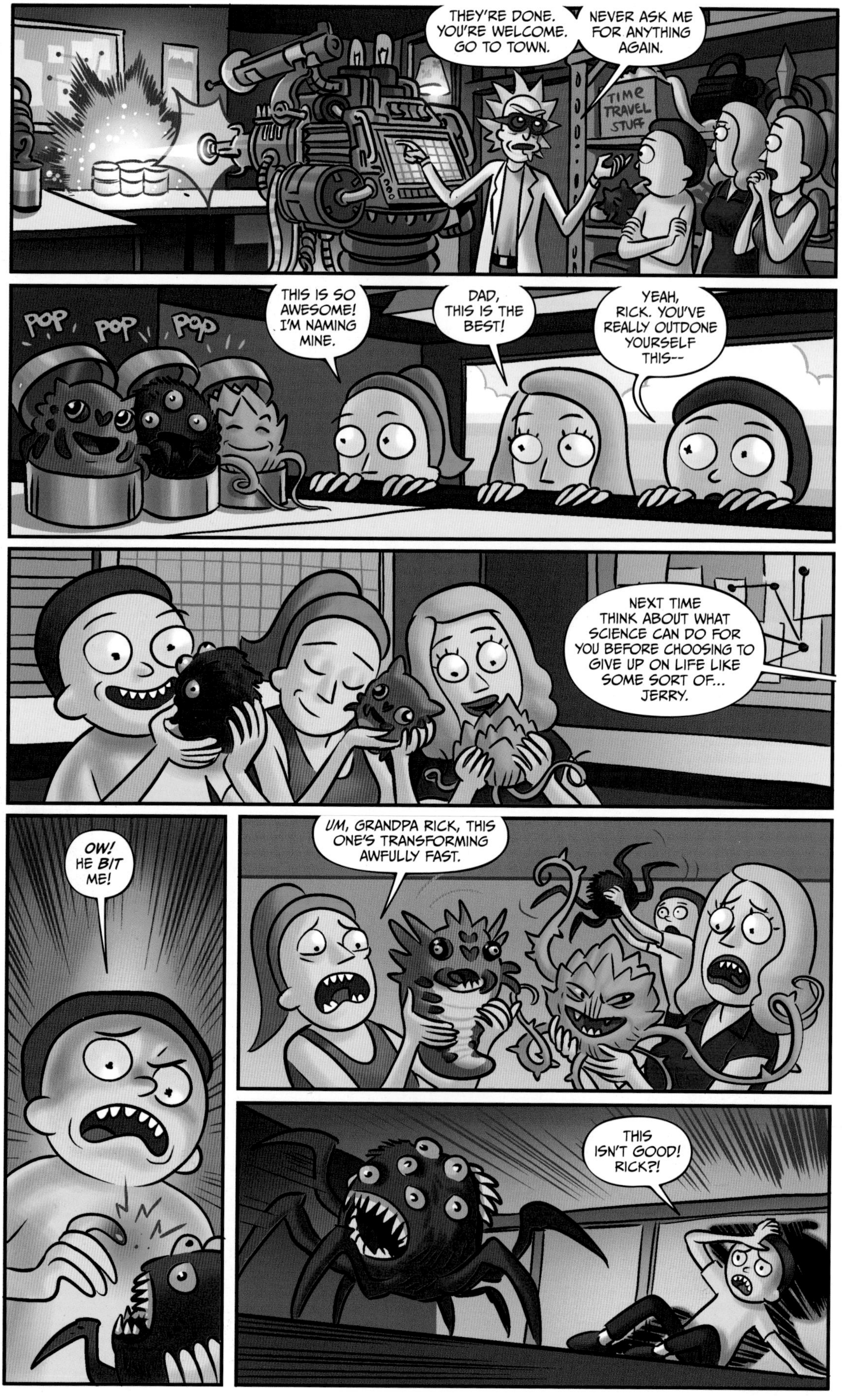
THEY'RE DONE. YOU'RE WELCOME. GO TO TOWN.
NEVER ASK ME FOR ANYTHING AGAIN.
TIME TRAVEL STUFF
POP POP POP
THIS IS SO AWESOME! I'M NAMING MINE.
DAD, THIS IS THE BEST!
YEAH, RICK. YOU'VE REALLY OUTDONE YOURSELF THIS--
NEXT TIME THINK ABOUT WHAT SCIENCE CAN DO FOR YOU BEFORE CHOOSING TO GIVE UP ON LIFE LIKE SOME SORT OF... JERRY.
OW! HE BIT ME!
UM, GRANDPA RICK, THIS ONE'S TRANSFORMING AWFULLY FAST.
THIS ISN'T GOOD! RICK?!

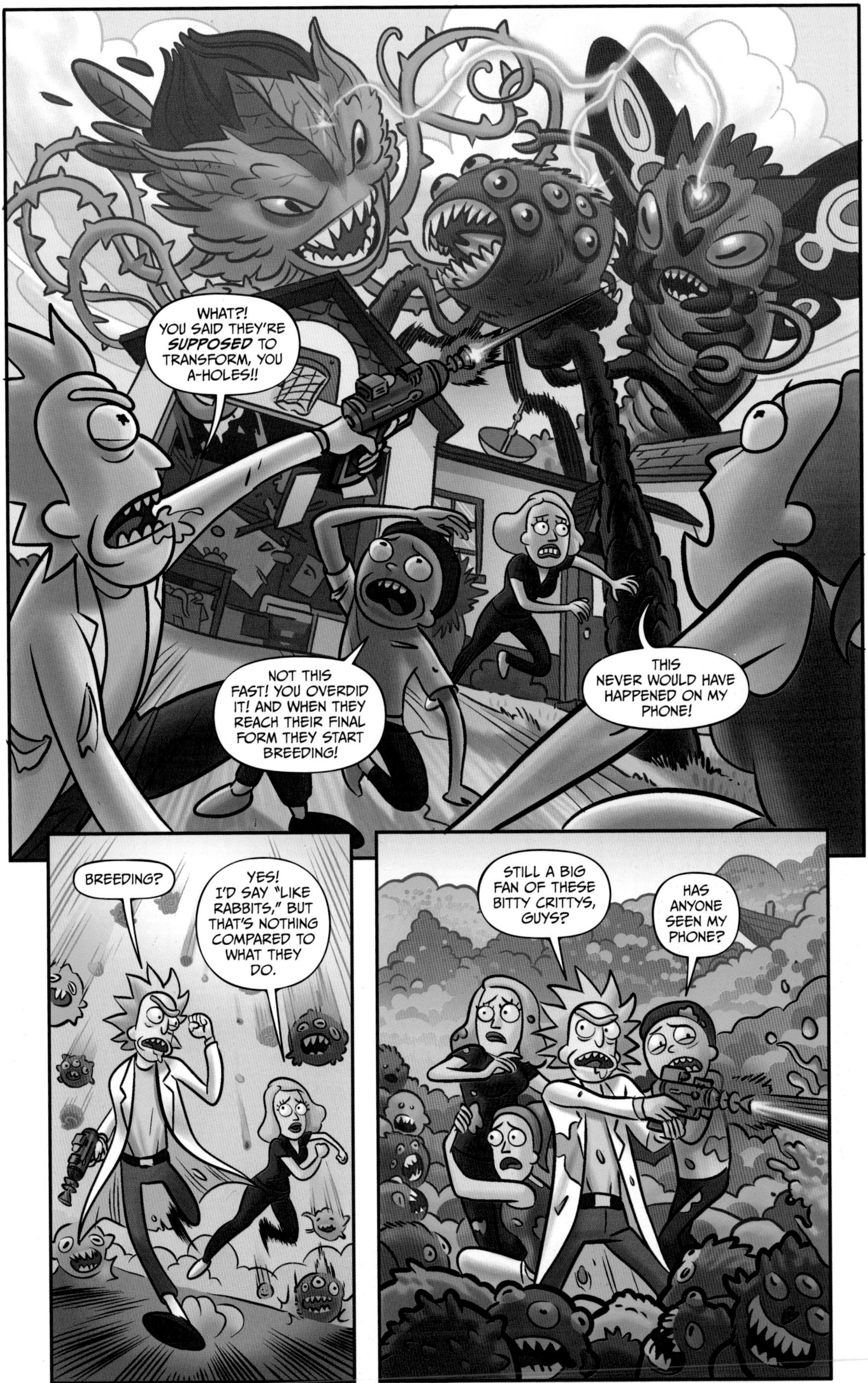
WHAT?! YOU SAID THEY'RE **SUPPOSED** TO TRANSFORM, YOU A-HOLES!!
NOT THIS FAST! YOU OVERDID IT! AND WHEN THEY REACH THEIR FINAL FORM THEY START BREEDING!
THIS NEVER WOULD HAVE HAPPENED ON MY PHONE!
BREEDING?
YES! I'D SAY "LIKE RABBITS," BUT THAT'S NOTHING COMPARED TO WHAT THEY DO.
STILL A BIG FAN OF THESE BITTY CRITTYS, GUYS?
HAS ANYONE SEEN MY PHONE?

***THE END?***

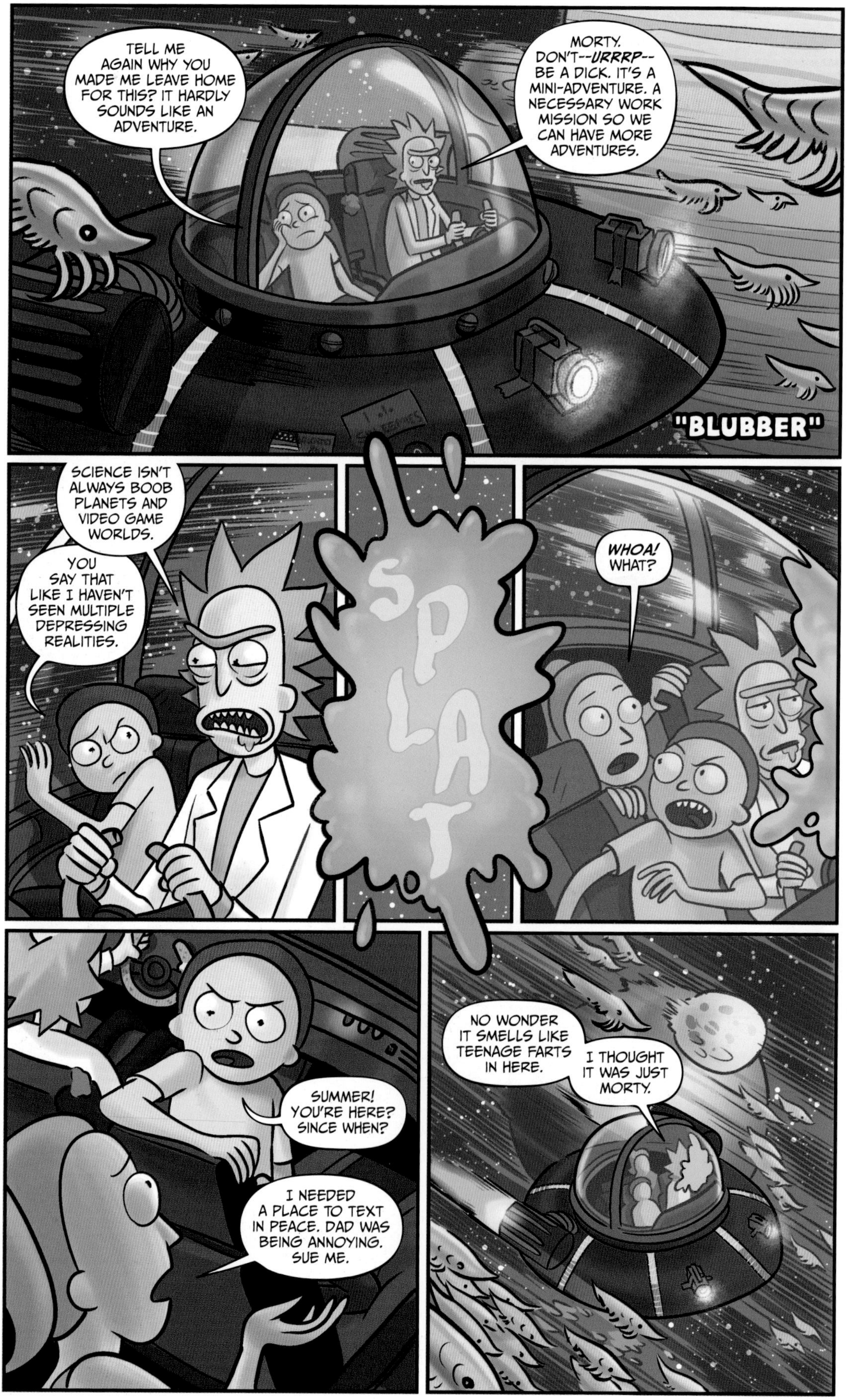
TELL ME AGAIN WHY YOU MADE ME LEAVE HOME FOR THIS? IT HARDLY SOUNDS LIKE AN ADVENTURE.
MORTY. DON'T--URRRP--BE A DICK. IT'S A MINI-ADVENTURE. A NECESSARY WORK MISSION SO WE CAN HAVE MORE ADVENTURES.
"BLUBBER"
SCIENCE ISN'T ALWAYS BOOB PLANETS AND VIDEO GAME WORLDS.
YOU SAY THAT LIKE I HAVEN'T SEEN MULTIPLE DEPRESSING REALITIES.
SPLAT
WHOA! WHAT?
SUMMER! YOU'RE HERE? SINCE WHEN?
I NEEDED A PLACE TO TEXT IN PEACE. DAD WAS BEING ANNOYING. SUE ME.
NO WONDER IT SMELLS LIKE TEENAGE FARTS IN HERE.
I THOUGHT IT WAS JUST MORTY.

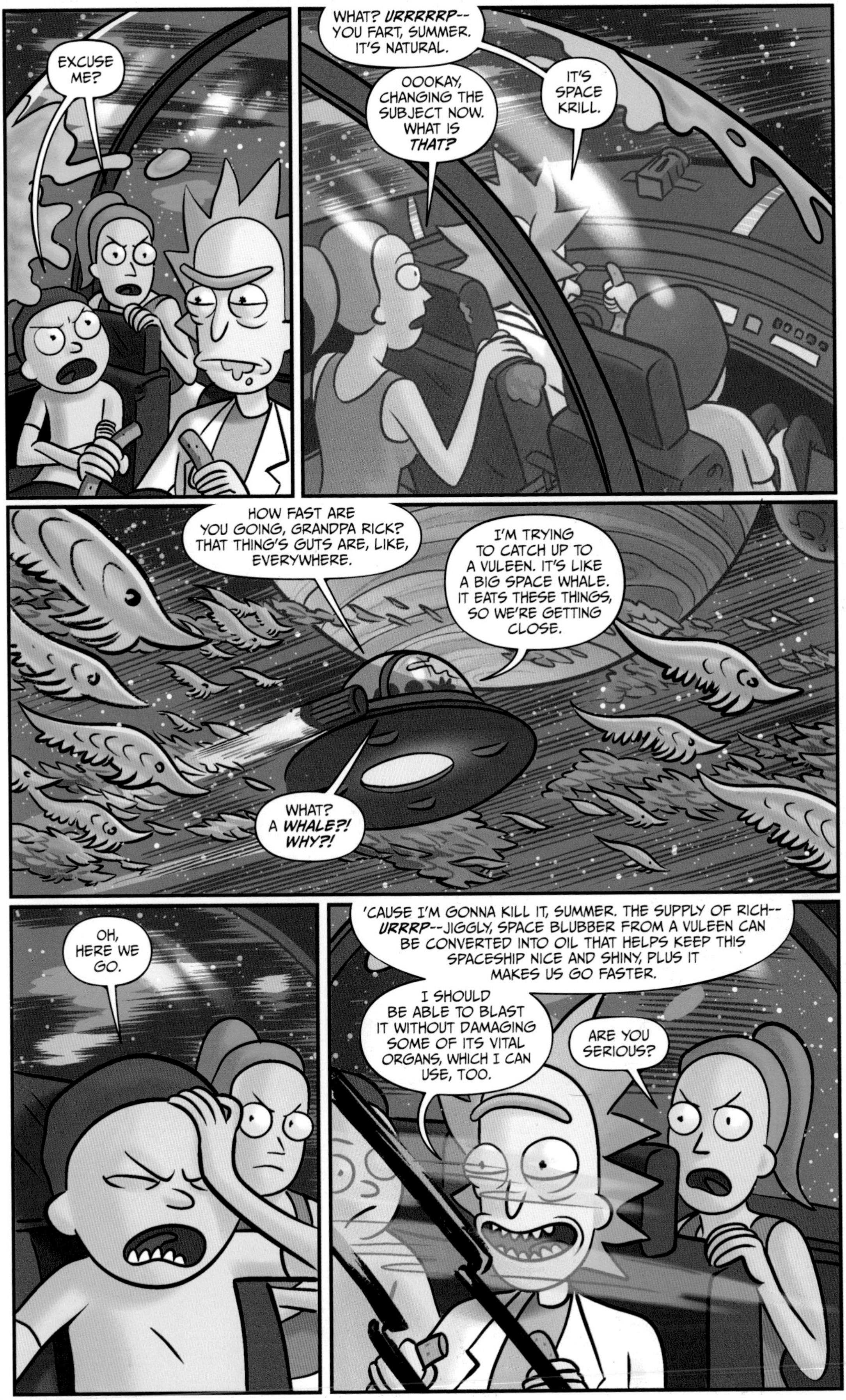
EXCUSE ME?
WHAT? URRRRRP-- YOU FART, SUMMER. IT'S NATURAL.
OOOKAY, CHANGING THE SUBJECT NOW. WHAT IS THAT?
IT'S SPACE KRILL.
HOW FAST ARE YOU GOING, GRANDPA RICK? THAT THING'S GUTS ARE, LIKE, EVERYWHERE.
I'M TRYING TO CATCH UP TO A VULEEN. IT'S LIKE A BIG SPACE WHALE. IT EATS THESE THINGS, SO WE'RE GETTING CLOSE.
WHAT? A WHALE?! WHY?!
OH, HERE WE GO.
'CAUSE I'M GONNA KILL IT, SUMMER. THE SUPPLY OF RICH-- URRRP--JIGGLY, SPACE BLUBBER FROM A VULEEN CAN BE CONVERTED INTO OIL THAT HELPS KEEP THIS SPACESHIP NICE AND SHINY, PLUS IT MAKES US GO FASTER.
I SHOULD BE ABLE TO BLAST IT WITHOUT DAMAGING SOME OF ITS VITAL ORGANS, WHICH I CAN USE, TOO.
ARE YOU SERIOUS?

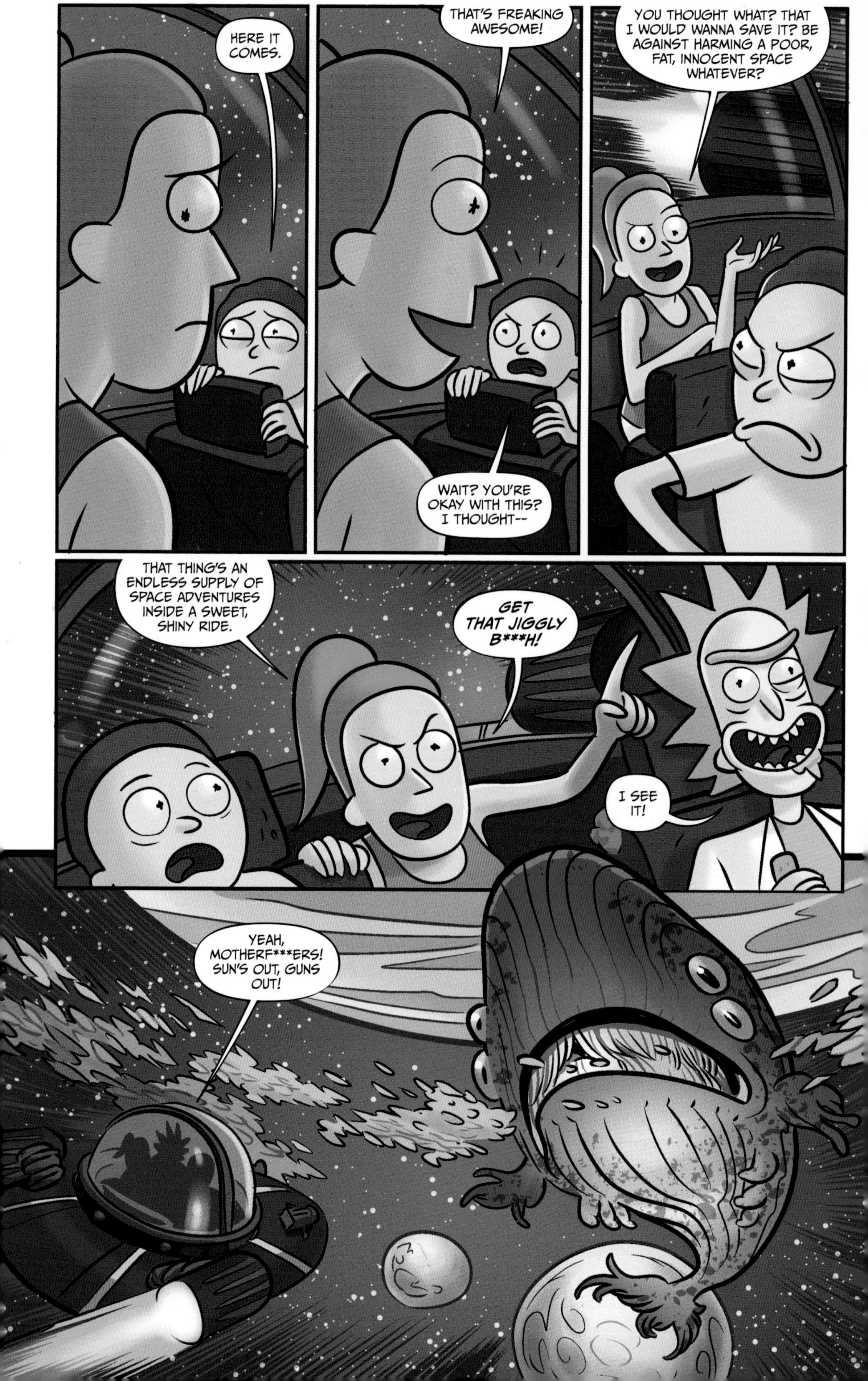
HERE IT COMES.
THAT'S FREAKING AWESOME!
WAIT? YOU'RE OKAY WITH THIS? I THOUGHT--
YOU THOUGHT WHAT? THAT I WOULD WANNA SAVE IT? BE AGAINST HARMING A POOR, FAT, INNOCENT SPACE WHATEVER?
THAT THING'S AN ENDLESS SUPPLY OF SPACE ADVENTURES INSIDE A SWEET, SHINY RIDE.
GET THAT JIGGLY B***H!
I SEE IT!
YEAH, MOTHERF***ERS! SUN'S OUT, GUNS OUT!

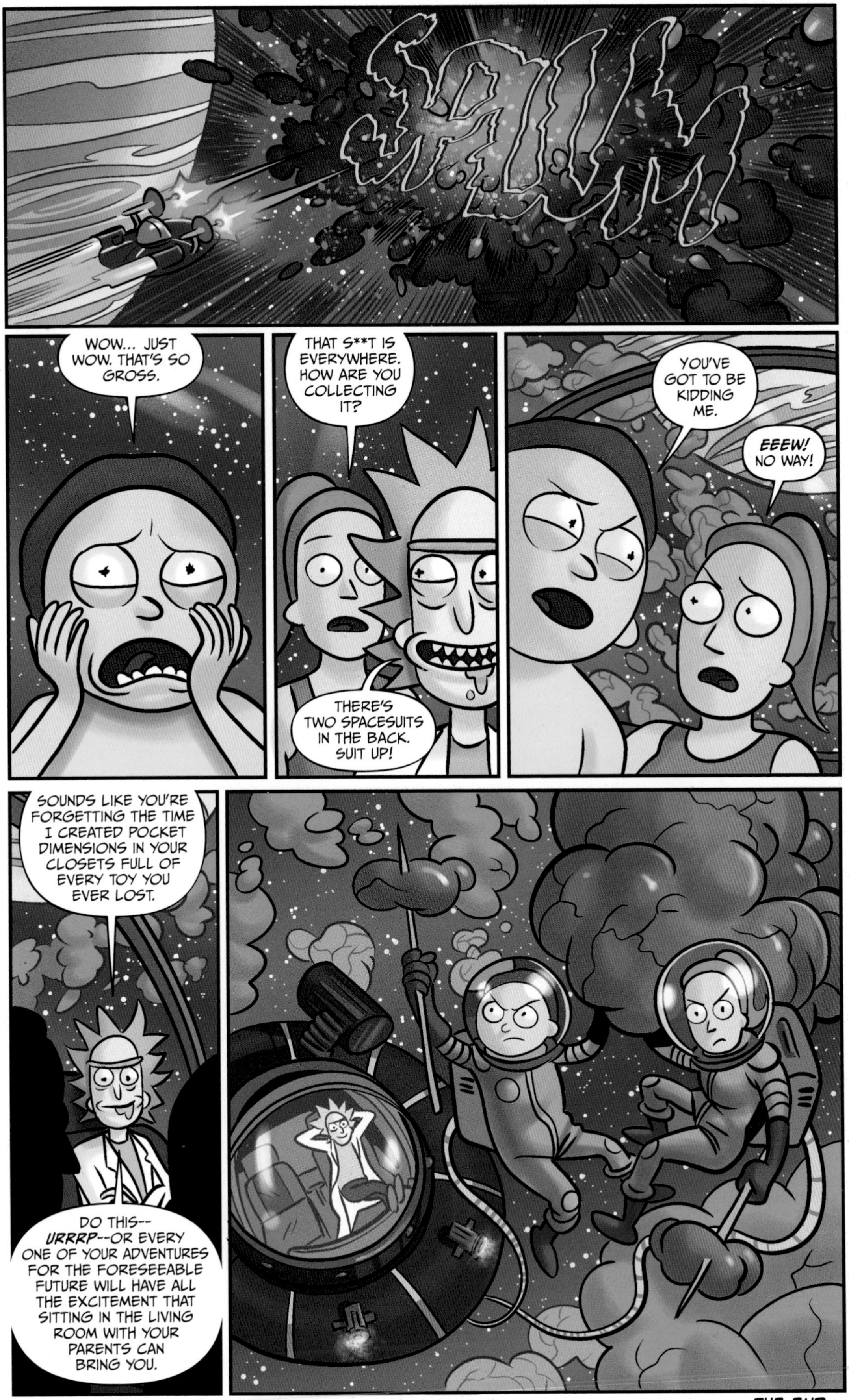
WOW... JUST WOW. THAT'S SO GROSS.
THAT S**T IS EVERYWHERE. HOW ARE YOU COLLECTING IT?
THERE'S TWO SPACESUITS IN THE BACK. SUIT UP!
YOU'VE GOT TO BE KIDDING ME.
EEEW! NO WAY!
SOUNDS LIKE YOU'RE FORGETTING THE TIME I CREATED POCKET DIMENSIONS IN YOUR CLOSETS FULL OF EVERY TOY YOU EVER LOST.
DO THIS-- URRRP--OR EVERY ONE OF YOUR ADVENTURES FOR THE FORESEEABLE FUTURE WILL HAVE ALL THE EXCITEMENT THAT SITTING IN THE LIVING ROOM WITH YOUR PARENTS CAN BRING YOU.

*THE END.*

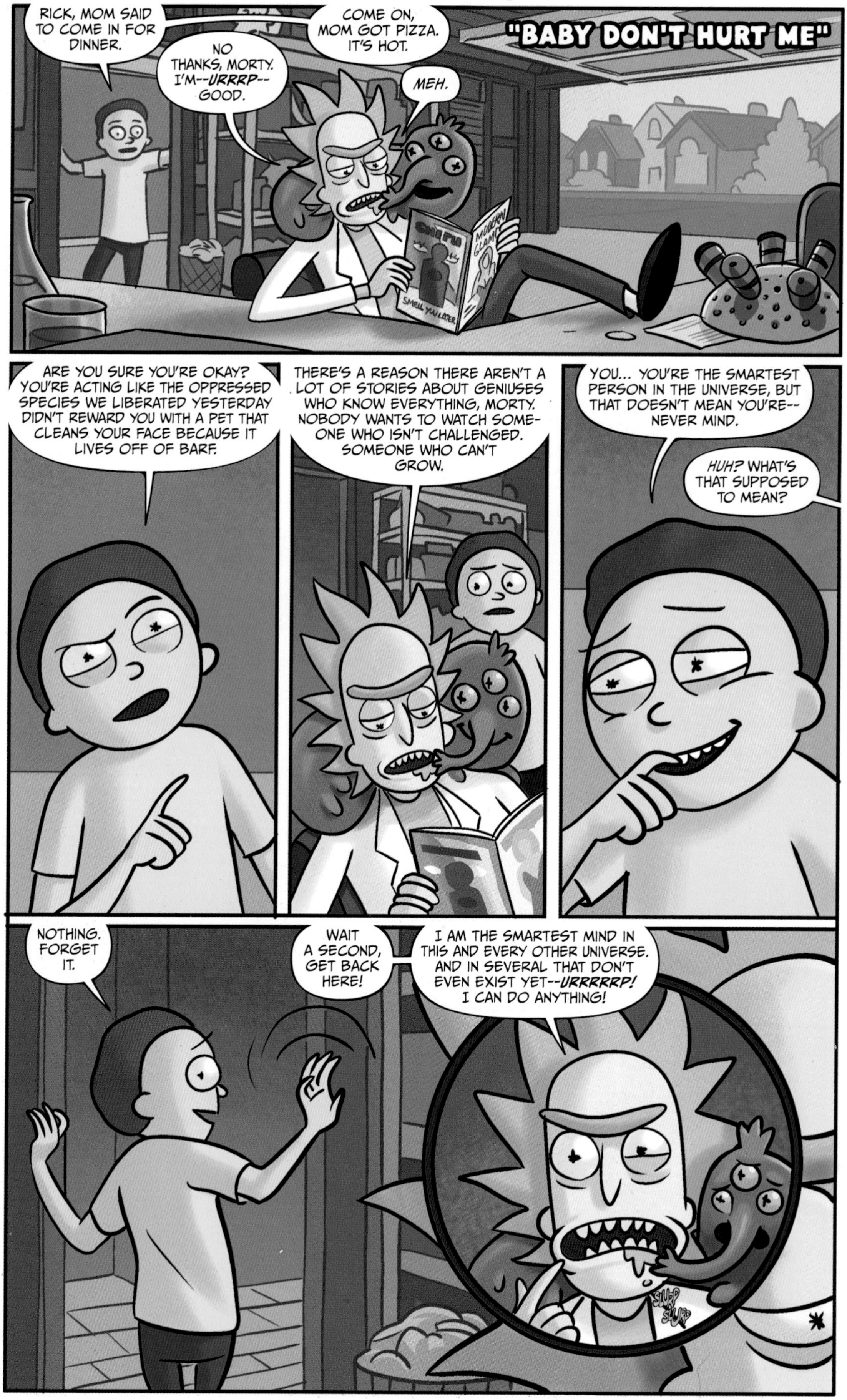
"BABY DON'T HURT ME"
RICK, MOM SAID TO COME IN FOR DINNER.
NO THANKS, MORTY. I'M--*URRRP*--GOOD.
COME ON, MOM GOT PIZZA. IT'S HOT.
MEH.
MODERN GLAM
SMELL YOU LATER
ARE YOU SURE YOU'RE OKAY? YOU'RE ACTING LIKE THE OPPRESSED SPECIES WE LIBERATED YESTERDAY DIDN'T REWARD YOU WITH A PET THAT CLEANS YOUR FACE BECAUSE IT LIVES OFF OF BARF.
THERE'S A REASON THERE AREN'T A LOT OF STORIES ABOUT GENIUSES WHO KNOW EVERYTHING, MORTY. NOBODY WANTS TO WATCH SOME-ONE WHO ISN'T CHALLENGED. SOMEONE WHO CAN'T GROW.
YOU... YOU'RE THE SMARTEST PERSON IN THE UNIVERSE, BUT THAT DOESN'T MEAN YOU'RE--NEVER MIND.
*HUH?* WHAT'S THAT SUPPOSED TO MEAN?
NOTHING. FORGET IT.
WAIT A SECOND, GET BACK HERE!
I AM THE SMARTEST MIND IN THIS AND EVERY OTHER UNIVERSE. AND IN SEVERAL THAT DON'T EVEN EXIST YET--*URRRRRP!* I CAN DO ANYTHING!
SLURP SLURP

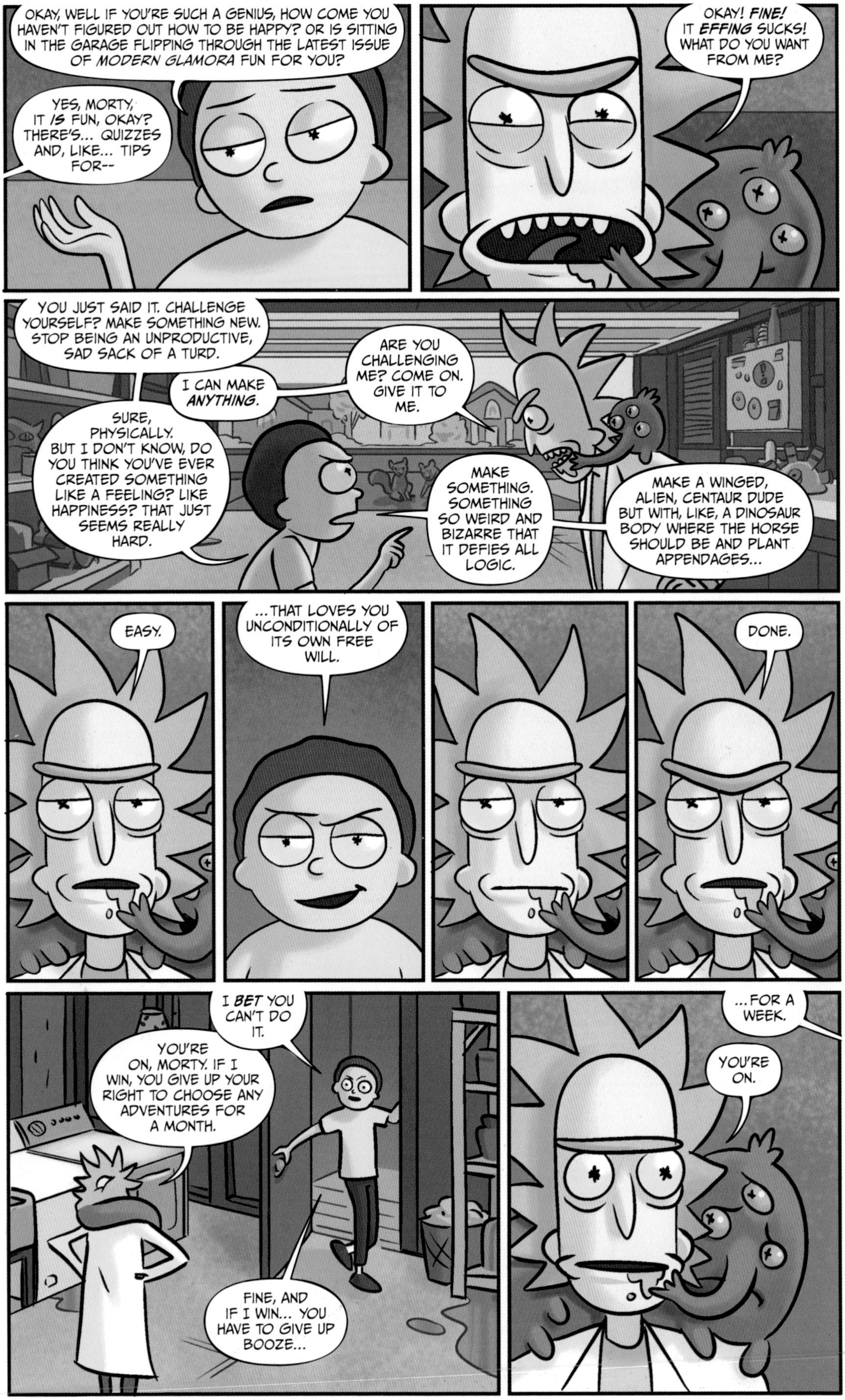

OKAY, WELL IF YOU'RE SUCH A GENIUS, HOW COME YOU HAVEN'T FIGURED OUT HOW TO BE HAPPY? OR IS SITTING IN THE GARAGE FLIPPING THROUGH THE LATEST ISSUE OF *MODERN GLAMORA* FUN FOR YOU?
YES, MORTY, IT *IS* FUN, OKAY? THERE'S... QUIZZES AND, LIKE... TIPS FOR--
OKAY! *FINE!* IT *EFFING* SUCKS! WHAT DO YOU WANT FROM ME?
YOU JUST SAID IT. CHALLENGE YOURSELF? MAKE SOMETHING NEW. STOP BEING AN UNPRODUCTIVE, SAD SACK OF A TURD.
I CAN MAKE *ANYTHING.*
SURE, PHYSICALLY. BUT I DON'T KNOW, DO YOU THINK YOU'VE EVER CREATED SOMETHING LIKE A FEELING? LIKE HAPPINESS? THAT JUST SEEMS REALLY HARD.
ARE YOU CHALLENGING ME? COME ON. GIVE IT TO ME.
MAKE SOMETHING. SOMETHING SO WEIRD AND BIZARRE THAT IT DEFIES ALL LOGIC.
MAKE A WINGED, ALIEN, CENTAUR DUDE BUT WITH, LIKE, A DINOSAUR BODY WHERE THE HORSE SHOULD BE AND PLANT APPENDAGES...
EASY.
...THAT LOVES YOU UNCONDITIONALLY OF ITS OWN FREE WILL.
DONE.
I *BET* YOU CAN'T DO IT.
YOU'RE ON, MORTY. IF I WIN, YOU GIVE UP YOUR RIGHT TO CHOOSE ANY ADVENTURES FOR A MONTH.
FINE, AND IF I WIN... YOU HAVE TO GIVE UP BOOZE...
...FOR A WEEK.
YOU'RE ON.

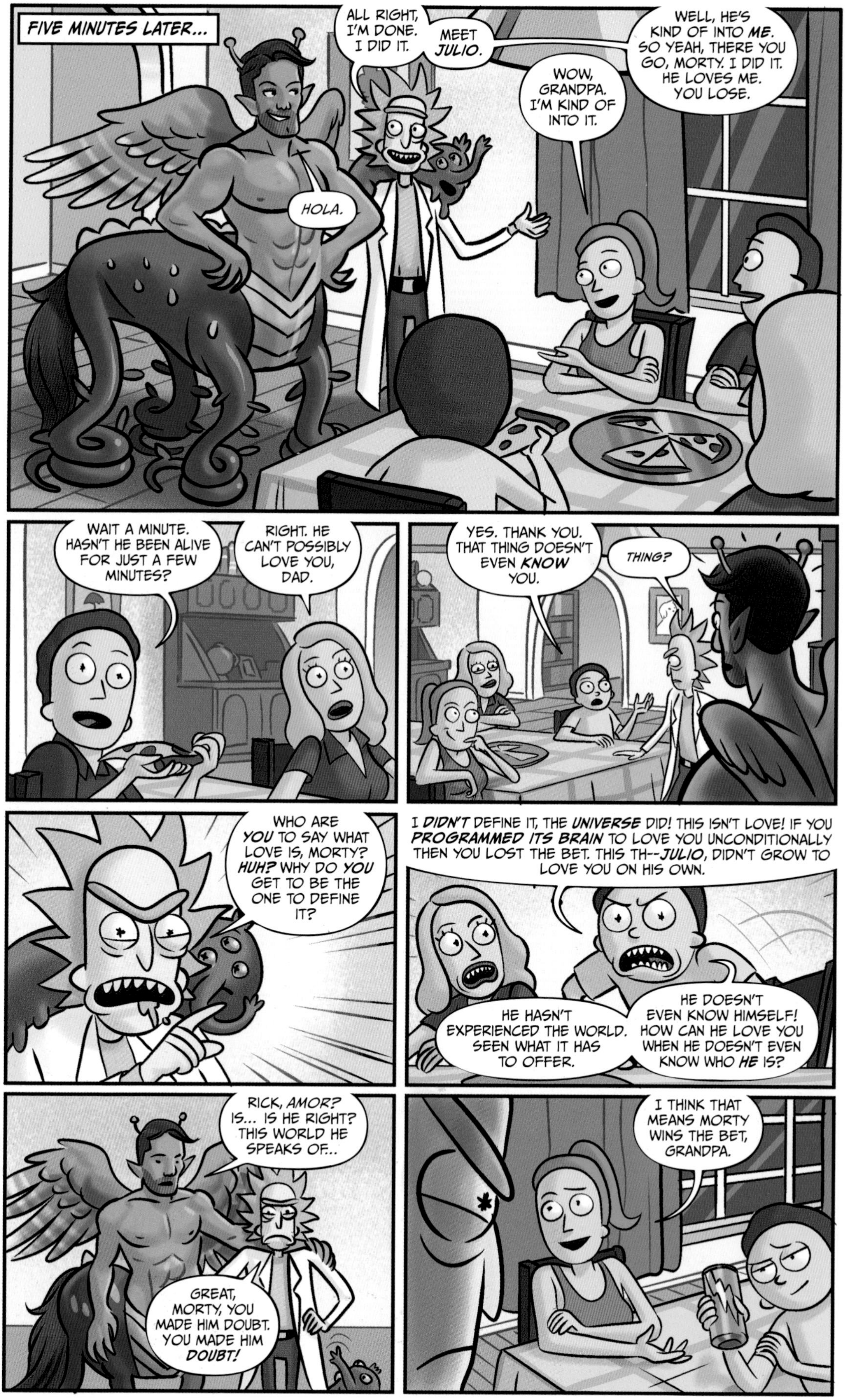
FIVE MINUTES LATER...
ALL RIGHT, I'M DONE. I DID IT.
MEET JULIO.
HOLA.
WOW, GRANDPA. I'M KIND OF INTO IT.
WELL, HE'S KIND OF INTO ME. SO YEAH, THERE YOU GO, MORTY. I DID IT. HE LOVES ME. YOU LOSE.
WAIT A MINUTE. HASN'T HE BEEN ALIVE FOR JUST A FEW MINUTES?
RIGHT. HE CAN'T POSSIBLY LOVE YOU, DAD.
YES. THANK YOU. THAT THING DOESN'T EVEN KNOW YOU.
THING?
WHO ARE YOU TO SAY WHAT LOVE IS, MORTY? HUH? WHY DO YOU GET TO BE THE ONE TO DEFINE IT?
I DIDN'T DEFINE IT, THE UNIVERSE DID! THIS ISN'T LOVE! IF YOU PROGRAMMED ITS BRAIN TO LOVE YOU UNCONDITIONALLY THEN YOU LOST THE BET. THIS TH--JULIO, DIDN'T GROW TO LOVE YOU ON HIS OWN.
HE HASN'T EXPERIENCED THE WORLD. SEEN WHAT IT HAS TO OFFER.
HE DOESN'T EVEN KNOW HIMSELF! HOW CAN HE LOVE YOU WHEN HE DOESN'T EVEN KNOW WHO HE IS?
RICK, AMOR? IS... IS HE RIGHT? THIS WORLD HE SPEAKS OF...
GREAT, MORTY, YOU MADE HIM DOUBT. YOU MADE HIM DOUBT!
I THINK THAT MEANS MORTY WINS THE BET, GRANDPA.

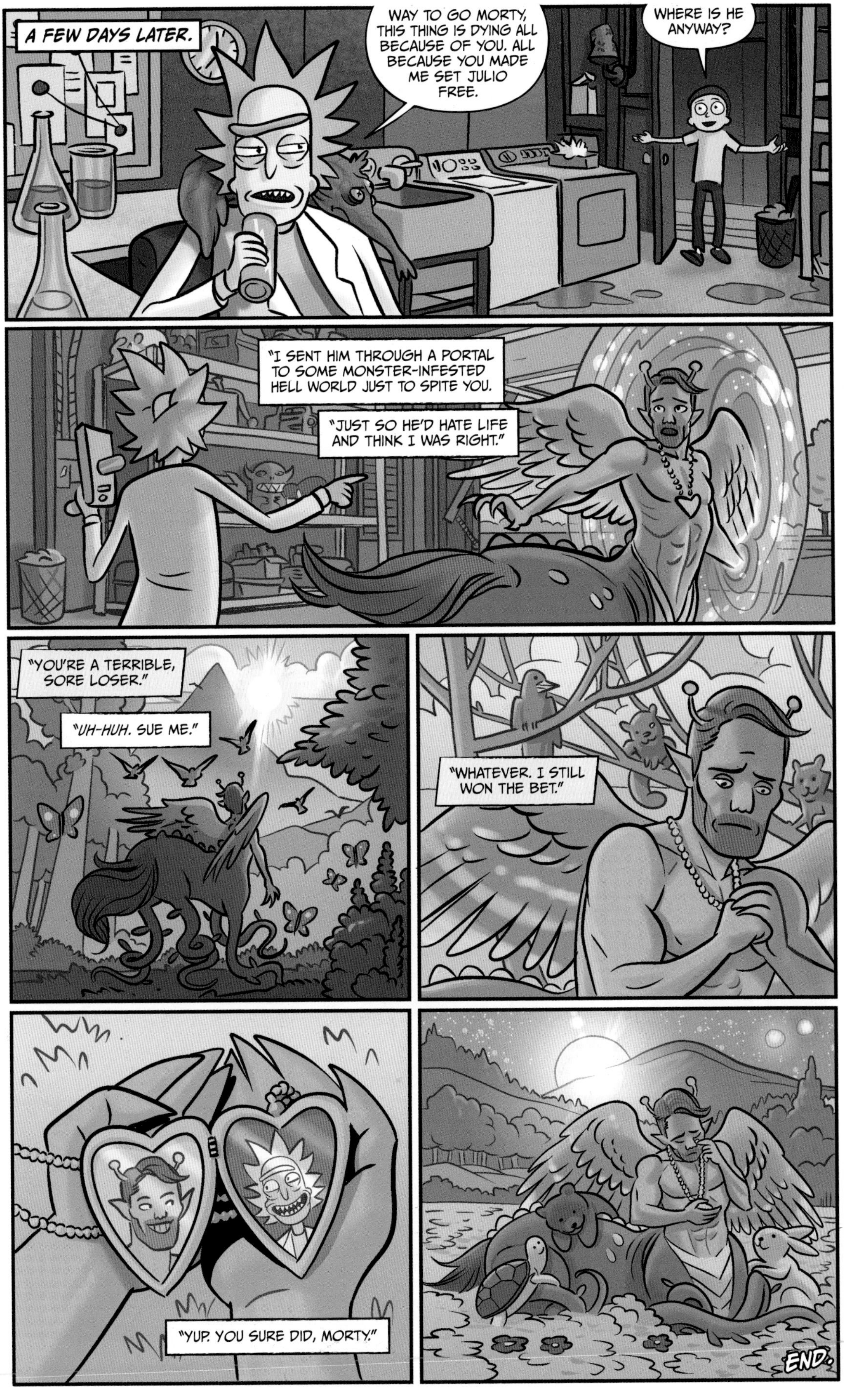
A FEW DAYS LATER.
WAY TO GO MORTY, THIS THING IS DYING ALL BECAUSE OF YOU. ALL BECAUSE YOU MADE ME SET JULIO FREE.
WHERE IS HE ANYWAY?
"I SENT HIM THROUGH A PORTAL TO SOME MONSTER-INFESTED HELL WORLD JUST TO SPITE YOU.
"JUST SO HE'D HATE LIFE AND THINK I WAS RIGHT."
"YOU'RE A TERRIBLE, SORE LOSER."
"UH-HUH. SUE ME."
"WHATEVER. I STILL WON THE BET."
"YUP. YOU SURE DID, MORTY."
END.

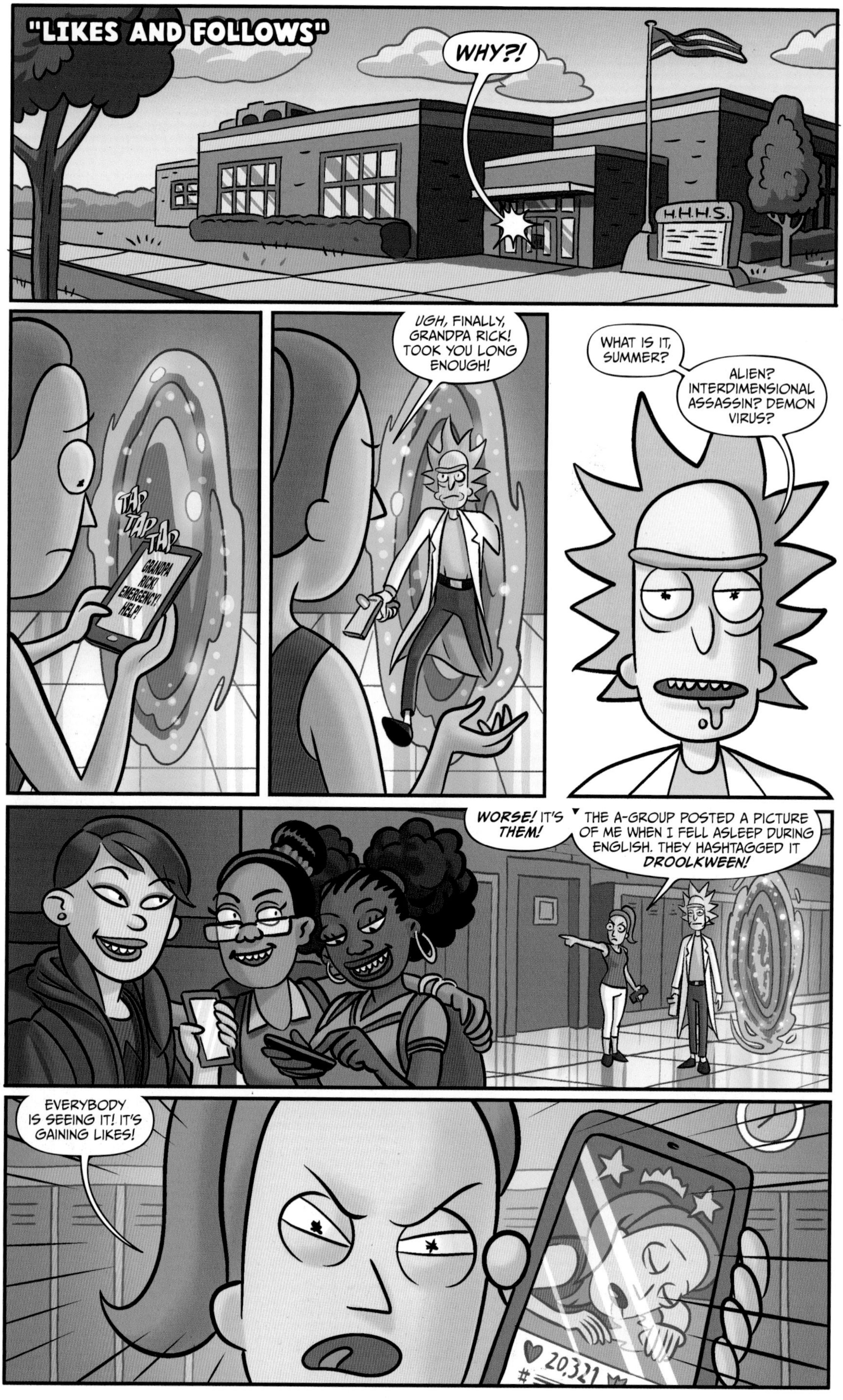
"LIKES AND FOLLOWS"
WHY?!
H.H.H.S.
TAP TAP TAP
GRANDPA RICK! EMERGENCY! HELP!
UGH, FINALLY, GRANDPA RICK! TOOK YOU LONG ENOUGH!
WHAT IS IT, SUMMER?
ALIEN? INTERDIMENSIONAL ASSASSIN? DEMON VIRUS?
WORSE! IT'S THEM!
THE A-GROUP POSTED A PICTURE OF ME WHEN I FELL ASLEEP DURING ENGLISH. THEY HASHTAGGED IT DROOLKWEEN!
EVERYBODY IS SEEING IT! IT'S GAINING LIKES!
20,321

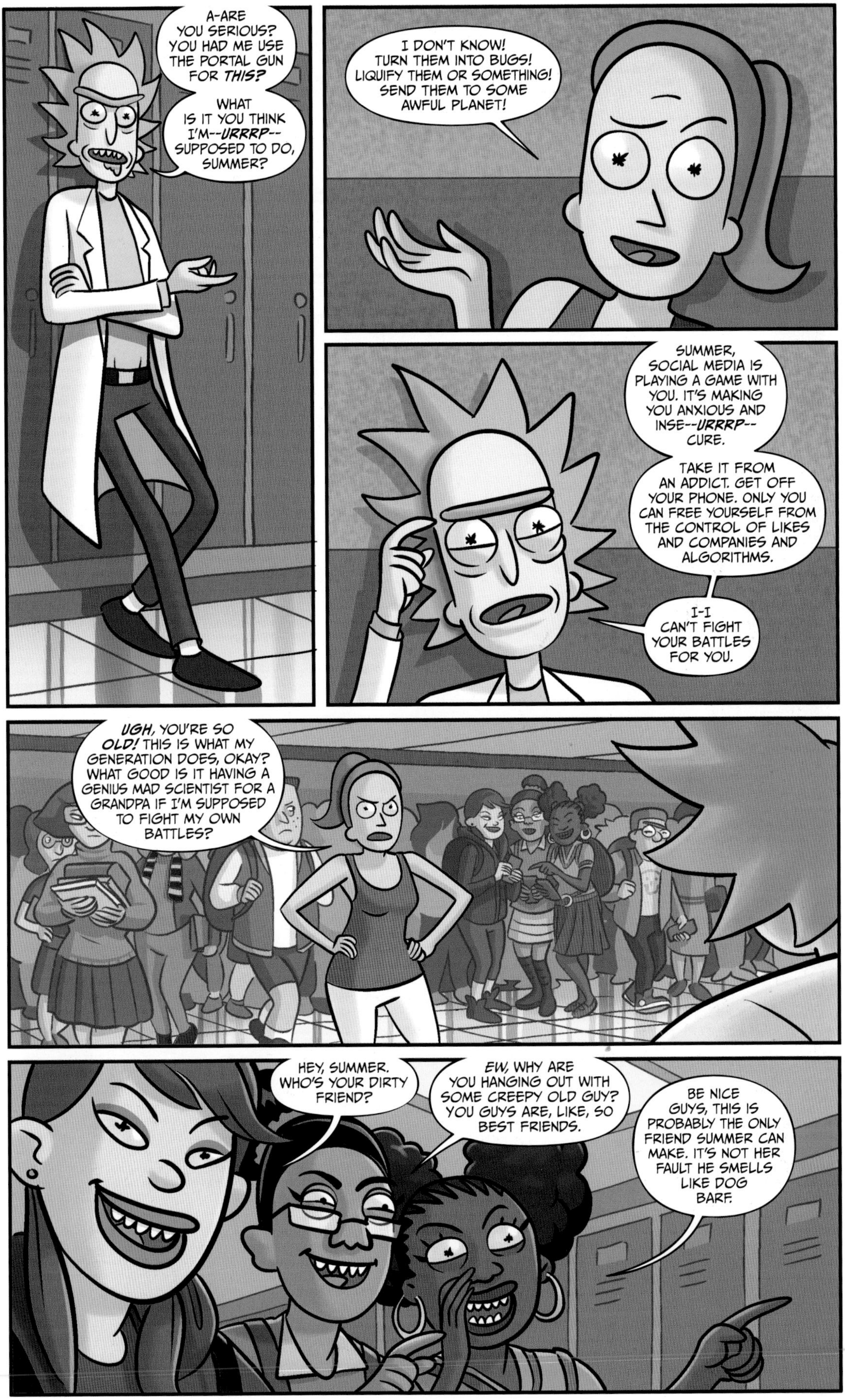
A-ARE YOU SERIOUS? YOU HAD ME USE THE PORTAL GUN FOR *THIS?*
WHAT IS IT YOU THINK I'M--*URRRP*-- SUPPOSED TO DO, SUMMER?
I DON'T KNOW! TURN THEM INTO BUGS! LIQUIFY THEM OR SOMETHING! SEND THEM TO SOME AWFUL PLANET!
SUMMER, SOCIAL MEDIA IS PLAYING A GAME WITH YOU. IT'S MAKING YOU ANXIOUS AND INSE--*URRRP*-- CURE.
TAKE IT FROM AN ADDICT. GET OFF YOUR PHONE. ONLY YOU CAN FREE YOURSELF FROM THE CONTROL OF LIKES AND COMPANIES AND ALGORITHMS.
I-I CAN'T FIGHT YOUR BATTLES FOR YOU.
*UGH*, YOU'RE SO *OLD!* THIS IS WHAT MY GENERATION DOES, OKAY? WHAT GOOD IS IT HAVING A GENIUS MAD SCIENTIST FOR A GRANDPA IF I'M SUPPOSED TO FIGHT MY OWN BATTLES?
HEY, SUMMER. WHO'S YOUR DIRTY FRIEND?
*EW,* WHY ARE YOU HANGING OUT WITH SOME CREEPY OLD GUY? YOU GUYS ARE, LIKE, SO BEST FRIENDS.
BE NICE GUYS, THIS IS PROBABLY THE ONLY FRIEND SUMMER CAN MAKE. IT'S NOT HER FAULT HE SMELLS LIKE DOG BARF.

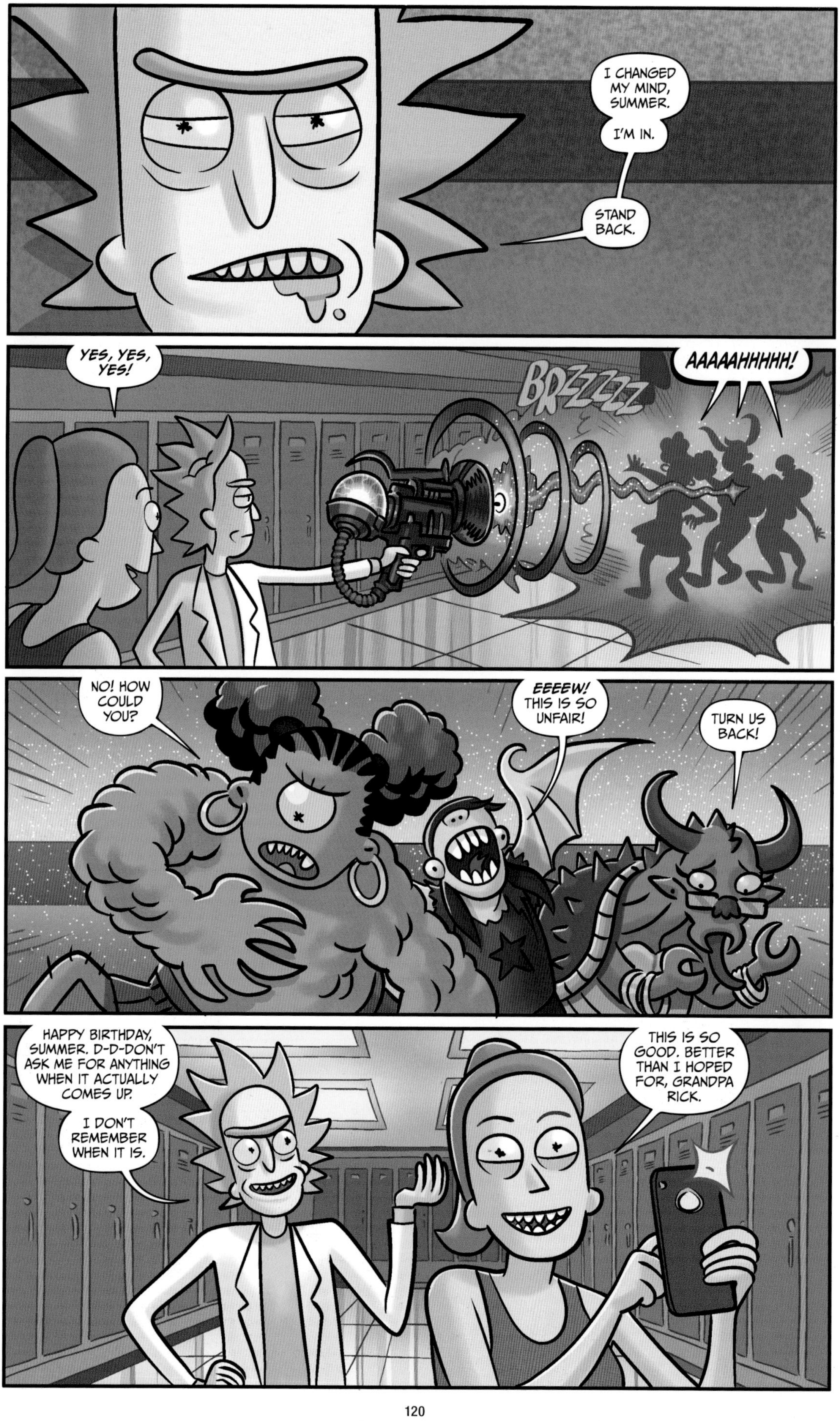
I CHANGED MY MIND, SUMMER.
I'M IN.
STAND BACK.
YES, YES, YES!
BRZZZZZ
AAAAAHHHHH!
NO! HOW COULD YOU?
EEEEW! THIS IS SO UNFAIR!
TURN US BACK!
HAPPY BIRTHDAY, SUMMER. D-D-DON'T ASK ME FOR ANYTHING WHEN IT ACTUALLY COMES UP.
I DON'T REMEMBER WHEN IT IS.
THIS IS SO GOOD. BETTER THAN I HOPED FOR, GRANDPA RICK.

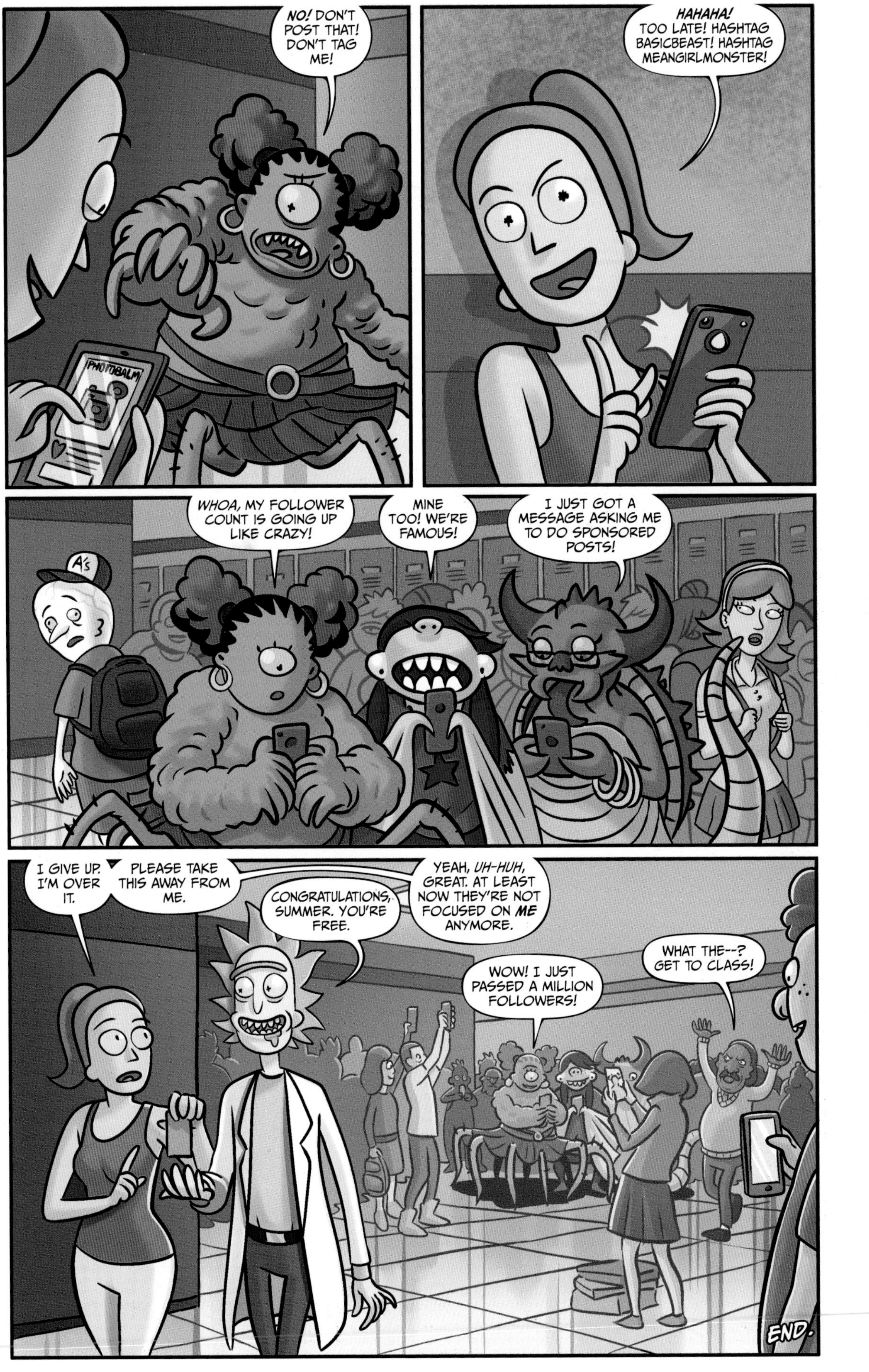
NO! DON'T POST THAT! DON'T TAG ME!
PHOTOBALM
HAHAHA! TOO LATE! HASHTAG BASICBEAST! HASHTAG MEANGIRLMONSTER!
WHOA, MY FOLLOWER COUNT IS GOING UP LIKE CRAZY!
MINE TOO! WE'RE FAMOUS!
I JUST GOT A MESSAGE ASKING ME TO DO SPONSORED POSTS!
A's
I GIVE UP. I'M OVER IT.
PLEASE TAKE THIS AWAY FROM ME.
CONGRATULATIONS, SUMMER. YOU'RE FREE.
YEAH, UH-HUH, GREAT. AT LEAST NOW THEY'RE NOT FOCUSED ON ME ANYMORE.
WOW! I JUST PASSED A MILLION FOLLOWERS!
WHAT THE--? GET TO CLASS!
END.

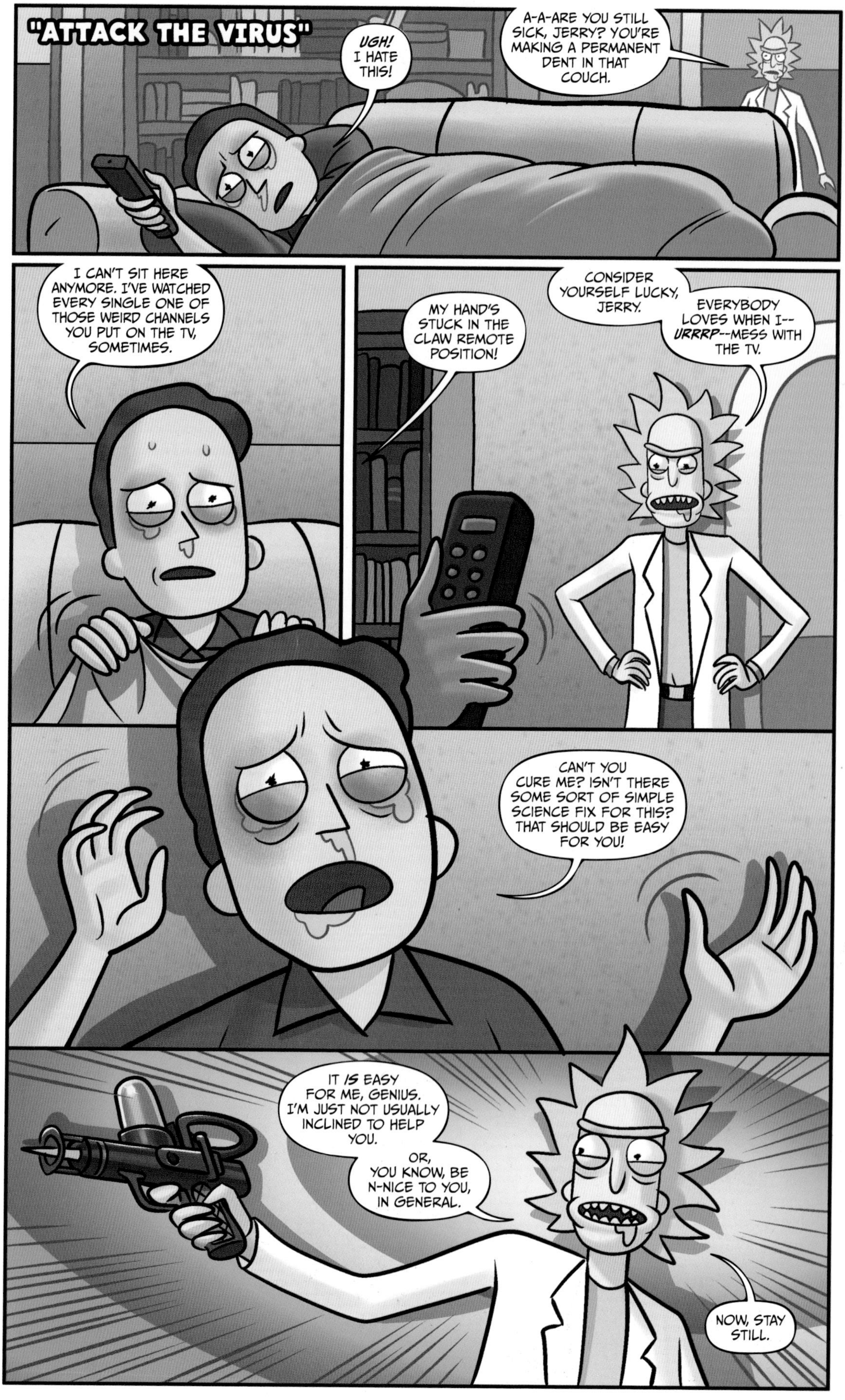
"ATTACK THE VIRUS"
UGH! I HATE THIS!
A-A-ARE YOU STILL SICK, JERRY? YOU'RE MAKING A PERMANENT DENT IN THAT COUCH.
I CAN'T SIT HERE ANYMORE. I'VE WATCHED EVERY SINGLE ONE OF THOSE WEIRD CHANNELS YOU PUT ON THE TV, SOMETIMES.
MY HAND'S STUCK IN THE CLAW REMOTE POSITION!
CONSIDER YOURSELF LUCKY, JERRY.
EVERYBODY LOVES WHEN I-- URRRP--MESS WITH THE TV.
CAN'T YOU CURE ME? ISN'T THERE SOME SORT OF SIMPLE SCIENCE FIX FOR THIS? THAT SHOULD BE EASY FOR YOU!
IT IS EASY FOR ME, GENIUS. I'M JUST NOT USUALLY INCLINED TO HELP YOU.
OR, YOU KNOW, BE N-NICE TO YOU, IN GENERAL.
NOW, STAY STILL.

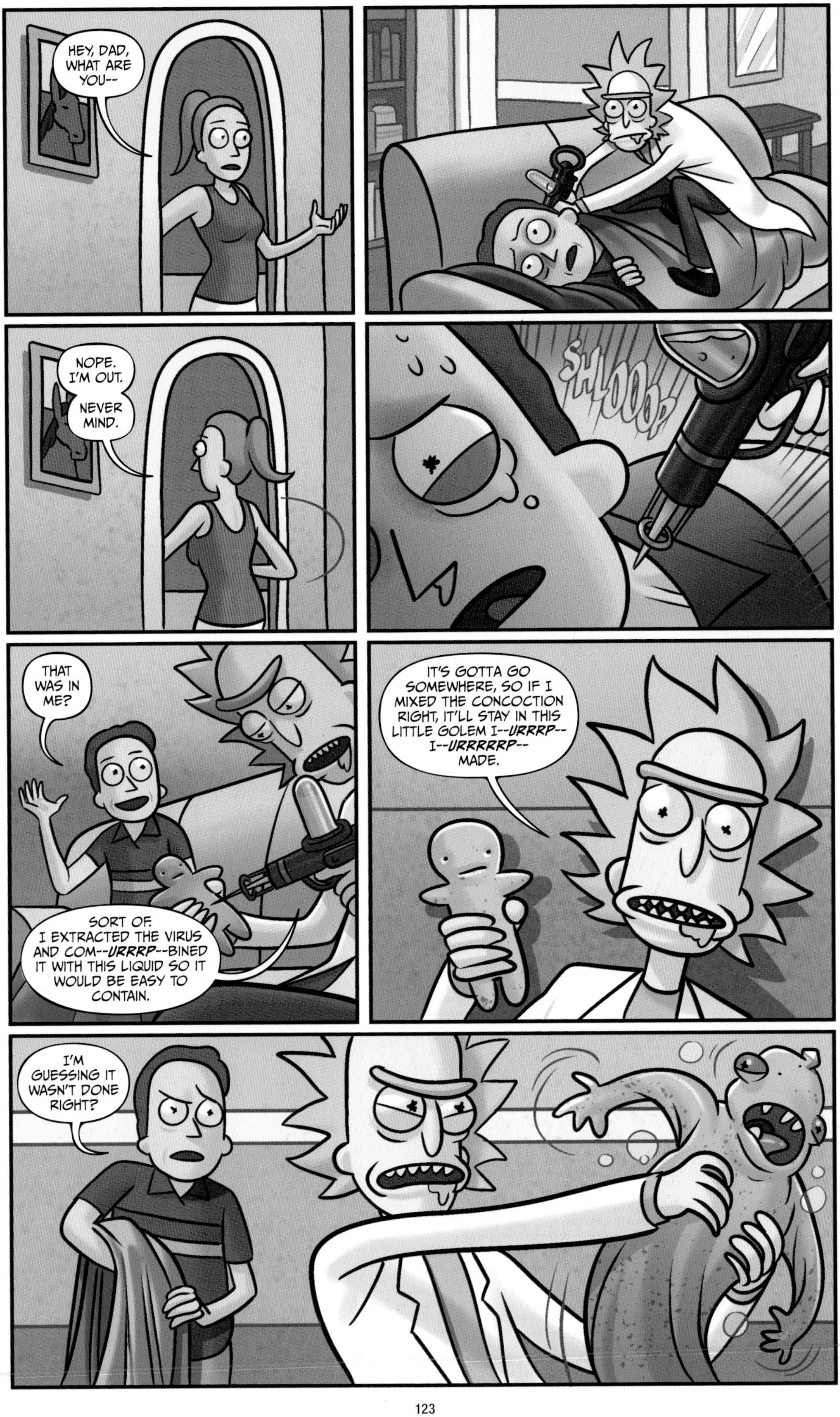
HEY, DAD, WHAT ARE YOU--
SHLOOOP
NOPE. I'M OUT.
NEVER MIND.
THAT WAS IN ME?
SORT OF. I EXTRACTED THE VIRUS AND COM--URRRP--BINED IT WITH THIS LIQUID SO IT WOULD BE EASY TO CONTAIN.
IT'S GOTTA GO SOMEWHERE, SO IF I MIXED THE CONCOCTION RIGHT, IT'LL STAY IN THIS LITTLE GOLEM I--URRRP--I--URRRRRP--MADE.
I'M GUESSING IT WASN'T DONE RIGHT?

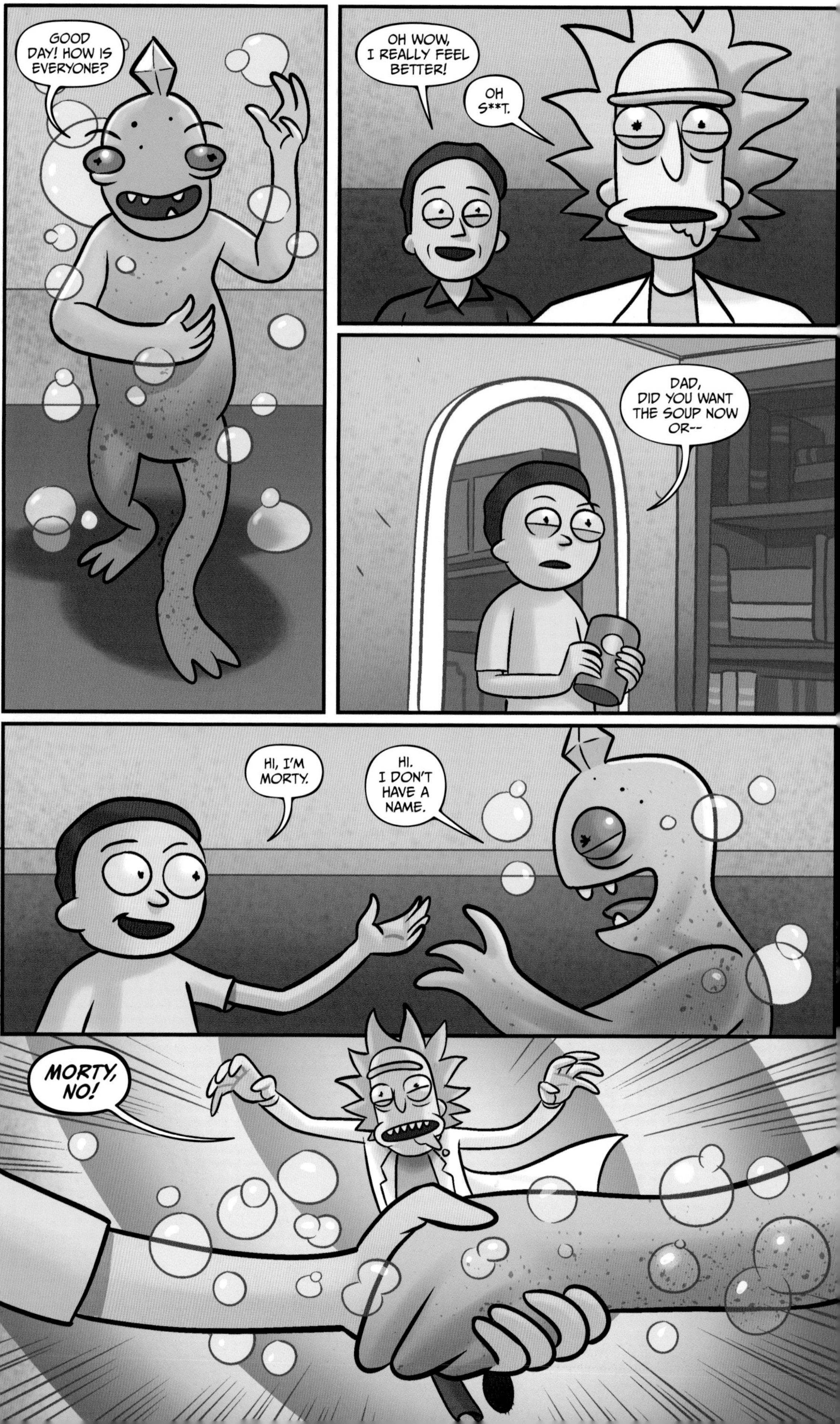
GOOD DAY! HOW IS EVERYONE?
OH WOW, I REALLY FEEL BETTER!
OH S**T.
DAD, DID YOU WANT THE SOUP NOW OR--
HI, I'M MORTY.
HI. I DON'T HAVE A NAME.
MORTY, NO!

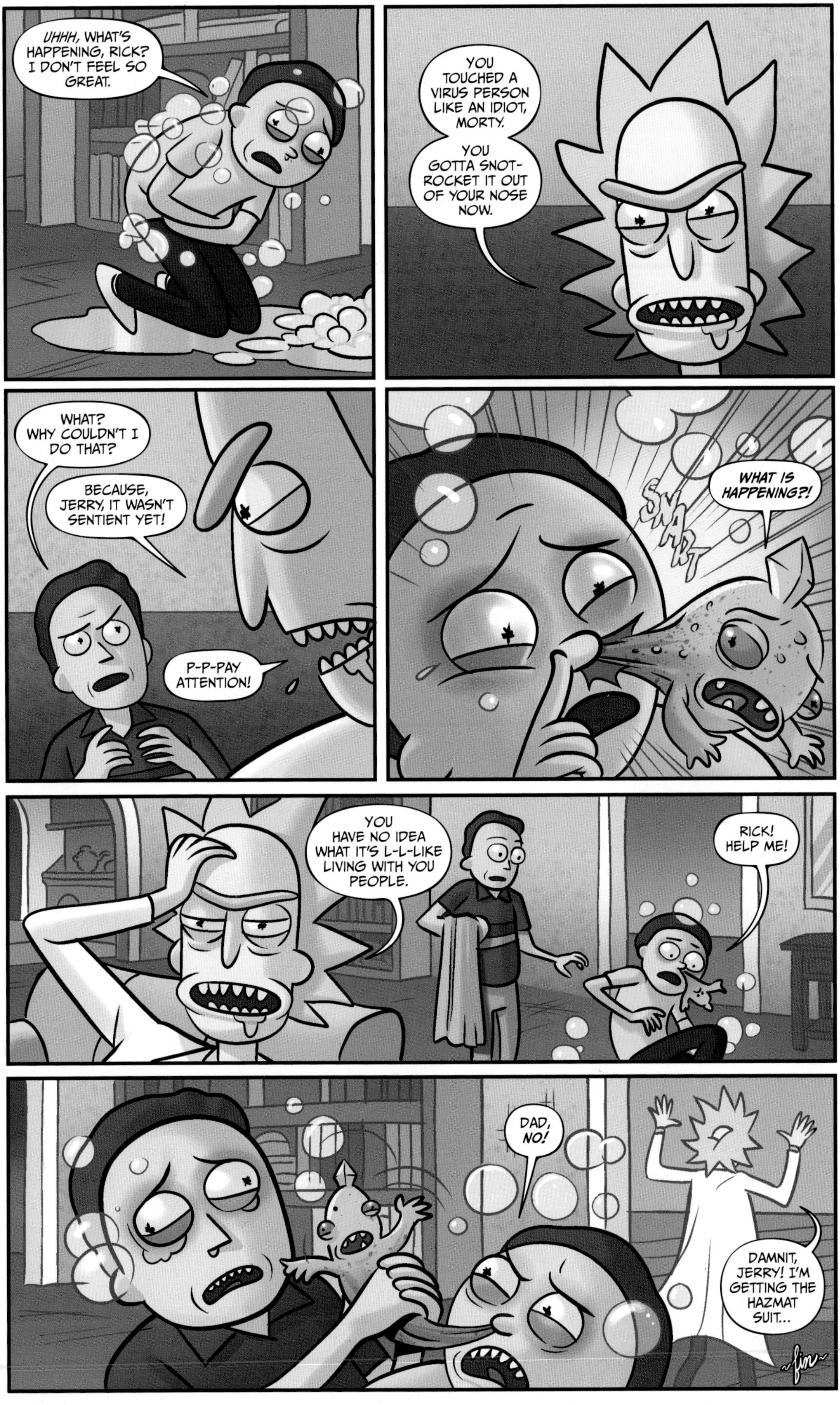
UHHH, WHAT'S HAPPENING, RICK? I DON'T FEEL SO GREAT.
YOU TOUCHED A VIRUS PERSON LIKE AN IDIOT, MORTY.
YOU GOTTA SNOT-ROCKET IT OUT OF YOUR NOSE NOW.
WHAT? WHY COULDN'T I DO THAT?
BECAUSE, JERRY, IT WASN'T SENTIENT YET!
P-P-PAY ATTENTION!
SNART
WHAT IS HAPPENING?!
YOU HAVE NO IDEA WHAT IT'S L-L-LIKE LIVING WITH YOU PEOPLE.
RICK! HELP ME!
DAD, NO!
DAMNIT, JERRY! I'M GETTING THE HAZMAT SUIT...
~fin~

**DAN HARMON** is the Emmy® winning creator/executive producer of the comedy series *Community*, as well as the co-creator/executive producer of Adult Swim's *Rick and Morty*™.

**JUSTIN ROILAND** grew up in Manteca, California, where he did the basic stuff children do. Later in life he traveled to Los Angeles. Justin also really hates writing about himself in the third person. I hate this. That's right. It's me. I've been writing this whole thing. Hi. The cat's out of the bag. It's just you and me now. There never was a third person.

**KYLE STARKS** is an Eisner-nominated comic creator from Southern Indiana, where he resides with his beautiful wife and two amazing daughters. Check out his creator-owned work: *Assaination Nation, Kill Them All*, and *Sexcastle*.

**TERRY BLAS** is an illustrator and writer based in Portland, Oregon. His auto-bio comics *Ghetto Swirl*, *You Say Latino* and *You Say LatinX* were featured on NPR, OPB, Vox.com and Cosmo.com.

Terry's work has appeared in the comics *Bravest Warriors, Regular Show, The Amazing World of Gumball, Adventure Time,* and *Steven Universe*.

His first graphic novel, *Dead Weight: Murder at Camp Bloom*, is a murder mystery set at a weight loss camp. *Dead Weight* was named by YALSA as a 2019 Quick Pick for Reluctant Young Readers.

His second graphic novel, *Hotel Dare*, is an all ages, fantasy, epic inspired by his childhood memories of his grandmother in Mexico. His third book, *Lifetime Passes*, is a summertime adventure set at a Southern California theme park and will be published by Surely Books.

**MARC ELLERBY** is a comics illustrator living in Essex, UK. He has worked on such titles as *Doctor Who, Regular Show,* and *The Amazing World of Gumball*. His own comics are *Chloe Noonan: Monster Hunter* and *Ellerbisms*.

**BENJAMIN DEWEY** grew up drawing monsters, robots and dragons in Cleveland, Ohio. He now lives in Milwaukie, Oregon with his wife, Lindsey, two cats, too many guitars and stacks of comics pages. Ben has drawn for nearly every major publisher and does his own webcomics whenever his schedule permits. In the rare moments he isn't drawing he enjoys playing in a band, exploring RPG video games and getting breakfast with his favorite people.

**SARAH STERN** is a comic artist and colorist from New York. Find her at sarahstern.com or follow her on Twitter at @worstwizard.

**CHRIS CRANK** letters a bunch of books put out by Image, Dark Horse, and Oni Press. He also has a podcast with Mike Norton (**crankcast.net**) and makes music (**sonomorti.bandcamp.com**).

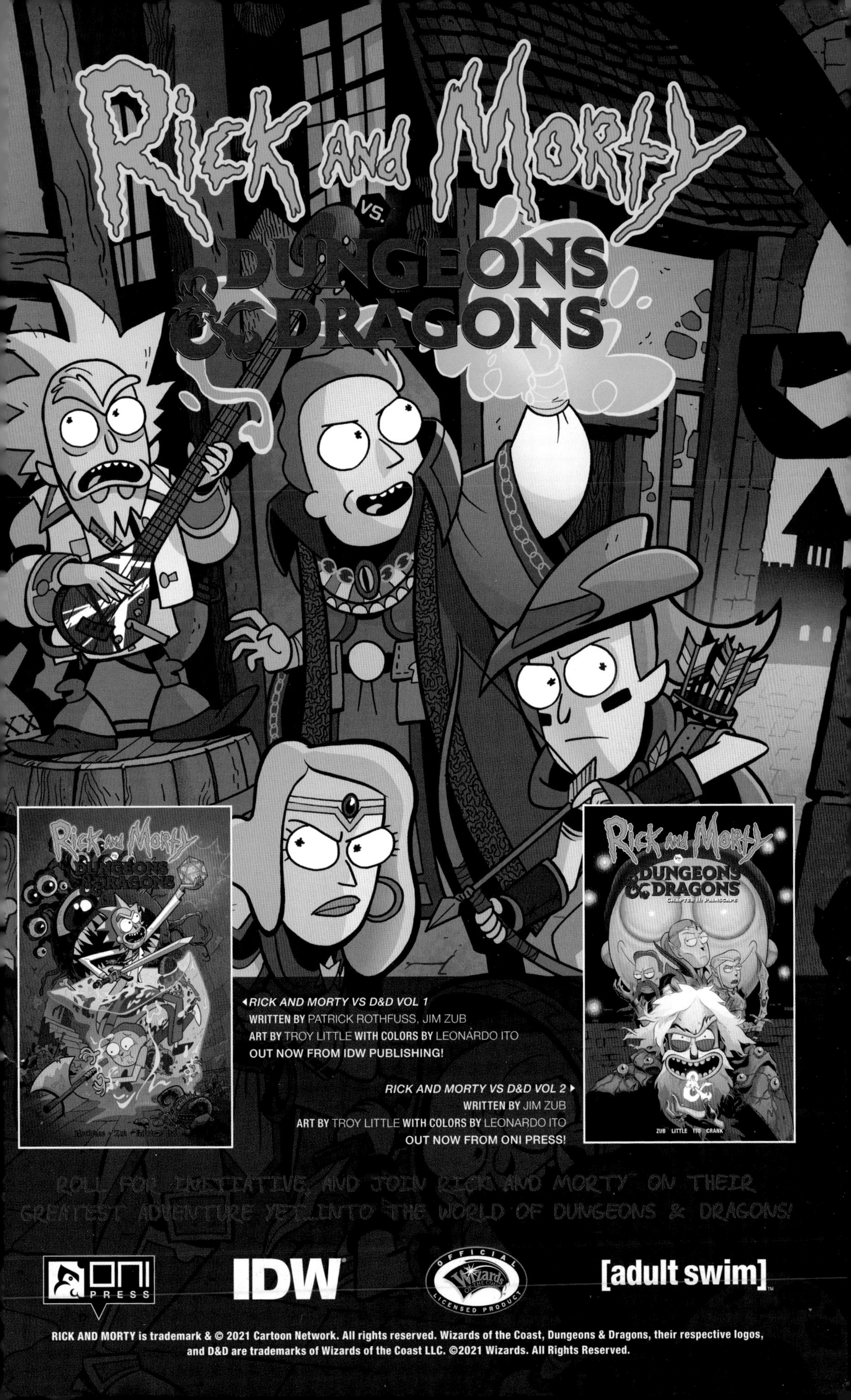
Rick and Morty vs. Dungeons & Dragons
◂ RICK AND MORTY VS D&D VOL 1
WRITTEN BY PATRICK ROTHFUSS, JIM ZUB
ART BY TROY LITTLE WITH COLORS BY LEONARDO ITO
OUT NOW FROM IDW PUBLISHING!
RICK AND MORTY VS D&D VOL 2 ▸
WRITTEN BY JIM ZUB
ART BY TROY LITTLE WITH COLORS BY LEONARDO ITO
OUT NOW FROM ONI PRESS!
ZUB LITTLE ITO CRANK
ROLL FOR INITIATIVE, AND JOIN RICK AND MORTY™ ON THEIR GREATEST ADVENTURE YET INTO THE WORLD OF DUNGEONS & DRAGONS!
ONI PRESS
IDW
OFFICIAL Wizards of the Coast LICENSED PRODUCT
[adult swim]
RICK AND MORTY is trademark & © 2021 Cartoon Network. All rights reserved. Wizards of the Coast, Dungeons & Dragons, their respective logos, and D&D are trademarks of Wizards of the Coast LLC. ©2021 Wizards. All Rights Reserved.

# MORE BOOKS FROM ONI PRESS

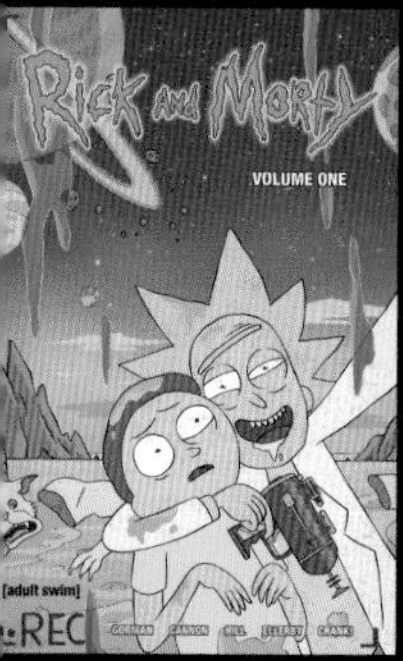
Rick and Morty
VOLUME ONE
[adult swim]

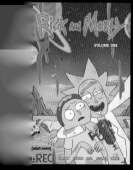

**RICK AND MORTY™, VOL. 1**
By Zac Gorman, CJ Cannon, Marc Ellerby, and more
128 pages, softcover, color
**ISBN 978-1-62010-281-7**

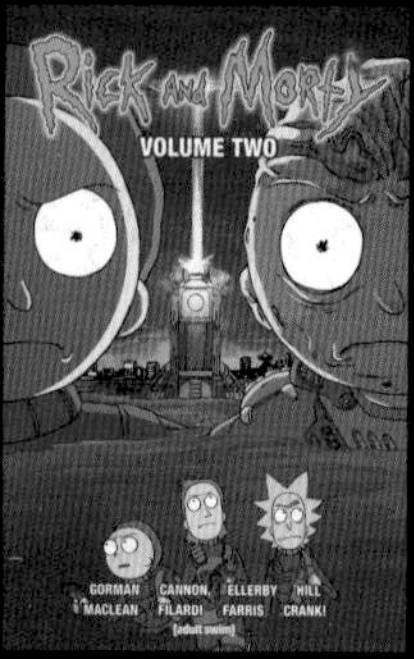
Rick and Morty
VOLUME TWO
[adult swim]

**RICK AND MORTY™, VOL. 2**
By Zac Gorman, CJ Cannon, Marc Ellerby, and more
128 pages, softcover, color
**ISBN 978-1-62010-319-7**

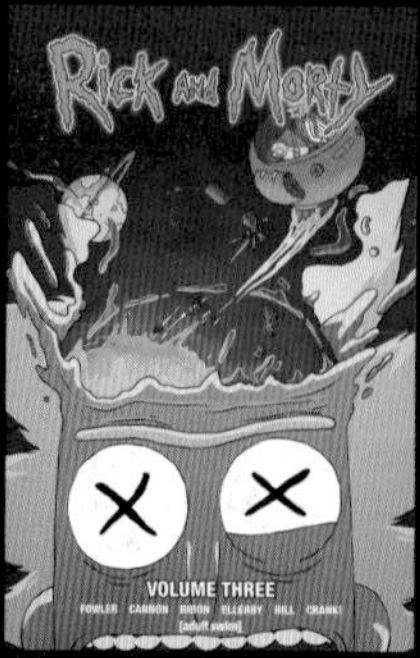
Rick and Morty
VOLUME THREE
[adult swim]

**RICK AND MORTY™, VOL. 3**
By Tom Fowler, CJ Cannon, Marc Ellerby, and more
128 pages, softcover, color
**ISBN 978-1-62010-343-2**

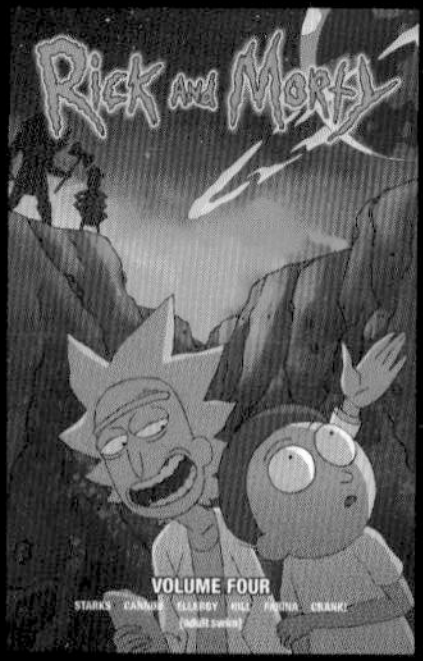
Rick and Morty
VOLUME FOUR
[adult swim]

**RICK AND MORTY™, VOL. 4**
By Kyle Starks, CJ Cannon, Marc Ellerby, and more
128 pages, softcover, color
**ISBN 978-1-62010-377-7**

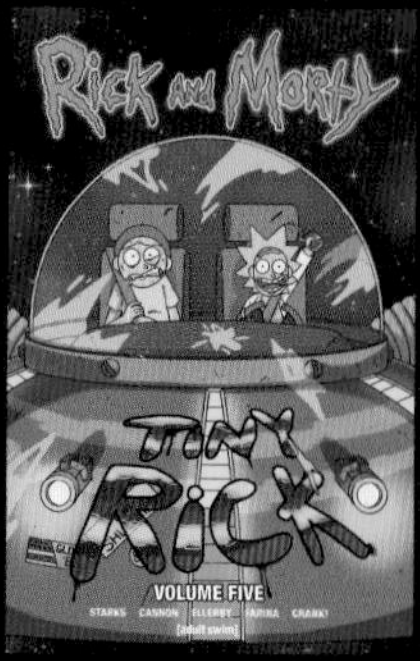
Rick and Morty
TINY RICK
VOLUME FIVE
[adult swim]

**RICK AND MORTY™, VOL. 5**
By Kyle Starks, CJ Cannon, Marc Ellerby, and more!
128 pages, softcover, color
**ISBN 978-1-62010-416-3**

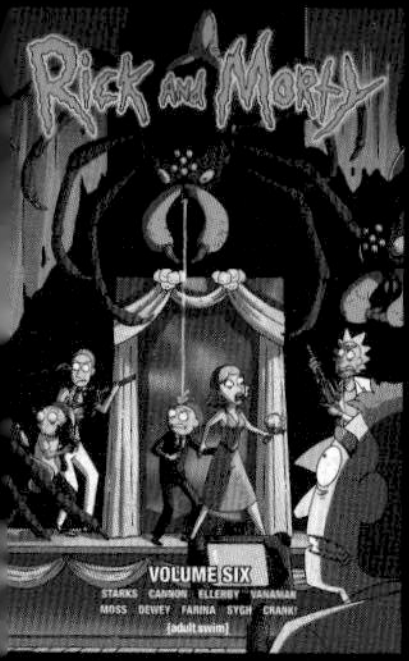
Rick and Morty
VOLUME SIX
[adult swim]

**RICK AND MORTY™, VOL. 6**
By Kyle Starks, CJ Cannon, Marc Ellerby, and more
128 pages, softcover, color
**ISBN 978-1-62010-452-1**

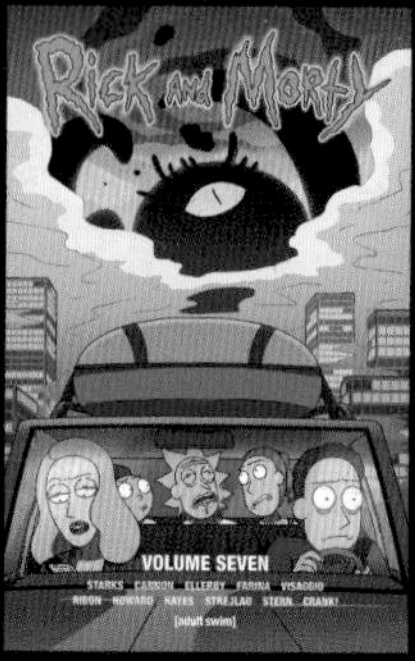
Rick and Morty
VOLUME SEVEN
[adult swim]

**RICK AND MORTY™, VOL. 7**
By Kyle Starks, CJ Cannon, Marc Ellerby, and more
128 pages, softcover, color
**ISBN 978-1-62010-509-2**

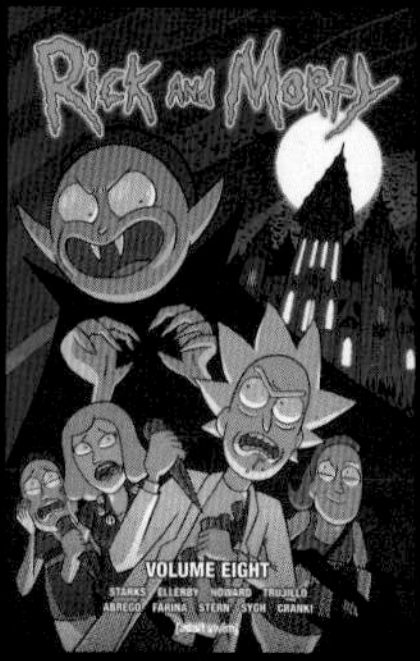
Rick and Morty
VOLUME EIGHT

**RICK AND MORTY™, VOL. 8**
By Kyle Starks, Tini Howard, Marc Ellerby, and more
128 pages, softcover, color
**ISBN 978-1-62010-549-8**

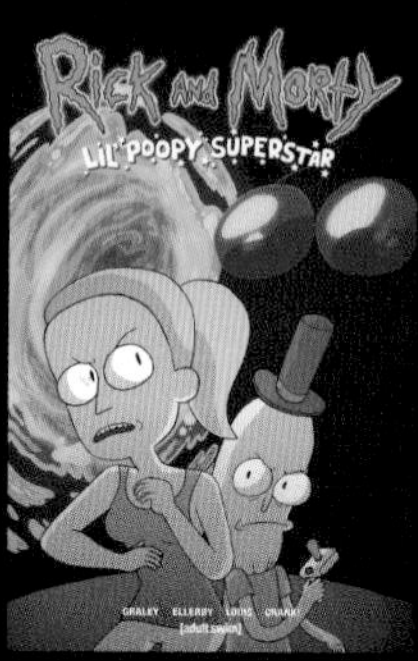
Rick and Morty
LIL' POOPY SUPERSTAR

**RICK AND MORTY™: LIL' POOPY SUPERSTAR**
By Sarah Graley, Marc Ellerby, and Mildred Louis
128 pages, softcover, color
**ISBN 978-1-62010-374-6**

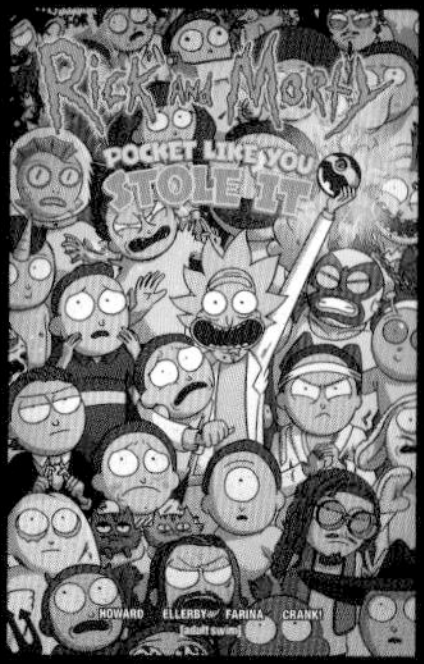
Rick and Morty
POCKET LIKE YOU STOLE IT

**RICK AND MORTY™: POCKET LIKE YOU STOLE IT**
By Tini Howard, Marc Ellerby, and Katy Farina
128 pages, softcover, color
**ISBN 978-1-62010-474-3**

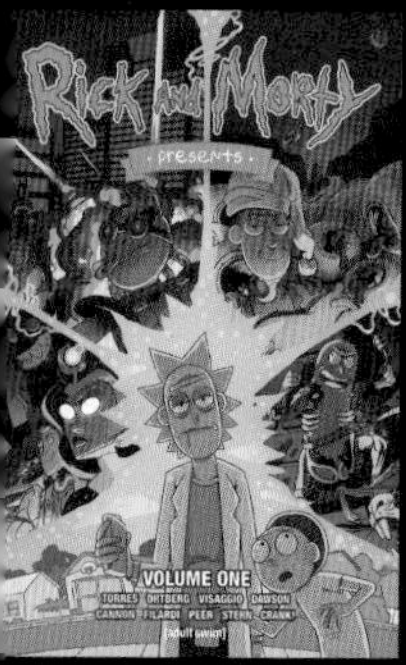
Rick and Morty
PRESENTS
VOLUME ONE

**RICK AND MORTY™ PRESENTS, VOL. 1**
By J. Torres, Daniel Ortberg, CJ Cannon, and more
136 pages, softcover, color
**ISBN 978-1-62010-552-8**

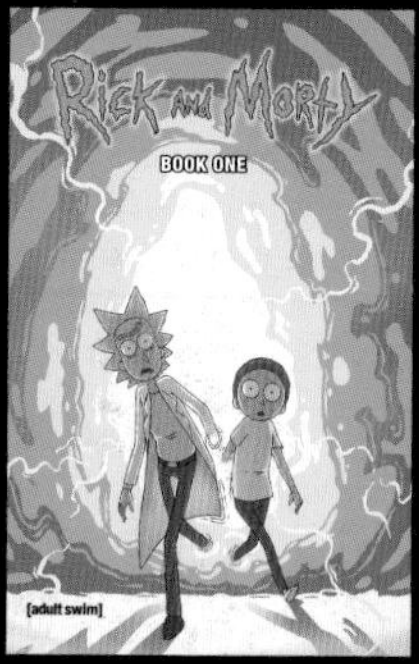
Rick and Morty
BOOK ONE
[adult swim]

**RICK AND MORTY™ DELUXE EDITION, BOOK ONE**
By Zac Gorman, CJ Cannon, Marc Ellerby, and more
296 pages, hardcover, color
**ISBN 978-1-62010-360-9**

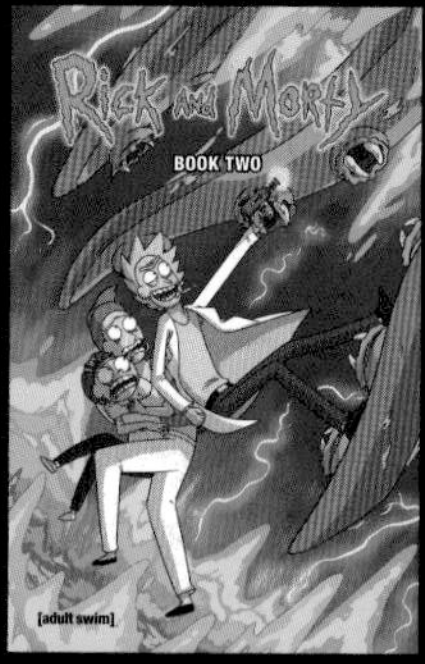
Rick and Morty
BOOK TWO
[adult swim]

**RICK AND MORTY™ DELUXE EDITION, BOOK TWO**
By Tom Fowler, Kyle Starks, CJ Cannon, Marc Ellerby, and more
288 pages, hardcover, color
**ISBN 978-1-62010-439-2**

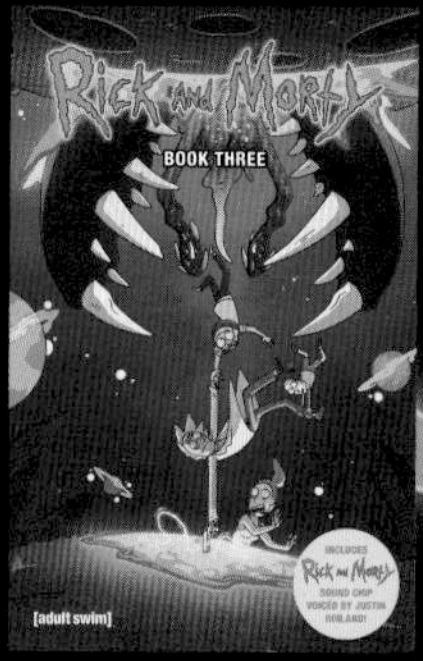
Rick and Morty
BOOK THREE
[adult swim]

**RICK AND MORTY™ DELUXE EDITION, BOOK THREE**
By Kyle Starks, CJ Cannon, Marc Ellerby, Sarah Graley, and more
288 pages, hardcover, color
**ISBN 978-1-62010-535-1**

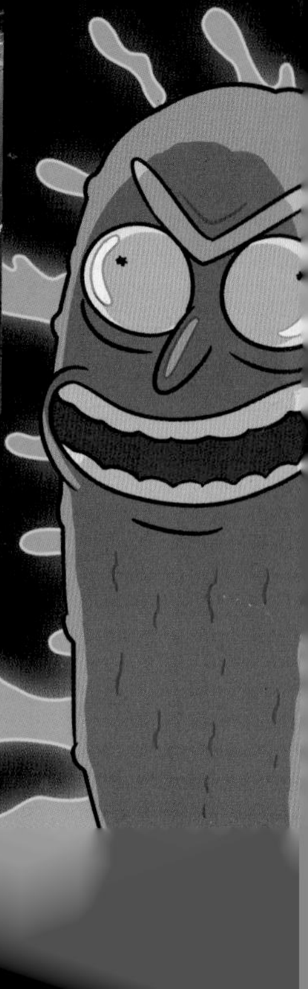

ONI PRESS

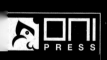

For more information on these and other fine Oni Press comic books and graphic novels visit **www.onipress.com.** To find a comic specialty store in your area visit **www.comicshops.us**